The Ethics of Social Research

ASPECTS OF MODERN SOCIOLOGY

General Editor: Professor Maurice Craft, Foundation Dean of Humanities and Social Science, Hong Kong University of Science and Technology

SOCIAL RESEARCH

THE LIMITATIONS OF SOCIAL RESEARCH
Marten Shipman

DATA COLLECTION IN CONTEXT
Stephen Ackroyd and John Hughes

THE PHILOSOPHY OF SOCIAL RESEARCH
2nd edition
John A. Hughes

READING ETHNOGRAPHIC RESEARCH
Martyn Hammersley

ETHICS IN SOCIAL RESEARCH
Roger Homan

FORTHCOMING:

SOCIAL RESEARCH AND SOCIAL POLICY
Roger Burrows

ASPECTS OF MODERN SOCIOLOGY

The Ethics of Social Research

Roger Homan

LONGMAN
London and New York

Longman Group UK Limited,
Longman House,
Burnt Mill,
Harlow,
Essex CM20 2JE, England
and Associated Companies throughout the world.

Published in the United States of America
by Longman Inc., New York

First published 1991

British Library Cataloguing in Publication Data
Homan, Roger
The ethics of social research. – (Aspects of modern sociology, social science).
1. Social sciences. research. Ethical aspects
I. Title II. Series
174.93

ISBN 0–582–05879–1

Library of Congress Cataloging in Publication Data
Homan, Roger.
The ethics of social research/Roger Homan.
p. cm. — (Aspects of modern sociology)
Includes bibliographical references and index.
ISBN 0–582–05879–1 : £8.95 (est.)
1. Social sciences—Research—Moral and ethical aspects.
2. Social sciences—Methodology—Moral and ethical aspects.
I. Title. II. Series.
H62.H5945 1991 90–6651
174′.93′0072—dc20 CIP

Set in 10/11 Times

Printed in Malaysia
by Percetakan Jiwabaru Sdn. Bhd.,
Bangi, Selangor Darul Ehsan

CONTENTS

EDITOR'S PREFACE

The first series in Longman's *Aspects of Modern Sociology* library was concerned with the social structure of modern Britain, and was intended for students following professional and other courses in universities, polytechnics, colleges of education, and elsewhere in further and higher education, as well as for those members of a wider public wishing to pursue an interest in the nature and structure of British society.

This further series sets out to examine the history, aims, techniques and limitations of social research, and it is hoped that it will be of interest to the same readership. It will seek to offer an informative but not uncritical introduction to some of the methodologies of social science.

Maurice Craft

PREFACE

In the spring and summer of 1977 I was a guest lecturer in the sociology department at Illinois State University, which I used as a base from which to extend fieldwork for my thesis on the language behaviour of old-time pentecostals. In Britain and Canada I had innocently adopted the method of covert observation. Such innocence was not allowed to pass in an American institution in which social scientists were keenly aware of ethical considerations constraining the conduct of their research.

Having done some of my fieldwork already, I was bound to be defensive of my disfavoured methods and my justifications of covertness and deception were largely retrospective. A lively debate followed the publication in *The Sociological Review* of a paper which drew on my covert observation (Homan, 1978). I fought my corner in that debate with conviction but came out of it with mixed feelings. It is hoped that those mixed feelings permeate this book. Its purpose is to keep open a debate which such formulae as ethical codes are inclined to close. The case against deception and covertness and other recognised offences is stated throughout the book but there are also vigorous and sustained challenges to the general assumptions of ethical principles and to the professional consensus. For example, it is normally supposed that open methods are more virtuous and that covert ones are unethical: that assumption is questioned by illustrating some of the undesirable effects of open methods and the informing of consent and by working out the rationale of covert methods in ethical terms. Our purpose is not to destroy ethical principles but to fulfil them by defining moral values appropriate to the conduct of social research.

In the early stages of this debate I was enormously supported by the correspondence and friendship of John Barnes, then Professor of Anthropology at Churchill College, Cambridge. His articulate defence of procedures that were so uniformly disapproved within the British Sociological Association was an inspiration to me at a time when I might otherwise have had half the debate to myself. I take this opportunity to acknowledge my gratitude and to salute him in his retirement.

Being more dependent than others upon the support of library staff, my debt to the libraries I have used is surely the greater and my thanks are the more heartfelt. In particular I should like to thank the librarians of the University of Sussex for extending to me their facilities for blind readers and to the staff of Brighton Polytechnic's Falmer library and the British Library of Political and Social Science who willingly searched catalogue systems designed for better-sighted users.

One of the few conventions that will go unquestioned in this volume is that of using the printed word to acknowledge a debt to one's spouse. Caroline willingly excused me for many long evenings and large parts of vacations to attend my desk and I hope that there will be an interval before the next project which will afford some overdue companionship.

CHAPTER 1

Introduction

1.1 THE MEANING OF ETHICS

Now to instruct each individual in what manner to govern his own conduct in the details of life, is the particular business of private ethics (Jeremy Bentham, 1789. In Burns and Hart 1982: 246).

In its grandest form, ethics may be recognised as a philosophical discipline 'primarily concerned with the evaluation and justification of norms and standards of personal and interpersonal behaviour' (Karhausen, 1987: 25). Ethics is the science of morality: those who engage in it determine values for the regulation of human behaviour. One of the general definitions given by the Oxford English Dictionary is 'the science of morals; the department of study concerned with the principles of human duty'.

When ethics is applied and developed within a particular professional context such as medicine or social research, it takes on a distinctive form and some of the general definitions of ethics that are to be found in dictionaries and philosophical accounts are not appropriate. For example, ethics is often treated as the study of moral questions and morality as the quality or standard of actual conduct (Pond, 1987: ln). However, the literature, debate and professional statements which pass for the ethics of social research are often highly prescriptive and closely applied to the realities of the research situation. Although 'morality' features more prominently and explicitly in medical research, which since the days of Hippocrates has been accustomed to share moral questions more openly with the wider public, there is little talk of morality in the literature treating the rights and wrongs of social research. In consequence there is a *de facto* distinction between morality and ethics in the context of social research in that morality is often thought of as being exogenous, whereas ethics refers to the standards established within the profession for the conduct of its members.

In the context of medicine Häring (1972: 24) has identified a professional ethos as 'those distinctive attitudes which characterize the culture of a professional group': ethics is then the systematic attempt to illuminate this ethos and to elaborate the perspectives and norms of the profession. In both medicine and social research there have developed ethical codes as an endeavour to foster and guarantee professional ethos and standards. It has happened that the spirit of codes has largely taken over the literature of social research ethics and will persist in this volume: in practice, ethics has come to be no longer the philosophical study of values such as the ethic of autonomy, the ethic of non-maleficence, that of utility and that of good consequences (Davis and Aroskar, 1983); for better or worse, the literature is now at the stage not of moving toward procedures to safeguard these ethics but of recognising consensual standards and judging examples of social research accordingly. For example, much of the literature and a chapter of this book are taken up with the principle of informed consent: this is not an ethic but a procedure widely agreed to safeguard the rights of human subjects to know that research is being conducted and to approve their own participation. The debate that continues is largely about offences, which can only be identified when the rules are agreed; the minor part of the debate in recent years has been about whether the rules effectively safeguard the values and rights they are intended to protect. One of the themes of this book will be the attempt to recover those values or ethics and this will imply challenges here and there to the rules or guidelines that are now in place within the professional associations.

This book will also be frequently occupied with the tension between personal moral standards and professional ethical norms and, in conclusion, it will be submitted that the notion of ethics is so hazardous and ineffective in the context of social research that thought should be given to establishing a professional morality. One level of morality is that which students bring with them as they enter the community of social research: they are entitled to find some research prospects uncongenial and unacceptable, such as observation in public lavatories or the adoption of covert roles to collect data by the methods of espionage. At the general and public level, there is an agenda of moral issues which is referred to the professional community and which cannot be resolved entirely independently of the prevailing view outside: matters such as research into genetic engineering and *in vitro* fertilisation have been widely debated in recent years and the trend in the teaching of medical ethics has been toward the discussion of these problems (Pond, 1987: 1–2). Between the public and the private levels of morality is situated the professional level: it is into the ethics of the professional community that the student is inducted. However, codes and contracts invariably form the basis of professional socialisation in social research so that the moral problems are not explicitly engaged as they are in medical education. The tension between individual morality and professional ethics is seen to be most problematic when legitimate scruples disqualify a student from taking up a research post or other opportunity. It is an indictment of the professional control of social research if it is a case of the survival of the least scrupulous. The individual may yet be called upon by a research team or professional obligation to respect an ethic that by the standards of individual and public morality is seen to be inferior: for example, the observer of criminal behaviour may be compelled by moral obligations to report but constrained by ethical principles to conceal (Bennett, 1967: 373).

1.2 THE RATIONALE OF SOCIAL RESEARCH ETHICS

One of the reasons why an individual may find that professional expectations conflict with what is publicly perceived to be moral or privately regarded as honourable is that ethical principles are established on the basis of a considerable measure of professional self-interest.

A distinction may be made between ethical issues which concern intrinsic or fundamental values including what are asserted as rights and those which have to do with the consequences of particular actions (Pring, 1984b: 9). In the event, most ethical issues involve elements of both kinds. When we look at the reasons that are set out for adopting ethical standards in the conduct of social research, we see that even when the concern professed is for the interests and rights of other parties such as human subjects or the wider public, there is invariably a suggestion that these should be respected for reasons of self-interest. The unethical treatment of subjects, it is suggested, yields poorer results than respect for them. Open procedures are desirable not merely because human subjects are entitled to know what is going on but because the research community will suffer and have less cooperative relationships in the long term if it is noised abroad that sociologists are lurking in disguise. What in moral discourse may be respected as ends in themselves are often treated as means in ethical guidelines. Such a rationale for the establishment of ethical principles is expressed in the *Code of Conduct* of the Market Research Society (1986: 7):

> Research is founded upon the willing cooperation of the public and of business organisations. It depends upon public and business confidence that it is conducted honestly, objectively, without unwelcome intrusion and without harm to informants . . . It is in this spirit that the Code of Conduct has been devised.

Jennifer Platt elaborates the interdependence of the ethical and the technical. She argues that if a subject senses an interviewer's manner to be unethical, whether in the mildest form of impoliteness or the more serious matter of impropriety, the approach is likely to be technically weakened, however much it squares with the ethical position of the investigator. In a similar way, an interviewer made uncomfortable by personal scruples is less likely to be able to carry out an enquiry as planned with appropriate coolness and persistence (Platt, 1981: 87).

Occupying an area of high moral ground, Baumrind (1971: 887) insists that if methodological rigour ever conflicts with the fundamental rights of subjects, methodology must be compromised. The difficulty here, researchers argue, is that a compromise or relaxation of methodological rigour threatens other rights asserted by parties also implied in social research, such as the public right to know. The right of human subjects to yield or withhold data must be set not only against the aspirations of social researchers to disclose and interpret but also against interests of members of the general public who may claim entitlement to information on the basis of which they can make wise decisions: typical groups include parents, policy makers, potential employers and social workers. The public right to know is therefore frequently invoked to justify the conduct of social research.

1.3 THE PUBLIC RIGHT TO KNOW

Social researchers are often puzzled that projects which seem to them to be so obviously in the public interest, and even in the interest of the particular community they hope to study, are not more cooperatively received by the intended subjects. This is partly because they assume that their own rationalisations of research will find credence with their subjects. The contrary is often the case. In an expression that betrays a keen sense of the conflict of interest between researcher and researched, Josephson comments from his own experience that 'projects dealing with the "pathologies" of slums or with deviant behaviour should be prepared for trouble' (Josephson, 1979: 96).

It is partly because the motives of researchers are complex that subjects are not easily or necessarily disposed to share their sense of the desirability of particular kinds of research. Just as investigative journalists may have a personal and economic interest in the discovery of a 'story' even if its publication may harm the individuals who are involved – and even, some would say, if a 'story' is not already there – so social researchers pursue ends to which the interests of their subjects are incidental. A dominant motive among researchers is the development of a reputation fulfilled by keeping one's name in the clear view of one's colleagues. Those seeking or established in academic posts come under peer and institutional pressures to keep publishing. Journal editors and referees apply criteria in accepting articles which might be expected to extend knowledge and break new ground; publishers of books, on the other hand, want to assure themselves of a sufficient market and those who propose books must take account of their commercial interest. The standard commendation of a book or article both to editors at the stage of submission and to fellow professionals to whom it is addressed, is that decades of serious research in cognate fields have left untouched one important subject which it has been the purpose of the author to investigate: the claim is that this is the last and vital piece of a jigsaw:

> We know a great deal about the health status and medical care needs of the very young and very old; but very little about those between childhood and adulthood (Josephson 1979: 98).

or,

> Our models also include another dimension that is usually ignored: to have coitus one must have a partner (Udry and Billy 1987: 841).

While there is a long and respectable tradition of social research as a response to human need, therefore, there is another approach to social research in which the researcher thinks in terms of what has not already been done, what will be of interest, what will strike oil in professional advancement, what will succeed in the competition for journal space. When human subjects feel that the interests of a researcher have come before that of a fair representation of their situation, they declare themselves to have been betrayed. Among the best documented of such subjects are the residents of 'Plainville' who thought that 'James West' had stressed the negative and backward features of their community because this made for a more interesting account; so acute was the sense of grievance felt by the postman in that small town that he took to his grave an unfulfilled desire to lay violent hands on 'West' (Gallaher, 1964: 288).

What is happening is that the knowledge to which the public is said to have a right is – according to aggrieved subjects – being distorted in the process of collection and communication. The professional structures and economic principles which bear upon this situation are not declared by researchers who seek consent upon rather more worthy if less credible warrants. The declared aims of research are so often not the real motives. The quest for consent might feature selected selling points thought likely to be persuasive with intended subjects and with which researchers might even have convinced themselves; however, subjects are likely to recognise ulterior motives.

Although the right to know is readily invoked in the justification of conducting and publishing social research, it should be noted that it has implications for the role of researcher in society. If the public has a right to know, the researcher has less of a right than an obligation to publish. Many researchers would want to retain some control over how they spend their time, what projects they choose, what aspects they pursue, what interpretations they offer; both they and their publishers would be inclined to omit from published reports fragments of data that do not have a perceived bearing on the main argument. But if the public has a right to know, the researcher may not be entitled to be selective.

1.4 THE PURSUIT OF TRUTH

It might be thought that honesty is so obviously a desirable virtue in scientific reporting that it needs hardly to be asserted in codes or discussed in textbooks such as this. Indeed, it does not arise in the influential Nuremberg Code which was prompted by other ethical concerns such as the responsibilities of researchers to their subjects. Nor is it a theme of the current ethical principles of the British Sociological Association.

Elsewhere, however, professionals are reminded that truth in reporting is a fundamental aspect of professional integrity: it is an axiom of social researchers' responsibility both to the public they serve and to the reputation of fellow professionals. For example, the latest code of ethics of the American Sociological Association (1989) states:

> Sociologists are committed to the pursuit of accurate and precise knowledge ... without personal and methodological prejudice and without ideological malice ... In presenting their work, sociologists are obligated to report their findings fully and should not misrepresent the findings of their research.

In Britain, a similar position is adopted by the Social Research Association (n.d.):

> While social researchers operate within the value of their societies they should attempt to uphold their professional integrity without fear or favour. They should also not engage or collude in selecting methods designed to produce misleading results, or in misrepresenting findings by commission or omission.

It may be noted that while there is a taboo upon research which is 'fixed' in the sense that methods are selected to produce particular results and close the possibility of alternative findings, there is no taboo upon the pursuit of a truth that is anticipated from or before the outset. Prior observation of a situation is a legitimate means of formulating hypotheses and the exposure of problems in a social situation is a respectable purpose of scientific research. The values of the researcher will probably be selection of a research agenda: social researchers who feel passionately about inequalities in respect of class, race and gender may be prompted by their concern to devote their energies to researching these problems. Again, sociologists preferring traditional forms of worship in the usage of the established Church have turned to opinion polling to demonstrate levels of popular support. What the public and profession is entitled to expect of such researchers is that they are open to the range of possible findings and that their methods are not loaded to produce the results they want to achieve. The same standard is true for those whose values are neutral to the findings of their work but whose interest in particular results is vested in career aspirations. 'Tendentious', then, is not a dirty word.

The most blatant form of dishonesty in reporting is the falsification of results: the profession achieves as great a consensus against cheating and falsification as against any transgression of ethical principle. Outrageous though it is considered to be, there have been some celebrated cases, of which none is better known than that of Sir Cyril Burt, a British psychologist who was knighted for research that was afterwards discredited. Burt was interested in the effects of environment upon intelligence. He claimed to have worked with over fifty sets of identical twins who had been separated early in life and brought up in situations that were socially and culturally independent. In spite of differential upbringing and environmental exposure, there was a reported high correlation between the twins' IQ scores, and this finding was taken to affirm the importance of genetic factors. As long as Burt's findings were believed – and even after they were discredited – they were influential in the system of streaming favoured in British schools. After his death, however, it transpired that Burt had an unusual concept of data: he had seen them as statistics that a researcher might invent in order to convince peers of a truth that seemed to him to be obvious. Many results had been faked. Co-authors did not exist. Data cited in later papers purporting to confirm earlier findings had also been used in the initial publications. Burt probably invented data in order to defend his case against critics (Diener and Crandall, 1978: 154–5).

If, as is commonly agreed, the fabrications of Cyril Burt were of this order they had the effects not only of lending scientific support to educational policy, but also of contaminating knowledge, getting psychology a bad press and occupying the energies of a number of other psychologists on the strength of spurious findings.

Sadly, however, it is not only at the top level that such fraud is perpetrated: students do it too. The pressures upon an established academic to consolidate a reputation and go for gold with the publication of epoch-making findings are matched by those upon an undergraduate student to complete a dissertation as swiftly as possible in order to release time for other studies. Diener and Crandall (1978: 157) tell of a student who, being pressed for time, collected some experimental data in the laboratory and fabricated others, a procedure known in the trade as 'dry labbing'. While his conscience inhibited him when it was suggested that he should publish, his professor wasted some time in a vain attempt to replicate the study.

Another hazard that besets the pursuit of truth is the glimpse of important findings at the end of a project. The author of this book has known the experience of working through over 200 questionnaires and noticing halfway through that a pattern is emerging that would be at least newsworthy. From that moment, he opened envelopes hoping for responses that would lend themselves to such findings. The temptation is to resolve ambiguous replies and illegible handwriting in one's favour. And when the intention had been to group respondents within five equal ranges on a 100-point scale, there was a temptation to regroup these in four categories covering the same range when a large number of respondents fell between 76 and 80. He hopes that he did not yield and the precaution against distorted interpretation was the retention of returned questionnaires for secondary analysis.

There is some evidence that dishonesty is rife. Azrin and colleagues endeavoured to replicate the study of Verplanck (1955) by asking graduate students to execute a field experiment which was impossible to conduct. Only one of sixteen students admitted to methodological problems while the others claimed – until they were tested – to have carried out the experiment. This exposed the dishonesty of Azrin's students and also cast doubts on the original work of Verplanck. Diener and Crandall (1978) cite a number of reports that suggest that falsification is common among research students and hired assistants and fear that 'a sizable proportion of published findings may be based on quicksand' (1978: 157).

If the desire for truth is an ethical principle distinguished by the consensus that supports it, it is also unique for its attendant sanctions. The consequences of detection are terminal. Shame and professional ostracism are the fate of a social researcher caught cooking the books.

CHAPTER 2

Codes and controls

2.1 THE MODEL OF MEDICAL ETHICS

2.1.1 The evolution of guidelines

Statements of principle among researchers in the social sciences have drawn heavily upon those developed within the medical profession which has always led the field in its attention to principle and pursuit of a professional discipline. The formulation of medical ethics goes back nearly two centuries – and rather longer if we take Hippocrates into account. In 1803 an English doctor Thomas Percival published a book *Medical Ethics* which was largely concerned with the responsibilities of professionals to see that they prescribed appropriate medicine. The first 'Code of ethics of the American Medical Association' appeared in 1847 and evidenced a clear debt to Percival's work (Schuler, 1982: 170).

But Percival was perhaps less concerned than Hippocrates with the moral dimension of the relationship between doctor and patient or experimenter and subject. This concern has been prominent and consistent in medical ethics since the Second World War. As so often in the evolution of ethical principles, it took something in the nature of a classic case – in this instance, even an atrocity – before principles were formulated. During that war, a number of Nazi doctors, of whom 23 stood trial at Nuremberg, had conducted experiments on imprisoned subjects who were supplied to them in batches: it was stated at the tribunal that they had received at various times lots of 200 Jews, 50 gypsies, 500 Poles suffering tuberculosis, or 1000 Russians (Phillips and Dawson, 1985: 57). The experiments used upon these victims included the infection of wounds, infections with malaria and typhoid, the freezing of subjects, experiments in pressure chambers and the use of poisons (Katz 1972: 292–306). On 19 August 1947 seven defendants were sentenced to death and others to terms of imprisonment. The positive outcome of the Nuremberg trials was the issue of ten rules nowadays known as the Nuremberg Code which can be seen to persist in ethical codes in medical research and for other experimental research such as psychological research, it is also adapted often fairly literally for the purposes of controlling the researches of social scientists.

The Nuremberg Code lays emphasis upon the need for those conducting experimental research with human subjects to be appropriately qualified in order to anticipate effects, to use only voluntary subjects and to relieve them of the pressure or pain of the experiment if this becomes excessive. The principle which the Code introduces, and which implies both that the researcher is cognizant of risks and that the subject is a volunteer, is that of informed consent. It is stated in the first of the ten rules as summarized below and affirmed in the others. Specifically, the Nuremberg Code provides:

1. that participation in experiments should be voluntary and that subjects should be fully apprised of risks: this implies that subjects must be told that the situation is experimental and there are implications in this clause for participation in experiments where this is a course requirement for students (Baumrind, 1964: 421);
2. that medical experiments are justifiable only if they serve an humanitarian purpose which cannot be served by other methods: this clause prompts social scientists to question whether the knowledge they seek is in a worthy cause;
3. that risk be calculated in proportion to the importance of the research for humanitarian purposes: researchers of all kinds should ask themselves whether the possible outcomes in terms of new knowledge justify the probable strain, discomfort or embarrassment of subjects;
4. that researchers should have a thorough knowledge of the nature of their experiments to be acquired through acquaintance with related research and, if appropriate, from pilot studies with animal subjects: it is no excuse not to have anticipated the hazards of an experiment if they were at least knowable from existing sources;
5. that measures should be taken to avoid physical and psychological injury: this provision places a heavy responsibility upon the researcher to consider the after effects of an experiment upon its subjects; and social researchers may recognise that interviews can be quite as harrowing as sessions in psychologists' laboratories;
6. that there can be no grounds for the expectation of a subject's death or disablement;
7. that the researcher takes all possible precautions to avoid harmful effects in medical and psychological research in recent years, such measures have included the maintenance of all equipment to a high standard of safety, the counselling of subjects by way of introduction and debriefing and the monitoring of experimental conditions so that these can be adjusted should they prove uncongenial;
8. that experimenters should be highly qualified and appropriately experienced: in the debates following particular cases such as that of Milgram (1974), experimenters have also been charged with the responsibility of consulting senior colleagues in the course of research design;
9. that subjects should be free and know that they are free to withdraw from an experiment, even once it is in progress: Milgram (1974) was criticised because the experimenter directed subjects to continue

administering electric shocks to a 'victim' even when they found this distasteful;

10. that a researcher should discontinue an experiment as soon as it is seen to cause undue discomfort or harm to a subject: Milgram was again criticised on this score and interviewers might apply this principle by breaking off interviews or omitting sensitive questions when they appear to cause distress to respondents.

It may be observed that the consent of subjects to participate in experiments is introduced in the Nuremberg Code in a context of obligations of experimenters. That the consent of subjects is secured is not a sufficient condition for the conduct of hazardous research: rather, experimenters are still committed to proceed on the basis of a concern for the welfare of subjects and to desist if that welfare is threatened. This principle is clarified in the World Medical Association's, 'Declaration of Helsinki':

> The responsibility for the human subject must always rest with a medically qualified person and never rest on the subject of the research, even though the subject has given his or her consent (reprinted in Phillips and Dawson, 1985: 213)

It is suggested in a later chapter (4.6) that this principle has sometimes been lost in social research in which the informed consent of subjects is taken as a licence to proceed without due care for the subject's interests, including the adverse effects of publicity.

The Nuremberg Code addressed the need to restrain medical research; but its agenda was confined to those possibilities of misuse which had emerged in the tribunal. The World Medical Association has since provided a number of regulations and declarations, some of them for specific situations such as war or in connection with capital punishment. These are helpfully collected and reproduced by Phillips and Dawson (1985: Appendix).

One of the major ethical principles of more recent guidelines that is missing in the Nuremberg Code is that of confidentiality. A Code of Confidentiality has been drawn up by a number of groups of medical professionals in Britain including the British Medical Association, nurses, dentists and health visitors (Phillips and Dawson, 1985: 193–206). By the standards of codes current among social scientists, the Code of Confidentiality of Personal Health Data is unusually specific in its prescription of procedures, its identification of levels of responsibility and its recognition of the exceptional cases in which personal data may be disclosed.

This greater specificity is possible because in a number of ways the code makers are better able to anticipate the circumstances in which research will be conducted and the particular problems that might arise. The structure and hierarchy of the medical profession and the relationships between groups within it are rather more formalised than within the indefinite field in which social research takes place. Seldom in social research are there established procedures between the various groups who act in the research as investigators, gatekeepers and subjects; in medicine. however, there are already principles of practice which form the basis of such principles for research. The membership of the professional community is already known in principle if not in practice and the sanction of exclusion from it is available in the event of improper behaviour; social researchers, by contrast, are an ill-defined community with several marginal types, no obligation to maintain membership of a professional organisation and no clear lines to draw between the bona fide social scientist and the journalist. Again, the Inter-professional Working Group which drew up the confidentiality code addressed a situation in which contingencies were much more predictable than in social research in which new methods might be deployed, new groups of subjects sought and the field for ever widened; thus it was possible to know from experience what circumstances might arise in which the principle of confidentiality might be tested, such as an order by a court of law or a request from the police for personal data that might assist in the detection and prosecution of crime or the identification of a dead person. We might observe also that there is a tradition of personal authority in medicine that has not prevailed in some of the social sciences so that the researchers to whom medical codes are addressed might be more receptive of some direction than members of an intellectual community unaccustomed to such leadership. For example, it is unlikely that students graduating in sociology would be either called upon or inclined to swear the oath of those entering the medical profession in the terms of the World Medical Association's Geneva declaration:

I WILL GIVE to my teachers the respect and gratitude which is their due (Phillips and Dawson, 1985: 211).

The World Medical Association's Declaration of Helsinki of 1964 and 1975 is one of the most widely cited of medical codes and is to be found reprinted in Reynolds (1979: 439–41), Phillips and Dawson (1985: 212–16) and Downie and Calman (1987: 252–6). It endorses the difference between biomedical research that is diagnostic and for the purpose of treating the patient who is its subject and that which is scientific, the results of which might not be applied to the subject's benefit. The desirability of medical progress is of course recognised and it is dependent upon research with animal and human subjects; but the worthy end is no justification of unworthy means and emphasis is placed upon the comfort and welfare of all subjects, animal and human. The object of the Declaration of Helsinki is to maintain professionally high standards in biomedical research and to set out procedures to ensure these. It stresses the need for competence by experimenters and for scrutiny of experimental design by qualified professionals. The consent of subjects should be freely given in the light of a full and honest assessment of the risks involved. The Declaration calls for respect for the privacy and welfare of research subjects and researchers are called upon to elaborate ethical issues as an element of the research design. The general tenor of the Declaration of Helsinki is to affirm in the case of medical research what is also prior in medical practice – concern for the welfare of the patient. This should never come second to scientific considerations:

> In research on man, the interest of science and society should never take precedence over considerations related to the well-being of the subject (Downie and Calman 1987: 255).

An appealing feature of the Helsinki Declaration is its affirmation of principles of moral behaviour for their own sake. The well-being of patients is a moral obligation of doctors whether in practice or research. It is not commended on a utilitarian basis – as it is in some guidelines for social research – as though to encourage subjects to volunteer for research because they know that no harm will befall them. The Declaration of Helsinki marks a broadening of the agenda of ethical issues and has with other medical research codes been normative in the ethics of social research but it only goes so far. There is a concern for the immediate welfare needs of the subject and the effects of participation upon a subject's well-being but there is no political sense of the consequences of publication except in that the magnitude of risk must be regarded in relation to the probable beneficial outcome. The first concern with the interests of the human subject is exclusive of a consideration of the rights of others such as sponsors who make claims over findings, researchers who invest their careers and those who may benefit by medical advance that affords the alleviation of suffering. The extension of the agenda of ethical issues has come about in the case of social research in which the resolution of conflicting interests has been less straightforward. The principles established in medical research have been adapted not only to the comparable conditions of psychological experiments but also to methods in which the investigator adopts a more passive role, such as interviewing and observation. In particular, the principle of informed consent, the taboo upon invading privacy, the assurance of confidentiality and precautions against injury and distress are widely recognised by social researchers and applied in practice.

One of the themes that has not been much developed in medical codes but which has greatly occupied and even animated social researchers is the place of lying or deception. There have been special considerations in medical practice such as the effect upon patients of information that is particularly distressing and which might conflict with the effect of therapy. Further, patients might not have about them the wits with which they protect themselves when healthy and so doctors might be inclined to make decisions for them and only share part of the full story. For these reasons, paternalistic lying to patients has seemed 'an especially excusable act' (Bok, 1978: 234) and the issue of lying has been skirted around in, for example, the World Medical Authority's 1948 Declaration of Geneva and the Principles of Medical Ethics of the American Medical Association. It has to be added that in recent years there has been a shift toward the telling of truth in medical practice, even in matters such as the diagnosis of a terminal illness (Bok, 1978: 246).

2.1.2 The profile of ethics in medicine

That ethical principles have featured so prominently in medical practice and research is attributable to a number of factors which distinguish medicine from social science and social research.

First, medicine is essentially a practice in the context of a human relationship in which one party is peculiarly dependent and vulnerable. Points of view are not equally valid if one results in recovery and the other in deterioration or death. While social research and the decisions based upon it sometimes have demonstrable consequences of a serious kind, they are rarely matters of life and death.

The serious responsibility which medical practitioners bear has always been expressed in terms of moral obligations. Medicine is a high vocation, transcending partisanship, personal considerations, feuding between nations or in the home, irrespective of all which life must be preserved, confidentiality maintained and honour upheld. Such is the spirit of the oath which dates from the time of Hippocrates in the fifth century BC and is attributed to him. From the fourth century AD it has been obligatory for doctors to take the Hippocratic Oath before entering into practice. In the terms of the Oath the sanctity of life is made explicit and the honour of the medical profession is implicit. Such prominence has never been given to what might be the fundamental values of the profession such as respect for truth.

The high profile of medical ethics has further been maintained, especially in recent years, by the succession of medical advances with ethical implications which have featured regularly in public debate. Being often charged with an emotional dimension they have provided appropriate topics for television debate and have been treated with all seriousness within the medical profession and in some instances by public inquiry. These issues include euthanasia, abortion, surrogate motherhood, artificial insemination, *in vitro* fertilisation ('test-tube babies') embryo storage, the prescription of contraceptives to patients below the age of consent, organ transplants including the possibility of brain transplants and the use of foetal tissues in the treatment of Parkinson's disease. These are issues on which political and religious opinions sharply divide. Pressure groups such as the Society for the Protection of the Unborn Child and opinion leaders such as the Roman Catholic Church have lobbied the public and contributed to the extension of live issues. The appointment of the Warnock Committee which reported in 1985 was an official recognition of the intricacy of legal and moral implications of interventions in human fertility, for which a shortage of babies for adoption made the demand more pressing.

2.1.3 Summary

There are, then, elements of the ethics of medical research and their application which, as we shall see, have been selectively borrowed and adapted in the conduct of social research; in particular, these are the development of ethical codes or guidelines, the quest for professional discipline, the establishment of ethics committees and the inclusion of ethics components in courses that prepare students for practice and research.

It is in the formulation of codes of practice that most progress has been made in the field of social research. However, while professional bodies in medicine may apply sanctions against offenders, those in the social sciences have few such measures at their disposal. The very diversity of social research inhibits the precise formulation of procedures. The ethical education of future practitioners is relatively systematic in medical training at the present time and by the same standards haphazard in preparation for social research. While a small number of the professional associations interested in social research have set up their own ethics committees, the committee practice has also been effective in universities and colleges of higher education in which an ethics committee is appointed to screen research proposals; where there is a medical faculty within the institution its influence may be seen to be normative.

The debt which social research owes to medical research is to be calculated not only with regard to the structure of the model but also in terms of content. The most conspicuous of the principles which are now current in social research is that of informed consent which implies the voluntariness of participation and the obligation of the research to counsel subjects in a comprehensive way. Some concerns of medical ethics such as the stress and possible harm suffered by human subjects and the need to anticipate and minimise this have in the past been considered inapplicable to social research. However, as methods in social research become even more innovative, it is important that the community of social research should monitor its practice against the standards prevailing in medical research.

2.2 INSTITUTIONAL REVIEW BOARDS: THE AMERICAN EXAMPLE

If social scientists have been less conscious and less concerned about ethical issues in research than colleagues in other disciplines, those operating in Britain have been particularly innocent of the issues and free from regulation. Robert Dingwall attributes our neglect of moral questions and regulatory institutions to 'a rather complacent set of practitioners' assumptions particularly in the UK, that ethnography is a priori on the side of the angels' (Dingwall, 1980: 873). It is therefore instructive to regard the operation of Institutional Review Boards which has been distinctive of the regulation of social research in the United States and to assess the appropriateness of this model in Britain.

It was – in the estimation of some commentators at least – the failure of the professional associations that necessitated the federal regulations that brought the Institutional Review Boards into being. The professional associations, including the bio-medical associations, had been unable to convince the public to trust their members or to believe that the associations were capable of controlling their members (Reynolds, 1982: 103). There are inherent limitations in professional associations as agencies of control, especially where membership is voluntary, the sanction of exclusion is weak and the fields of research which they aim to control have indefinite boundaries. They were and are, therefore, poorly equipped to offer the kinds of control upon social research for which a public clamours when publicity is being given to harmful cases.

The purpose of federal initiatives in the United States has been to provide the kinds of protection for human subjects which the professional associations are unable to guarantee. The significant element of these has been the constitution of Institutional Review Boards which control the research in their respective institutions (mainly universities) and to which outsiders may be appointed. Those intending to conduct research involving human subjects must submit their proposals to the Institutional Review Board which scrutinises proposals according to certain criteria, largely to do with application of standards of informing consent, which is estimated to occupy 75 per cent of IRB time (Tanke and Tanke, 1982: 136) and with the assessment of risk. These procedures apply to research funded or contracted by various government departments, which includes some research paid for by private money (Reynolds, 1982: 104).

That Institutional Review Boards (IRBs) have screened only proposals to conduct research for government departments and according to a limited range of ethical principles, however, are incidental to the significant feature of the American model which is the mandatory requirement for the prior and meticulous review of social research proposals by groups that are representative of a wider constituency than the research community. Certain kinds of research are exempted from this requirement: the use of interviewing, in which consent is implicit, and of the observation of public behaviour are exempt except where they touch on sensitive data or where subjects are likely to be identifiable from the record; classroom observation and the use of educational testing do not require IRB clearance, nor do certain uses of data for secondary analysis. There are also certain research activities which are deemed suitable for expedited review by a small sub-committee of the Board: because the list is designed to cover medical as well as social research, it includes the collection of hair and nail-clippings in a non-disfiguring way, the collection of excreta and external secretions, voice recordings for such purposes as research on speech defects, moderate exercise by healthy volunteers and the observation of certain forms of group behaviour where the investigator does not manipulate volunteers. The full list of exemptions and cases that qualify for accelerated clearance appears in the *Federal Register*, 26 January 1981. The effect of these lists is to distinguish research procedures which are safe or relatively safe and they reflect experience of difficult and risky cases in the past.

It is suggested by Tanke and Tanke (1982) that the clearance of research proposals is neither the only nor the most important function of the Institutional Review Board: it must be seen as having a valuable educational role. While the appointment of IRBs serves a purpose in allaying public fears about social research and their interventions may inhibit or prevent some adverse effects, the real value of the Institutional Review Board is in setting and making researchers generally aware of certain ethical standards. They have, therefore, a normative potential: they establish the criteria on the basis of which researchers must proceed if they want the big money from government departments. They are thus likely to be more influential than moralisers in books and journals and professional associations whose lead may not be followed even by their members.

The most obvious limitations of the IRB model are those of practice rather than principle. If they are called upon to control only research for government departments, they will have only an indirect impact on research which is privately sponsored and that which is conducted by students as requirements of degree courses. Their agenda has been as narrowly confined as the public concerns which they were established to allay but there is no reason why they should not broaden their terms of reference to include other sensitive issues such as the invasion of privacy. Another criticism made by Wax and Cassell (1981: 226) is that government may exploit the decentralised model to pass from itself to the institutions the responsibility of turning down otherwise promising proposals: while this complaint may make sense in the American context, there are many social researchers in Britain who are worried about an increase of government control and would welcome more devolved procedures.

The feasibility of vesting ethics committees in British institutions with statutory powers such as those enjoyed by IRBs in the United States is a complex matter, but one worth considering. It may only be in the wake of an outrageous case of harm or intrusion that sufficient public interest could be commanded to support the appropriate legislation. In recent years, the issues that have been more pressing with government departments involved in social research have not been those relating to the interests of the individual but the control of information available to the public: eligibility for funding is in the current economic climate determined not by the satisfaction of ethical standards but by the relationship of the proposal to government policy. When and where external-funding is the bread and butter of institutions of higher education, institutions may be disinclined to appoint boards with the remit of turning down offers of sponsorship on the basis of ethical scruples. This may well be a short-term view and social research, it can be argued, will suffer in the long term if it does not take good care of its reputation.

2.3 CODES AND COMMITTEES

2.3.1 Professional codes

Most of the major professional associations with interests in social research issue codes and guidelines for their members. These documents vary in weight. The Social Research Association (SRA) has produced a 28-page paper which engages and discusses a comprehensive range of problems and includes an extensive bibliography. The Market Research Society (MRS) (1986) has a printed *Code of Conduct* produced in booklet form. The British Sociological Association (BSA) issued a statement of principles in 1973 which was revised in 1982. The British psychological Society has a 'code of conduct for psychologists', which appeared in its *Bulletin* in 1985 and related to professional practice in general, and a more specific statement of 'Ethical principles for research with human subjects' which was agreed at its annual meeting in 1978. The British Educational Research Association offers no code or guidelines although its members are much exercised on matters of principle and, as will be seen below, codes are often developed and applied by particular groups and on particular projects.

There is a common core of ethical issues which is to be found in all the professional codes. This includes access to subjects, the acquisition and informing of consent, rights of subjects such as privacy and confidentiality, precautions to be taken in the interests of the reputation of the profession, obligations to colleagues and sponsors and care to be taken in reporting, speaking and publishing. While the professional organisations which offer guidelines make some statements in respect of each of these issues, they do not speak with a single voice. The SRA addresses the issues in a problematic rather than authoritative way and is studious in its avoidance of easy answers to complex questions, while the BSA and BPS are prepared to express themselves in terms of hard and fast rules, albeit recognising here and there that ideal practices are not always possible and accepting reasonable compromises on the part of the investigator.

Beyond these core issues there are particular problems and emphases which correspond to the type of research practised by each of the professional associations and their members. The BPS statement treats in detail of the hazards of experimental methods which may involve stress or pain; researchers in psychology are required to take counsel from experienced professionals in order to estimate the degree of stress likely to affect subjects and in order to decide whether an experiment in process should be abandoned if this degree is exceeded. This requirement is expressed in absolute terms and it clarifies the responsibilities of the investigator which were thrown into highlight by the work of Stanley Milgram (1974) summarised later in this book (7.1). This exemplary concern for the welfare and safety of subjects is not expressed in the guidelines issued to other professionals in as elaborate a style; this is partly because a more succinct reference serves its purpose where the risks to subjects are not regarded to be as acute and partly because codes are shaped by experience and reflect the cases of abuse or disapproved practice which have happened, rather than those which might yet occur. However, since there is a prevailing (if contested) view that children are particularly vulnerable subjects of research, it is perhaps regrettable that educational researchers are not supported with guidelines of a kind available to sociologists, anthropologists, psychologists and market researchers.

Another variation between the professional codes is explained in terms of normative methodology. The MRS mainly addresses problems which arise in survey techniques and interviewing while the SRA and BSA are more occupied with observational methods, which are attended by a number of particular ethical problems such as role pretence, disguise and covertness.

There are differences too in the rationale of guidelines. Each of the professions uses the notion of professional practice and control to enhance its status and image. None of the social research professions wants a public image characterised by deceit, betrayal, dishonesty, the failure to honour obligations and the inflicting of harm, discomfort or embarrassment upon unsuspecting subjects. The professional associations are able to rally their members around the avoidance of an image of that kind There is a kind of piety in the way that social research professionals view investigative journalism which is clearly not subject to the taboos which obtain in social research. Market researchers are more conscious than others of what they have to lose by a bad press or by being otherwise exposed as dishonest or unreliable: the MRS code is more than others conscious of 'the client', upon whose commissions the continuation of business depends. Market research organisations may compete with each other for work but they have a common interest in enhancing the image of their profession. This is to a lesser extent true for psychologists and sociologists, in whose guidelines the economic factor is less explicit.

Professional codes are also distinguishable by their teeth. The Market Research Society (1986: 23) is able to withdraw the facility and dignity of membership or take other disciplinary action if it finds that a member has in any way breached its code of conduct. The British Psychological Society (1985) enjoins psychologists to report misconduct 'without malice and with no breaches of confidentiality other than those necessary to the proper investigatory processes', The British Sociological Association formerly received complaints to be heard by its Ethics Committee (a function now assumed by its executive); one of the difficulties was that it could exercise no sanctions over non-members except by writing letters of disapproval where it judged ethical principles to have been violated. In cases where an individual has to be a member of a professional body in order to practise a particular profession – such as law or medicine – the appropriate conditions exist for a code to be applied with some force but this is not generally true in social research where clients may commission whom they choose.

Whether proclaimed authoritatively as a 'code' or more loosely as 'guidelines', the principles of the MRS, BSA and BPS are designed to be regulatory: that is, they provide a basis for discipline among social researchers and prescribe acceptable practice on the assumption of a professional consensus. One of the difficulties with regulations of all kinds is that the values which they are designed to protect may give way to the rules themselves. In a particular situation an observance of the letter of the law may contradict its spirit or the spirit of another rule that is also important. Regulations cannot always anticipate circumstances and in this book we cite a number of cases in which there has been a conflict between letter and spirit.

The statement of the SRA, however, is not regulatory but educative: it raises the issues and recognises the difficulties in formulating prescriptive rules to safeguard values such as individual rights to privacy and public rights to know. The effect of this is to place greater moral responsibility upon the researcher who must decide how best to safeguard certain values in the conduct of the enquiry. It is suggested below (4.6) that some investigators take cover behind the principle of informed consent but belie that principle by encouraging respondents to forget the research context of their transactions; an educative code establishes consensual values and obliges researchers to honour these throughout their work.

2.3.2 Ethics committees

Committees which are constituted to regulate social research according to ethical principles are of two basic types. First, such committees are established at the institutional level to maintain standards of research conducted by members, whether by staff or students. These correspond to the Institutional Review Boards in the United States (2.2), although in Britain they appear to be less frequently established in universities and polytechnics than in hospitals (Downie and Calman, 1987: 236–7). As with codes so with committees, those institutions of higher education which include faculties of medicine and departments of psychology tend to lead the field in the appointment of ethics committees and those are the dominant disciplines reflected in membership and terms of reference. By the same token, a useful incidental function of institutional ethics committees has been the development of contacts between disciplines that are able to benefit from the experiences of each other.

Ethics committees of the second type are to be found within professional associations which refer to them various assignments including the formulation of guidelines and the adjudication of alleged offences. The effectiveness of ethics committees in professional bodies is constrained by the factors that also affect the operation of codes, notably the voluntariness of membership and the difficulties of delineating the professional group. Barnes (1981: 19) observes that the former ethics committee of the British Sociological Association had to do with the rights of members as academics but not as sociologists. There were never within that association any successful moves towards ‘credentialism’, or its negative form, professional censure; the British Sociological Association has never offered a certificate of good standing and there has been nothing for a committee to withdraw except membership, which professionals can perfectly well do without (Barnes, 1981: 18). A rather different atmosphere may obtain in other forms of social research such as market research and opinion polling where clients seek to invest in accurate and reliable results rather than – as is increasingly the case in government-sponsored research – results that will lend support to policy intentions.

However, responsibility for ethical issues does not always rest with a committee having that as its principal purpose. In institutions there is often a research committee or research degrees committee to which cases of dispute would be referred and whose members might pick up ethical issues at the screening stage; their prior commitments are to other matters such as registration, quality control, institutional validation and the attraction of funding. Similarly, some professional bodies do not have an ethics committee that is separate from the general council; there was formerly a professional Ethics Sub-committee in the British Sociological Association but its responsibilities have now passed to its executive. The obvious disadvantage with this is that what purports to be a higher level system of control is a less effective one because members are not specialists in ethical issues and are therefore less likely to be vigilant. Against that, ethics committees may meet infrequently and there may not be sufficient special interest within an institution to staff these, so that they may be or have been less effective in practice than in principle.

Ethics committees may be charged with one or more of three major functions, the first of which is screening. Members may review research proposals in order to assess likely hazards, raise questions of which the proposer may have been unaware and suggest alternative strategies to steer clear of trouble. They may exercise this function in an advisory capacity only, as a service to the student or researcher, or they may operate in a system in which no research is allowed that is not properly cleared; in the second case, they may be acting in the service of the institution to avoid the deterioration of relationships in the field that might prejudice those who might want to make subsequent use of those contacts. Screening also provides the opportunity to disapprove research proposals in which individuals have agreed to compromise values such as truth and the right of publication; however, in the present economic climate it takes a courageous moral stance to resist funding on the basis of such principles.

Second, an ethics committee may have the purpose of keeping ethical issues under review and referring appropriate matters to the association or institution in general. For example, the ethics committee of the British Sociological Association (1974) made a special study of the terms and conditions of employment of research fellows, research officers, research assistants and research students and issued recommended guidelines. An alternative strategy for the periodic review of current issues is the appointment of a group or sponsorship of a seminar on an *ad hoc* basis; this strategy was recently deployed by the British Educational Research Association at a time of urgent concern over aspects of sponsor control (Elliott, 1989).

Third, professionals look to committees as the best hope for the enforcement of codes and other principles (Jorgensen, 1971: 19). As we have explained, committees within professional associations have powers of leadership only in certain conditions. However, they may enjoy a different kind of authority in institutions where they are vested with powers of approval and rejection and may have an explicit responsibility to protect the reputation of the institution.

2.4 INSTITUTIONAL CONTROLS

Within universities, polytechnics and colleges of higher education, there operate a variety of controls by which students in the social sciences are appraised of ethical problems and their proposals to conduct empirical work are screened. An enquiry was made into the practice of 58 such institutions, of which 48 responded (83 per cent). The focus was upon the control of educational research but responses were often made at the institutional level and controls had been developed to cover all social research in a number of institutions (Homan, 1990).

Although there were variations in style and emphasis, the pattern that emerged was general. Guidelines operated within the institutions were less systematic and comprehensive than those offered by the professional bodies – except, of course, in the case of educational research; and the practice of establishing codes and ethics committees was rather less standard in institutions in the United Kingdom than in the United States. The colleges and universities which had most formalised their practice tended to be those which had a medical faculty or department of psychology from whom the initiative came. General codes or statements of principle had been formulated in only one in ten of the institutions responding; the same number reported the existence of ethics committees with a general overview; and such a proportion included ethical issues in the methodology components of social science courses, usually only at postgraduate level. In some cases they were the same institutions which had set more than one of these controls in place so that the great majority had none. This is a sharp contrast with university practice in the United States where the existence of an ethics committee is standard and ethical principles are not allowed to elude investigators in training.

The system of control most widely used in the colleges and universities preparing students for fieldwork, whether at undergraduate level or as part of a higher or research degree, was the observance of formal clearance procedures. The common requirement was that before going into the field, even to make initial contact, students should have their proposals screened and approved, either by supervising tutors or by a responsible member of the department such as the Reader. Although departments in the colleges and universities affirmed their confidence in the adequacy of such procedures, they needed to be examined carefully. Like codes and guidelines in the institutions, tutors' declared conceptions of ethical problems tended to be narrow, for example being confined to a single issue such as confidentiality or in one case to the dangers of commercial exploitation. Whether tutorial judgement which is not exercised on the basis of a comprehensive statement of principles is an effective safeguard against offence is questionable. Further, the brief given to tutors concerning the clearance of proposals was seldom expressed in terms of ethical issues; they were primarily concerned with methodological problems such as validity and reliability and with the relationship of the proposed research to existing knowledge. In defence of such a system of control, a number of departments volunteered the information that there had been no complaints in the past which arose from offences against ethical principle. This perhaps highlights the way in which social research ethics has developed on the basis of case law and the difficulty of anticipating offences not yet committed; codes evolve in response to classic offences such as those of Festinger, Humphreys and Milgram.

The absence within institutions of a systematic apprehension of ethical problems raises questions, then, about the wisdom of relying upon the judgements of tutors. It also pervades departmental guidelines, where they exist, and contributions to methods courses. A number of departments issue booklets giving information helpful to students embarking on field projects. These are largely taken up with matters of house style, interviewing techniques, questionnaire design, statistical methods, the use of historical documents, establishing contacts, self-presentation and so on. Ethical issues are inherent in many of these topics but – whether for lack of time or space or whatever – they are begged. Ethical issues are not treated throughout the counsel given to students but, if at all, as a separate topic, selectively studied as the subject of consent or privacy or the rights of subjects. The content of guidance on ethics thus varies from one institution to another.

On the subject of conserving the environment for the benefit of future researchers, departments in colleges and universities usually take an authoritarian line motivated by self-interest. Departments of education, psychology, sociology and others have often cultivated networks of contacts such as schools and hospitals which are prepared to admit students researching for dissertations. The risk is that if a student appears in school improperly dressed or occupies a parking place or chair in the staff room notionally reserved for a resident colleague the relationship will be in jeopardy and that placement may not be available next year. This is a microcosm of the wider world of social research in which the non-cooperation of potential subjects is the sanction that responsible investigators must endeavour to avert. Another consideration in the development of departmental procedures was the need to regulate the placement of students so that particular fields would not be overloaded; some departmental protocols were formulated by consultation or in negotiation with local authorities.

While each type of control has its strengths, it must be emphasised that it is unwise to place all eggs in the one basket. The constitution of an ethics committee to govern research in all disciplines within a university or polytechnic has the potential merit of acquainting researchers in one discipline with the scruples of those in another: where medical research is represented, for example, its highly developed ethical principles may be an inspiration to others working with human subjects who have been accustomed to proceed less cautiously. On the other hand, some ethical principles may be seen as specific to one discipline and not relevant in another: as with codes so with committees, guidelines relating to the use of drugs under experimental conditions and to the safety of equipment may not engage the anthropologist or educational researcher. The norm is for committees established across institutions to meet on a termly basis, or at any rate infrequently; they do not operate to screen all proposals, many of which have an urgency which the ethics committee does not share; its schedule is better suited to advising on matters of principle than in adjudicating proposals.

The inclusion of an ethical principles component in all social science courses at undergraduate as well as postgraduate levels has the potential advantage of exposing all students to the range of relevant issues and of exploring these in a way that is specific to their own field of study. It is desirable that ethical issues should be recognised from the earliest stages of training in the social sciences, as they are in medicine. The constraint of time has the effect of forcing a narrow definition of ethical problems which are then only selectively addressed. This is a particular hazard if ethics is regarded as a separate topic. However, it is submitted here that there are responsible and irresponsible alternatives facing investigators in whatever methods they choose: ethical problems are not escapable and are certainly not confined to celebrated cases that happened long ago or in the United States.

The treatment of ethical issues in undergraduate courses is also desirable as a means of induction into respective professional communities whose codes and principles tend to penetrate only as far as their own members. The appreciation of professional standards is an aspect of professional socialisation which is seriously neglected in the social sciences when compared with other fields such as medicine and law. If undergraduate courses are to be means by which students are introduced to a community of professionals they must feature more prominently the problems which pervade research and the principles in which these are commonly resolved.

However, where departments issued guidelines to their students or referred them to the literature they tended to do so in a highly prescriptive way. If time is of the essence, there may be opportunity only for acquaintance with established principles and not for discussion of them in a problematic way. It is the purpose of this book to broaden the agenda of ethical problems, to re-open questions that in many places have been closed and to discover practices that satisfy the letter of the law and yet are arguably unprincipled; it is to explore the ethics of social research as an extensive subject for undergraduate debate which arises whenever and wherever research is being attempted or assessed.

It has to be recognised that in its current state the literature on ethical issues in social research is unsupportive of more extensive teaching and a more systematic application of principles. The situation yet again contrasts sharply with that of medical ethics where a burgeoning of public interest is reflected in a growing literature. Whereas in the social sciences the application of ethical principles occupies the odd volume here and there (Sjoberg, 1967; Barnes, 1979; Reynolds, 1979, 1982; Sieber 1982a, 1982b), medical ethics is now so developed that books are given to particular specialisms such as health promotion (Doxiadis, 1987), ethical issues in death (Beauchamp and Perlin, 1978) and dilemmas in nursing (McCloskey and Grace, 1981; Davis and Aroskar, 1983). The literature not only informs and stimulates public debate but renders medical ethics accessible as a course of study, both by intending medical practitioners among whom ethics has always been offered as a course or component but also at sixth form level: for example, medical ethics features in the Cambridge board's syllabus for GCE Advanced level Religious Studies. It is for the purpose of systematic study and at such audiences that some of the literature is now pitched (Downie and Calman, 1987). The featuring of medical issues from the earliest stages of medical training contrasts with practice in the social sciences in which it is found that these are introduced if at all only in further and higher degree work, and then often narrowly conceived.

2.5 CONTROLS BY SPONSORS

2.5.1 The case of Camelot

One of the cases most frequently cited in the literature to raise the ethical problems of sponsorship – and government sponsorship in particular – is that of Project Camelot. In the 1960s Camelot was conceived by high-ranking members of the United States army and funded by them to the extent of between four and six million dollars (Horowitz and Katz, 1975: 102). The purpose of the research was to 'make it possible to predict and influence politically significant aspects of social change in the developing nations of the world' (quoted by Horowitz and Katz, 1975: 102). The study was to focus upon particular countries, initially those of Latin America. The research was contracted to the Special Operations Research Office which was located in the American University of Washington DC. The university connection gave some legitimacy to project Camelot although the prevailing view in accounts by social scientists is that SORO was little more than an intelligence agency generously sponsored and at the disposal of the US army (Horowitz and Katz, 1975: 102–4; Burgess, 1984: 185).

To sell the warrant of social science even at so high a price – to the security forces to be used for such dubious purposes is regarded by many as an act of intellectual prostitution. However, few social scientists have been observed to raise their voices against this practice. Horowitz and Katz (1975: 105–6) attribute this partly to the availability of large government grants for research for which those who might want to compete are wise not to damage their chances of success, and partly to the likelihood that most or many social researchers would see nothing wrong in this use of social science research. One of the lessons of Project Camelot, then, is that the effect of competition for funding is likely to be some compromise of ethical and professional standards.

One of the more serious of Camelot's contemporary critics, Herbert Blumer (1967) was concerned with the consequences of the project for the integrity of social science research. He observed that the projects' staff were being used as representatives of their disciplines although, with the exception of critical commentary by Horowitz, 'scarcely any references to the Camelot affair are to be found in the professional journals in social science' (Blumer, 1967: 154). While some leading American sociologists were concerned with the implications of Camelot for the status of social science in the eyes of federal government, its principal sponsor, Blumer was rather concerned with the commitment of those who practised the discipline to the precepts of science: he was concerned less with public standing than with scientific integrity (Blumer, 1967: 56). He recognised specific threats in agency-directed research:

> (1) the restraints imposed on the scientific pursuit of truth, (2) a disrespect of the rights of the human beings being studied and (3) an unwitting corruption of scholars engaging in agency-directed research (Blumer, 1967: 157).

It was anticipated at the end of the 1960s that the effect of Camelot would be to 'divorce academia from government'; there were moves among anthropologists to prohibit fellow professionals from undertaking certain types of government-sponsored policy research abroad. Students on American and British courses and younger academics had expressed considerable discontent with the involvement of their institutions in some forms of government policy; research prohibition by professional organisations and institutions was seen to be a way of ensuring campus peace as well as maintaining academic and professional integrity, albeit also as an infringement on academic freedom (Madian, 1969: 328–9). In the event, those likely consequences have not been realised.

2.5.2 Trends in sponsor control

Research Projects that are conducted by students as part of degree requirements are subject to the constraints of ethical and professional principles according to the extent to which the students are familiarised with these. Students commonly design these projects themselves, choosing the field of study and working out the appropriate methodology. They may need to be conducted on a budget limited by the students' own resources and human subjects may need to be found within the local community. Those practical constraints apart, student research enjoys relative freedom in the subject of study, the research method and the lack of constraint on whether to publish and if so, how. Moreover, doors are open to students by virtue often of their youth that are not open to more seasoned investigators who have grown into a more formal style. For example, the author of this book has recently supervised empirical studies by undergraduate students which involved in one case interviewing AIDS activists, in another observing relations among the homeless through the role of a dispenser of soup and in a third exposure to the recruitment procedures of one of the new religious movements.

In each of these cases the supervisor stressed that he could not have practised the methods deployed by his students. In the first two cases he might have been perceived too much as an establishment figure to develop effective rapport and in the third, he knew that he passed the upper age limit of the target group!

There are, however, other constraints upon the kind of research that is conducted by social scientists in academic posts. These projects have resource implications for which approaches must be made to funding bodies and, as Orlans (1967: 4) observes, 'money does not come free'. Those who offer grants for research have purposes and interests of their own which include a desire to achieve and maintain Public legitimacy, the cultivation of a favourable reputation, a particular commitment to certain disprivileged groups and a vested interest in specific policy outcomes.

Funding bodies are often charitable foundations, sometimes established by individual benefactors and in other cases deriving their resources from industry and commerce. In the United States social researchers look to the Guggenheim Foundation, the Carnegie Corporation and the Ford Foundation, together with others; major non-statutory foundations in the United Kingdom include trusts like Cadbury, Rowntree, Leverhulme and Runnymede.

Apart from certain government departments, the major statutory body funding research in the United Kingdom is the Economic and Social Research Council which was set up in 1965 following the recommendations of the Heyworth Committee on social studies. It was at that time called the Social Science Research Council and changed its name in 1984. It is funded through the Department of Education and Science and is required by Royal Charter to encourage and support work in the social sciences.Increasingly, it gives its resources not to applications for funding made by academics, as it were, out of the blue but to projects which are designed in response to its advertised priorities for any given period. The writing of proposals is a time-consuming activity for those who depend on research contracts and like other sponsors the ESRC has its own form and style. In its favour, the ESRC has sustained the policy on publication set out by its predecessor the SSRC: it encourages dissemination, requires a copy of the study and welcomes a share of royalties but, according to its own statements, it does not require a preview of material which grant-holders are about to disseminate (Economic and Social Research Council, 1984: 10–11).

Elsewhere, however, funding bodies have been tightening their grip upon publication emanating from projects they have supported. Peter Willmott (1980: 9–10) sets out clauses from successive Department of the Environment research contracts which indicate a tightening of controls upon the freedom of the researcher. In the 1972 version it was the intention of the Department that the results of the study should be published freely in accordance with academic practice, albeit after consultation with the Department. In the 1975 version the Secretary of State lays claim to the ownership of results. In the 1977 and 1980 versions of the contract the researcher is required to submit a draft of any report for approval by the Department before publication. Noticing that the trend toward tighter control has persisted under both Labour and Conservative governments, Willmott argues that these clauses 'constitute a severe limitation on the rights of a researcher to communicate his findings, and in that sense represent a constraint on intellectual freedom' (Willmott, 1980: 10). According to these contracts, the only circumstances in which the Secretary of State might want to prevent or embargo publication are those in which dissemination might be judged to damage 'the national interest'; here begins a series of questions concerning the public right to know.

More recently, Nigel Norris (1988) has observed the continuity of the trend toward greater control by statutory sponsors. Projects funded by the Department of Health and Social Security are now subject to the condition that any publication of research material or results must be approved by the Secretary of State (Norris, 1988: 2). Norris goes on to cite the introduction of such clauses in the research contracts issued by the Department of Employment, the Manpower Services Commission, the Health Education Authority and the Department of Education and Science.

In 1988 health and social service researchers protested to the government's Chief Scientist over the new clause and were followed by educational researchers who were gathered by the British Educational Research Association to resist what was perceived to be a threat to academic integrity. It was reported that researchers who had produced controversial findings were coaxed into rewording their reports by civil servants (Caudrey, 1988: 12).

The ethical implications of these constraints are clear. Social scientists are morally committed to the pursuit of truth and the advancement of knowledge. The right of approval asserted by government departments allow for manipulation and massage so that the truth and knowledge derived from the project will either be withheld from public access or else will be distorted. Further, it is critical to the integrity of social researchers that they should not, whether wittingly or unconsciously, be committed to the pursuit of specified conclusions.

The merits of the sponsor system are, inevitably, more easily appreciated by those outside the research community than those within it. Government departments and other bodies dispensing public funds have an obligation not to be wasteful and so take a narrowly utilitarian view of social research. For researchers themselves, other things will be 'useful' than those which are relevant to immediate policy intentions. Work may be useful for the light it throws upon the methods used, for example. Again, some grant-making authorities also operate as agencies for advice: the ESRC is charged in its Royal Charter to provide advice (although it maintains a policy of giving no feedback to its unsuccessful applicants). In the recent financial climate, sponsorship by government and other agencies has been vital to the survival of research in institutions of higher education and many have been grateful for it; but this does not mean that an alternative system of dispensing research funds would not be preferred and many social researchers would welcome the greater independence of official funders from the departments of central government.

First, researchers would desire greater influence in determining the agenda for research. Problems identified by civil servants are not necessarily the priorities of those working within the social science disciplines.

For example, the vogue topics for educational research in 1988 were assessment and testing; in health they were AIDS and community care. On the other hand, there were taboo research topics such as the link between health and poverty. At Newcastle University, Tony Edwards received an ESRC grant to study the government's scheme of giving assisted places in independent schools to children who stood to benefit; he found that the scheme favoured middle-class children, contrary to the government's claims. Edwards noticed an official reluctance to have the scheme independently researched in the first place and a hostility when he released findings. Helen Simons conducted a survey on mother-tongue teaching for young children which the local education authority tried to withhold from the public, including parents. One of the methods used to control the development of research projects sponsored by government bodies is the appointment of a steering committee, even for relatively small-scale enquiries (Caudrey, 1988: 12).

Second, there is a fear that the control of publications and the selection of a few successful applications might be related to a tendency to pre-empt findings, a function which is anathema to social scientists:

> Social researchers should not accept contractual conditions that are contingent upon a particular outcome from a proposed inquiry (Social Research Association, n.d.: 7).

Researchers in the social sciences have considered a number of strategies for survival in this uncongenial situation. They may boycott government agencies altogether. In the United States the Institute of Policy Studies has adopted such a course and the Brookings Institute was prepared to keep government funding to a minimum (Orlans, 1967: 8). That might be possible where there is scope to find alternative sources of funding as from private bodies. It might also be realistic if all those who were eligible to apply for funds were bound by a single professional code, offence against which involved some kind of disciplinary action. In Britain the Market Research Society sets out standards that must not be compromised but its clients have a palpable interest in the same high standards and do not want to invest in research that is unreliable. By contrast, there is no such professional control upon educational researchers: if one institution declines to seek funding from a particular body on a point of principle relating to its expectations, another institution is free to undercut the first and secure the award. What is not sufficiently recognised in this instance is that sponsors, like clients in market research and opinion polling, invest in researchers for the quality of the product and for its credibility. The cumulative effect of accepting constraints such as those discussed here is that such credibility will diminish.

Another strategy relates to the enforcement of institutional and professional codes in the negotiation of grants and their contracts. Institutions are in most cases the official receivers of grants from sponsors. The institution may adopt a code of practice which takes the SRA line on pre-emption of findings quoted above and the grantee may honour a code which does not allow him or her to accept the conditions offered. Again clauses asserting the freedom to disseminate findings will enhance the standing in the research community and the self-respect of the institution which adopts them. Some undercutting of principles may well persist but it will be in the interests of sponsors to seek investment in the more reputable institutions.

2.6 EDUCATIONAL RESEARCH: A CASE OF NEGLECT?

2.6.1 Current situation

Educational researchers have seldom taken a leading role in the recognition of ethical problems. Psychologists, anthropologists and sociologists have always been the more inclined to recognise problems and propose principles to avert or resolve them. In Britain the major contributions to the literature on social research ethics have been made by sociologists and anthropologists like John Barnes (1963, 1979, 1981) and Martin Bulmer (1982a, 1982b). Such awareness has not been achieved among educational researchers: the British Educational Research Association, for example, has hitherto had no guidelines setting out probable ethical issues and commending procedures. Robert Burgess, in whose work on field methods in social research there has invariably been a concern with ethical problems (Burgess, 1982, 1984) has recently collected a number of papers which represent the first serious application of ethical problems to educational research in Britain (Burgess, 1989).

The state of the art at institutional level was the subject of an enquiry conducted in 1987 and reported as part of a symposium at the 1988 annual conference of the British Educational Research Association (Homan, 1990).

As outlined above (pp. 23–27) the study of ethical controls in British universities and polytechnics revealed a partial apprehension of ethical issues and unsystematic structures for their management. Moreover, educational research was marked by a still more haphazard and *laissez-faire* system of control than was to be found in other disciplines, or in similar institutions in the United States and other countries.

If departments seldom addressed more than one issue, they seldom deployed more than one strategy of control, tending to put all eggs in one basket such as the establishment of an ethics committee or the issuing of agreed guidelines. Devolutionary policies, such as the dependence upon tutorial discretion, allowed considerable variations of practice within a single institution which were not balanced by normative strategies such as investment in codes and committees.

Ethical controls of educational research were found to be no more developed by research foundations than by the professional bodies in educational research and by the institutions. For example, the National Foundation for Educational Research in England and Wales has no formal guidelines but expects high standards of it researchers and routinely guarantees privacy to research participants. The Council for National Academic Awards with which many Polytechnic students register their research degrees, issues no guidelines; the responsibility of vigilance is assumed to rest with research degree sub-committee in the polytechnics themselves, although ethical issues are not kept in clear view when these sub-committees screen proposals. For the fuller report of this enquiry see Homan (1990).

In the majority of responding institutions there were reported to be no provisions of any kind regarding educational research and ethical guidelines. A number of respondents reported that the very enquiry made to them had drawn a shortcoming to their attention and action had been initiated. In others, the intention was to let sleeping dogs lie. From one of the universities came the response:

> We have had no complaint in this Department since I came and we prefer therefore to leave matters as they are rather than draw up specific guidelines.

It may well be the absence of complaint or publicised offence against propriety that accounts for the lack of ethical concerns among educational researchers. In modern times it was the indiscriminate use of human subjects by doctors in prison camps that prompted the Nuremberg Code and the notorious obedience experiments of Stanley Milgram that clarified the issue addressed in guidelines current among psychologists. There has been no such outrage in educational research that might have activated researchers to protect the reputation of their profession. The conduct of Cyril Burt might have had considerable influence in British educational policy but it was within the discipline of psychology that his work was done. That ethical principles are not widely established among educational researchers, then, may be attributed to the situation in which so little has yet happened to raise ethical issues as a problem.

However, there is within the labyrinth of educational research one cell where professionals have become extraordinarily sensitive of a number of ethical issues. This is the conduct of action research in the classroom and educational evaluation and this exception to the general pattern may be attributable to a number of factors. First, it is a field in which researchers find themselves observing their own professional type: the research act is thus visited with a good deal of fellow-feeling and goodwill and ethical principles of consent and non-intrusiveness are already established as norms of professional behaviour between teachers. Second, the principles that have been developed are associated with some compelling personalities such as those of Barry MacDonald and Helen Simons who have made their principles the more credible by applying them to their own practice. And third, the momentum for a discussion of ethical principles has been established not by the publication of isolated fragments in obscure journals but in the context of communities of researchers such as the Classroom Action Research Network whose members are in face-to-face contact and are (or were) engaged in very similar kinds of research. The procedures associated with this movement are characteristically 'democratic', afford research participants an unusually high degree of involvement in negotiations and accord exceptional rights of ownership of data; for further detail and discussion, see section 4.3. What is evident from the foregoing survey of initiatives at the professional level and practice in the institutions is that the conscientious principles of the few have not been embraced by the many.

2.6.2 Interpretation

This picture lends itself to a number of interpretative comments. First, if prevention is better than cure, there is a need for the development of ethical and moral principles to serve the particular kinds of educational research that are being conducted. That other fields of research have had to learn from their own mistakes is not a good reason for waiting to do the same. In the 1990s, with the likelihood of accelerating trends in the directions of accountability and litigation, it would be foolhardy not to take pre-emptive measures on the basis of what indiscretions are imaginable. In some respects, action at professional level is already too late. Public sponsors are increasingly calling the tune of educational research and the Department of Education and Science makes absolute claims upon the ownership of data collected in projects it sponsors and controls publication of reports from such projects (Social Research Association, 1980: 13). Such controls by sponsors are seen to weaken the integrity and intellectual freedom of researchers; a possible antidote would be the insistence by professional associations upon certain standards of freedom. Educational researchers have been slower than others in wanting to establish professional standards of this kind.

Second, in the absence of a professional lead of a systematic kind, the agenda of educational issues that is set out in departments of education is strangely eclectic and reflects the influences of other forms of research active in the institutions. For example, in a university with a strong department of psychology, ethical guidelines issued to education students consisted largely of advice about the safety of apparatus. The ranges of what were perceived as ethical issues were variously selective, eccentric and distorted. That ethical guidelines can be occupied with good counsel on the hazards of commercial exploitation without a word about the consent of subjects let alone of the special considerations affecting research with children, is symptomatic of the devolution of the ethics of educational research; individual interests and experiences feature conspicuously and the conception of problems is greatly derived from other disciplines.

Third, in the light of these deviations in the conception of ethical issues, a serious view must be taken of leaving ethical issues to be treated by tutors supervising students' research. If departmental policies and guidelines were selective and unbalanced, it cannot be safely assumed that tutors' grasps of ethical problems will be any more comprehensive. Insistence in highly generalised terms upon 'propriety' and 'high standards' is only convincing if all parties have a reasonably broad view of the possible pitfalls.

Fourth, the definition and traffic of what are perceived to be ethical problems for social researchers has largely come into educational research from other fields. They have imported freely and offered little in return. One of the lost opportunities to redeem this adverse balance of payments has been the exploration of the special issues relating to research with children, whose consent has been either assumed or granted by a teacher acting *in loco parentis*. The selection of information as a basis for consent is adjusted to supposed levels of understanding. While researchers in other fields have endeavoured to apply basic principles with children as they would with adults, educational researchers have at times neglected even to entertain children as participants. The effect of pursuing consent as a contract between professionals may have been to exclude the interests of children, who are equally the subjects of classroom research. This is one of the themes that would need to be prominently featured in an ethical or moral formula addressing the particular conditions of educational research.

2.7 PROBLEMS WITH CODES

The notion of a code of practice or statement of principles which was first explored and applied in medical practice has since appealed to a wide range of professional groups including other therapeutic professions, social workers, lawyers, psychologists, travel agents, estate agents and newspaper editors. In each case the code is introduced to serve a peculiar balance of purposes such as the enhancement of the group's reputation, and guarantees to potential clients as will secure their confidence and safeguards against the need for professionals to compromise the moral principles that they bring from their personal to their working lives. The code is more appropriate in some conditions than in others: if it is to relate to conduct, it can only be enforced if the professional authority has at its disposal some such sanction as suspension or exclusion for example. Again, a community of professionals competing for commissions will have different needs to secure public confidence or comply with the expectations of sponsors from those who act with statutory authority. The purpose of this section is to explore aspects in which the notion of an ethical code does not easily fit the conditions which apply in social research.

First, a code implies some means of obligation to behave in a particular way, not least for the sake of other members of the professional group. That in turn implies that the professional group is definable and that there is a clear line dividing members from outsiders. In other occupational groups the drawing of a line may be possible. Medicine is a relatively autonomous profession with medical education and training confined to identifiable and registered institutions; those training and those entitled to practise are all listed and the entitlement may be withdrawn by the appropriate medical authority. In other contexts a franchise system may be operated to control participation in an occupation; under local by-laws, taxi drivers can only operate with hackney-carriage licences and those so licensed will be vigilant of those who are not. The notion of who is and who is not a social researcher cannot be so defined. Membership of the professional association appropriate to one's discipline is not a realistic criterion since many eminent social scientists have developed their careers without such membership. Undergraduate study in a subject like sociology does not signify entry into the sociological profession but merely the choice of an inspiring subject for a three-year period. Whatever the profession is, it is clearly much wider than the community of those who occupy teaching and research posts in the social science disciplines; there are social researchers who operate independently, or part-time; interdisciplinarity further confuses the issue. Again, there are those who conduct research in similar fields but upon a different warrant, such as investigative journalists; this makes it difficult to apply principles to those who are notionally 'social researchers' but to exempt those who operate in the margins of social research or beyond. At the present time unprincipled social research practice is not regarded as a serious prospect of the order of unscrupulous medical malpractice and so the law of the country does not lend its support to the principles of the profession. Nor are the clients and audiences of social research yet sufficiently attuned to the differences of good and bad practice for the one to be utterly credible and worth the investment and the other to be dubious, reflecting less of an objective truth than the interests of its sponsors and barely worth the paper on which it is written. Such are the conditions of social research in which ethical codes may be of limited utility.

The first problem, then, is that in our field ethical codes have no teeth. Some commentators like Robert Dingwall (1980: 883) have appealed for a code with built-in penalties but this is not feasible unless the sanction of exclusion has more serious implications than a slight stigma among a small group of professional peers. As the case of Boas shows, an eminent anthropologist can be expelled from his professional association for having incurred the disfavour of other professionals and the offence does not have to be anticipated in the form of a code (Weaver, 1973: 51). Anthropology and sociology are not closed shops and exclusion from membership of the professional association does not carry a prohibition upon practice. While at the professional level the enforcement of ethical codes in social research is either impracticable or inconsequential, however, they may be applied with some force at regional and institutional levels where principles enshrined in codes may be adopted in screening research projects for clearance and funding (Schuler, 1982: 169).

A second set of problems in installing an ethical code in the context of social research inheres in its likely aspiration to be authoritative or in some sense final. Individuals are called upon to show a code appropriate respect merely because it is framed in a good cause such as the reconciliation of the interests of researchers and their subjects (Dingwall, 1980: 884). The problem with such a deference to established codes as Dingwall encourages is that it demands an excessive trust in the code-writers for the statement of what is ethical whereas the procedures they do not approve may often be more sensitive of the interests of subjects and of the reputation of social research. A code which is authorised by a professional association may be of palpable disservice in the identification and encouragement of morally responsible procedures.

In the exploration of ethical issues in social research the contribution of a code may be seen to be not so much facilitative as pre-emptive. First, it may, by expressing authoritative resolutions to dilemmas, close a discussion that would have been better had it been allowed to continue. Codes appear at particular times and are often prompted by cases that raise questions in respect of certain issues but those who produce them attempt to be comprehensive and so conclude prematurely questions that have barely been addressed. Howard Becker (1964: 410) opposed the introduction of a code in the American Sociological Association on these grounds, arguing that its effect would be to obscure rather than illuminate issues and pleading with Fredson (1964: 410) for the alternative strategy of a symposium that would afford a fuller discussion of the issues. The periodic revision of codes and guidelines is an effective way of allowing a continuing debate to contribute to the terms in which they are expressed.

As well as cutting off an important debate, codes may also preempt what might have been a more effective system of professional regulation. A compelling example of the deliberate use of a code in this way is the introduction and agreement of a Code of Practice relating to the invasion of privacy, to which the editors of all national daily newspapers subscribed in November 1989. According to the code, newspapers would only reveal private details about individuals if these were of public interest, would allow a right of reply, would only use information obtained by straightforward means and so on. What had concentrated the minds of editors so wonderfully was the prospect of legislation that would secure rights for individuals by means that would deploy legal controls instead of professional autonomy. In a similar way, sociologists in Britain took account of the recommendations of the Younger and Lindop reports on privacy and in the early 1980s there were moves within the British Sociological Association so to put the house in order that the need of government intervention would be forestalled. Such, in some but not all cases, are the politics of professional codes: the formulation of a code is in these instances prompted not by a sudden respect for the interests of subjects but by an urgent need for self-protection.

A third problem, associated with the claim to authority and partly arising from the organisational and cultural diversity of the community of social researchers, is the questionable assumption of a professional consensus. Downie and Calman (1987: 244) doubt whether a sufficient consensus can be achieved for the operation of codes in the relatively cohesive and unified profession of health care, in which authority and orthodoxy are more powerful factors in professional control than in the conduct of social research. While codes can relate confidently and easily to points on which there may be little or no argument – such as the convention that a professor's name take second place to that of a student who is the principal author of a paper – they tend to be equivocal (Becker, 1964: 409) on more complex issues such as the use of covert methods, or else they regulate without recognising the force and value of contrary views.

Fourth, there are hazards with codes – as with other legislative measures – in attempting to enshrine values in the form of rules and procedures. The commandment 'Thou shalt not kill' was sufficient in its day for the protection of life but it needs to be elaborated if it is to be applied in the event of a patient's life being dependent upon a machine. Again, as Bonhoeffer considered in the plan to assassinate Hitler, what if by killing one person we can save the lives of millions? The ethical codes offered by the professional associations tend to be prescriptive of procedures which in some cases contradict the interests they are designed to safeguard. Throughout this book we raise questions about the procedures that have through codes become the conventions of 'ethical' research and we suggest in conclusion that there is a need to recover sight of the values on which recommended principles of practice were founded.

When codes prescribe procedures, they invite practitioners to find loopholes and 'play the system'. The professional formulation of what is acceptable displaces judgement at the individual level: codes can 'undercut the sense of personal accountability and, hence, of the importance of personal integrity' (Payne, *et al.*, 1981: 249).

A fifth and related limitation of codes is that they cannot cover every eventuality , especially if they are formulated in a prescriptive mode, and they cannot offer procedures that will ensure all kinds of desirable outcome. A code of practice may be more appropriate in medical than in social research because a very different epistemological regime applies there and the situations in which professionals may need the support of a code are more frequently and explicitly ones in which received wisdom is being applied:

> Are we to choose the American Dental Association for our model, or are we to choose scholarly and scientific societies? Is the sociologist's identity to be primarily that of one who renders personal services to a helpless and ignorant clientele and whose work consists largely of the practical application of knowledge discovered and refined by others? Or is it to be that of one who is devoted to scholarly and scientific investigation and to

communicating his work to his scarcely helpless and ignorant colleagues? (Fredson, 1964: 410).

Fredson recognises that the code has a place as an instrument of professional control but not in the complex conditions of social research.

This discussion has hitherto assumed that codes have the intention of direct professional control and it is such a function that most codes offered for the guidance of social research are designed to have. However, codes are not necessarily of this kind and the principles of the Social Research Association are an exception to the rule. Roger Jowell usefully distinguishes three types of code. First, he identifies an 'aspirational' type which is a catalogue of ideals to which everybody can subscribe but by which nobody is compelled to abide; it is, in his word, 'ineffectual'. Second, there is a 'regulatory' type specifying in the form of rules what is and what is not allowed: it is, as we have argued above, 'unworkable'. So Jowell elaborates a third type, the 'educational' code, which sets out to inform, is partly aspirational but also recognises conflicts between aspirations (Jowell, 1982: 49). In this spirit, the Social Research Association (n.d.) raises the issues, identifies values and discusses strategies alongside a useful list of references for further exploration.

CHAPTER 3

Privacy

3.1 THE NOTION OF PRIVACY

If dictionary definitions are indicative of current use, it is evident that the notion of privacy which prevails in popular understanding is in many respects different from that which is recognised in the literature of the social sciences and in particular in such passages as are concerned with cultivating a respect for it.

In the *Oxford English Dictionary* privacy is regarded as a state of seclusion or withdrawal from the society of others; it is a spatial concept applied to a private place or place of retreat; or it may denote the absence or withdrawal of publicity. Chambers settles for the same range of meanings and, with Collins, stresses the opposition of the private to the public. *Private* is variously defined as personal, secret and confidential.

One of the helpful features of dictionary definitions of privacy is that they recognise it signifies both a territorial concept and a domain of transactions: this is an important consideration for the social researcher committed to respect privacy, for the concepts of private space and private data will be found to be independent. However, one of the ways in which the dictionaries vary from textbook definitions in the social sciences is in regarding privacy as an objective phenomenon, as though there are recognised boundaries and categories of data which count as private. With the exception of recognising privacy as a condition achievable by withdrawal, the dictionaries fail to acknowledge the occupant of a private domain as the principal agent in the delineation of its boundaries. By contrast, formulations in social science textbooks and codes recognise the variable quality of privacy from one place to another and from one person to another. In Britain it has been customary to regard income as a private matter, along with voting behaviour and sexual activity; interviewers are therefore briefed to approach these subjects circumspectly. In Sweden, however, income is a matter for public information and there is not the tradition of treating it with caution. Similarly, sexual behaviour is an activity which individuals may prefer not to divulge; however, there is a variety of persons with whom they may be willing to talk including general practitioners, counsellors, peer groups and social researchers, each of these with or without the assurance of confidentiality.

In recent years, following an American trend, more people have been prepared to talk about such potentially private matters on television. What is happening is that the boundaries of the private domain are being controlled not by hard and fast principles about what is private and what is not but by those whose privacy is at issue. The notion that privacy varies with the degree of protection or insulation which he or she wants to enjoy is implicit in the helpful definition of Sissela Bok:

> I shall define privacy as the condition of being protected from unwanted access by others – either physical access, personal information, or attention (Bok, 1984: 10–11).

The Lindop Committee, which is thought by many to have addressed the problem of privacy more effectively than its successor the Younger Committee, decided that privacy should be defined

> in relation to a data subject, as his interest to determine for himself what data relating to himself shall be known, to what other persons and upon what terms as to the use which those persons may make of those data (Martin, 1982: 5).

For James Michael privacy is

> the control of information about natural living persons, by those persons (Michael, 1984: 135).

Michael argues that individuals should have the right to control not only false information and unfavourable true information but also favourable true information. Bulmer (1979: 4) and Reynolds (1982: 52) are among those who cite with approval the definition of Westin:

> the claim of individuals, groups or institutions to determine for themselves when, how and to what extent information is communicated to others (Westin, 1970: 7).

This fashionable emphasis upon self-control as an essential element of privacy has a number of implications in the conduct of social research. First, it implies that research subjects be recognised and consulted as the gatekeepers to their own privacy. If individuals are to control access to their own private domains they must know who are those who approach them and what is their purpose. This in turn requires that researchers declare their interests. So it is that the ethical principles of informed consent and openness rest upon the concept of privacy. Of course, it is also arguable that in certain conditions subjects may have no right to exclude access and that the pursuit of knowledge is so desirable that it should not be subject to the whims of participants; the right to privacy is discussed later in this chapter (3.7).

A second implication of the subject's control of privacy concerns the complexities of the researcher's role. In a situation in which there is a stable and generalisable definition of the extent of privacy that an individual may enjoy, the researcher may enter a field knowing the rules. There will be particular spaces that are considered as private such as the bathroom and particular areas of subject matter such as bank balances. The researcher honours his or her profession by not trespassing in this area. However, it may well be that an investigator has a place within the private domain of a research subject by virtue of another role and it is in that capacity that the researcher has been granted admission. The researcher may exploit a rapport established in one role in order to negotiate the boundaries of privacy in his or her favour. For example, Sutherland used her role in the community as a teacher in order to gain access to the closed and highly secretive Rom community in California (Sutherland, 1975: 30). Robert Burgess draws attention to the ambiguities of the role of teacher-researcher: children may trust their private world to a familiar teacher but not want to open it to a researcher (Burgess, 1980: 168). To illustrate the degree of confidence that female respondents may have in female researchers, Ann Oakley reproduces a letter she received from a woman who was concerned about bleeding after sexual intercourse (Oakley, 1981: 49–50); that data are transferable from the role of confidante to that of reporter is evident from Oakley's publication of the letter.

A third concern relating to subjects' control over their own privacy is that it may have the effect of weakening their defences rather than affording greater protection. The subject negotiates the bounds of privacy with a researcher whose training and practice provide experience in pressing the line as far as possible in the subject's direction. The counsel of textbooks is not to take 'no' as an answer and some premium is placed upon data that are difficult to acquire. These techniques are elaborated below (3.5). The point here is to recognise that in the negotiation of the boundaries of privacy researcher and subject will often have conflicting interests and that the researcher is likely to be the more practised and powerful negotiator. Further, when the subject is notionally in control, penetration of the private sphere is effected with the subject's consent; to that extent, what is regarded as invasion when norms are fixed now passes for a legitimised essay into formerly private territory and with the compliance of the subject. When the subject is given notional control over privacy, the researcher revokes moral responsibility for protection. As we argue below, the behaviour of the researcher toward the privacy of the subject may be less moral rather than more so.

Hitherto, this discussion of the concept of privacy has been based upon the subjective quality of definitions that are current in the textbooks. A further limitation of dictionary definitions that is important in recent public debates about privacy and as the basis of professional guidelines concerns its political context. Privacy is not merely the counterpart of a public arena of behaviour but is seen as a sphere of human activity with appropriate rights and freedoms that are threatened by a burgeoning of public or state control. The anxieties that have activated debate in recent years have stemmed from the experience of totalitarian states, both Nazi and communist, from a recognition of the potential of computers to store and disseminate private data and from invasions of privacy by the mass information media (Younger, 1972: 5–6). In a survey of public opinion commissioned by the Younger Committee, the protection of privacy was rated as a more important issue than the freedom of the press; the aspect that caused most alarm was the prospect – as it then was – of computerised storage of personal data. Respondents to the survey had been asked to consider the possibility that data such as family circumstances, financial situation and political views could be centrally stored and the information made freely available: Rhodes is critical of the question for conjuring up 'nightmarish possibilities' (Rhodes, 1980: 117) but such an arrangement has proven to be technically possible and only professional scruples and the Data Protection Act have inhibited the trading of private information.

3.2 PRIVATE SPACE AND PRIVATE DATA

3.2.1 Privacy in public places

The conceptions of privacy which social scientists bring with them to their research are in any case so complex that they defy attempts to formulate simple definitions. They recognise private space in public places. Personal data are not necessarily private data and data acquired in a private setting may be neither private nor personal. The Younger Committee surveyed definitions of privacy in its quest for a workable formula and in the end gave up trying (Younger, 1972: 18).

The delineation of public and private domains was always problematic for ethnologists but in modern times it has been rendered even more complex by the seminal insights of Erving Goffman. Private spaces, we now appreciate, are to be found in public places such as on beaches and in railway trains. After Goffman (1971: 28–61) we must take account of conventions used by actors to establish private territory in places that are in a formal sense public, of the signals used to discourage direct observation and of the adjustments between 'back' and 'front' behaviour according to the actor's understanding of the character and purposes of those with whom the situation is shared. Irrespective of any legal view of what space belongs to whom, the placing of a towel on an empty beach or of a newspaper on a seat in a train are socially acceptable assertions of space, such that occupying a place close to them before the beach or train has reasonably filled is interpreted as an intrusion. There are also conventions affecting the observation of behaviour on beaches. There may be a taboo upon staring at persons who are having difficulty changing clothes in a modest way and it may be expected that other bathers will politely look in another direction until the embarrassment has passed. The implication of this taboo is that certain behaviours in public places are respected as private. That does not stop their being observed by assiduous students of human behaviour such as Douglas (1977) who has produced a detailed account of intimate encounters on a nudist beach in California. In a similar way, Laud Humphreys (1975) studied sexual encounters in men's lavatories or 'tearooms' which he recognises as 'public places'; the behaviour observed, however, is marked by some very private qualities. Both Douglas and Humphreys find a role and posture in which their subjects allow them to observe behaviours that are not made available to hostile observers: Douglas would not have been able to collect his data had he sat on the beach fully dressed with a telescope, nor Humphreys had he not found and assumed the credible role of lookout-voyeur or 'watchqueen'. Even in public places, then, territories are guarded and behaviour may be observable only upon the satisfaction of certain conditions.

Nor are they only deviant groups, such as those observed by Humphreys and Douglas, who display private behaviours in public places. Places of worship are to all intents and purposes public. Many display invitations to enter at times of religious worship and the more evangelistic assure the keenest welcome to visitors. Every evidence suggests to the researcher that he or she is entering a public space. However, religious worship includes a variety of behaviours each allowing an appropriate element of observation. A sermon or address is viewed and the faithful may themselves make notes, albeit rarely of a sociological kind. However, during times of prayer certain postures are encouraged which preclude observation and are intended to enhance the application of the worshipper. Eyes may be closed, silence kept by all but the leader; those present may kneel or lower their heads or crouch between pews, obscuring both their own view and that of others present. In such moments, looking at other worshippers is improper and the attempt to record transactions would, if noticed, be regarded as invasive. The public space of the chapel is thus broken down, if only for a short time, into many private spaces. The welcome is conditional upon a respect for certain norms; the visitor is expected to recognise that some transactions are private and one must secure for them what seclusion one can. In Goffman's terms, preaching is front behaviour and prayer is back behaviour.

It is then instructive to speculate about what kinds of data a social researcher might want to gather in such a situation. The symbolic behaviour by which individuals signify their expectation or desire of solitude might well interest a Goffman. The situation might be compared with a public changing room in a clothing store or swimming bath. The researcher could look for common rituals to establish the boundaries of a compartment and signs that avert the gaze of others. One might study the techniques by which potentially ambiguous messages are clarified or 'defined', as did Joan Emerson (1973) in gynaecological examinations. Whether the research act is to observe interaction during the prayer meetings of a religious sect (Homan, 1978) or consultations with a gynaecologist, the space and the behaviour are notionally private: the place may be public, but the behaviour *pro tem* defines the space as private. The data that are gathered, however, are not personal. Neither Homan nor Emerson were interested in knowing who were their subjects, even for the purpose of checking across files. Nor was Goffman's insight personal or peculiar to the individuals he observed. The data are not about individuals but about human behaviour as a phenomenon. The data collected from private situations, therefore, need not be recorded or regarded as private data.

One of the immediate problems with this distinction between the quality of data and the context in which they were collected is that it may sanction some practices that are widely disapproved. It would follow that it is permissible to eavesdrop or bug rooms or tap telephones as long as it is only for the relatively innocent purpose of studying the number of subordinate clauses in a sentence or some other aspect of English grammar. Before these technologies became available, Henle and Hubble (1938) stowed themselves under beds in student dormitories to monitor tea time conversations that were uninhibited by the awareness of an audience. The spectacle of two mature researchers with clip-boards and torches fearing lest the dust should cause one of them to sneeze is as bizarre sixty years later as it is outrageous. They were not proven voyeurs but social psychologists interested in egocentricity and the offence of their enterprising methodology was in the invasion of space rather than in the plundering of personal data.

In conditions in which subjects themselves determine what spaces and transactions are public and what are private, however, it does not require the stealth of Henle and Hubble to effect an invasion: the risk is that privacy can be more innocently abused. We have seen from the studies of Douglas and Humphreys that subjects open their worlds to observers on particular understandings, in those cases of an implicit rather than explicit kind. Whether the space is public is relative to the definitions of those who occupy it. Vidich claimed that what he wrote about the small town of

'Springdale' was public knowledge there; but difficulties arose because what was public within 'Springdale' was not intended to be public outside it (Vidich and Bensman, 1968: 398–9). This represents a considerable hazard for the social researcher: if ethical principles demand that subjects' definitions are to be respected to this extent, the researcher may be warned even against quoting from printed sources such as provincial newspapers. Younger (1972: 35) and other sources regard unwanted publicity as an aspect of invasion: whether and in what conditions subjects are entitled to be free from it is of course a matter for discussion (see 3.7).

3.2.2 Public behaviour in private domains

So far in this section we have taken examples of social research to illustrate claims to privacy that might be made or assumed within fields that are commonly regarded as public. We now turn to the reverse of that problem and examine briefly cases in which privacy or immunity is claimed for behaviour that is public in that it might be sponsored from public funds or be a matter of public interest. The purpose here is to register a problematic aspect of the claim to privacy which will be revisited in later discussions on the right to privacy (3.7), the case for covert methods (5.4) and the ownership of data (6.1).

The problem arises particularly but not exclusively when individuals are to be researched in their professional role. Although teachers have no right to refuse Her Majesty's Inspectors of schools the opportunity to observe them in the classroom – or else it would be at their peril that they asserted such a right – educational researchers have tended to proceed only with the consent of teachers. This means that they have observed only those transactions which teachers have been willing to share and particular arenas such as classroom or staff meeting may be closed to them. Whether for the sake of educational researchers or government inspectors, teachers are inevitably free to modify their behaviour and to withhold such behaviours as they choose not to expose. Closures of these kinds, upon the undertaking of research *per se* and upon the exposure of normal behaviour once researched, were introduced in studies of policing (Holdaway, 1982: 63) and long-term imprisonment (Cohen and Taylor, 1977).

One of the most fiercely debated of invasions upon the privacy of a public group which was effected in the name of research was the study of jury deliberations conducted some years ago in Wichita, Kansas (Amrine and Sanford, 1956). For this study a judge gave permission for the covert tape-recording of the deliberations of juries in five civil cases; the jurors did not know that they were being recorded until some time after the event and anonymity was protected. Such was the heat of the public debate that followed that a law was passed to prevent such research in the future (Reynolds, 1982: 90n). The debate addressed two ethical issues: first, the right to trial by an impartial jury was held to imply that the privacy of the jury should not be violated; second, knowledge of jury transactions was held to be more desirable than ignorance and conducive to the operation of a just system (Barnes, 1977: 23). Both arguments are pertinent to the problem of privacy. The first may be developed by supposing that the freedom of jurors to speak conscientiously could be impaired by the very awareness that the jury room could be bugged. The second argument invokes the principle of accountability and it may be contended that elements in a public system can be enhanced only by scientific scrutiny. Against that, the American jury system had not been deemed to be in need of review and what could be learned from five civil cases in the Wichita district was not necessarily generalisable to cases elsewhere and to criminal trials (Reynolds, 1982: 91). The justification of jury tapping on the grounds that knowledge is desirable assumes also that the same insight cannot be derived by non-invasive methods, such as simulations of trials.

3.3 DATA PROTECTION

The public debate about privacy which has in its time been referred to the Lindop and Younger Committees has settled on a wide range of possibilities for invasion including intrusions of the home by unsolicited mail and telephone calls, the pursuit of the media, unwanted publicity and the potential of computers to store and disseminate personal data. The legislative outcome of this debate took the form of the 1984 Data Protection Act and addressed the problem of privacy more narrowly by addressing the specific questions of computerised data. International pressure and economic interests were major factors in ensuring that at least this aspect should be controlled in British law. This is recognised under section 37 of the Data Protection Act which notes that Article 13 of the European Convention binds member states to render each other certain kinds of support and cooperation; the Act designates a Data Protection Registrar to furnish partners relevant information about data protection law in the spirit of this Article (Gulleford, 1986: 123–4). The Act is commended as a condition necessary for the exchange of information between European partners and for trade purposes (Gulleford, 1986: v).

It is argued in this section that the Data Protection Act takes a narrow view of data protection and a still narrower view of privacy, anxieties over which it was intended in some measure to allay. Therefore we will not restrict ourselves to a consideration of the provisions of the Act but will treat also of other forms of data protection practised by social researchers; this section has to be read in conjunction with those on confidentiality (6.4) and the ownership of data (6.1).

3.3.1 The Data Protection Act 1984

Even before the 1984 Act there were some legal safeguards for individuals established mainly by case law and there were statutory provisions controlling the dissemination of certain kinds of data. For example, in 1967 the Duchess of Argyll obtained an injunction restraining a newspaper from publishing marital confidences disclosed by the Duke of Argyll (Savage and Edwards, 1984: 6). The Franks Committee of 1972 found over 60 statutory provisions affecting the disclosure of data, but these mostly protected information in the possession of government; perhaps the best known example is the Official Secrets Act of 1911 which relates to the disclosure of state secrets by government employees (Savage and Edwards, 1984: 3).

There is an important difference between these two kinds of constraint. It is in consideration of a supposed public interest that data are designated as secret but it is on account of the rights of and potential harm to an individual that checks are made upon the disclosure of information with which individuals can be identified. The Data Protection Act is a measure intended to control the use of personal data. In its definition of personal data, however, the Act loses sight of the concept of privacy which was so central to the debate which led toward its passing.

If privacy is that sphere in which an individual might want to enjoy freedom from interference, private data would be those data which that individual might not want to be known or circulated. However, personal data are defined not with respect to the sensitivities of the person to whom they relate, but with reference to factors unrelated to the notion of privacy such as the form in which data are stored.

The terms used in the Data Protection Act are strictly defined. *Data* means 'information recorded in a form in which it can be processed by equipment operating automatically'; that is to say, information recorded manually, however private or personal it may be, is not afforded the protection of the 1984 Act. *Personal data* is information so stored that relates to a living individual who may be identified, either from that information or from other information in the possession of the data user. Data cease to be 'personal data' upon the death of the individual to whom they relate. Nor are data classified as personal data if the person to whom they relate is a legal person, such as a company or institution; the emphasis is upon data which relate to individuals (Data Protection Registrar, 1989, 2: 4–6).

Much personal data such as full names, addresses and names of other members of household are thus afforded protection by the 1984 Act; but this protection is pointless because such information is in any case available to the public from other sources such as the electoral register. The Act does not control the storage of much more sensitive information by researchers and others because it allows them to hold private data on handwritten or typed pages or to have the identities of subjects held in such form by an individual who is not the data user.

The Act is supposed to work by requiring 'data users' (who may be 'persons' in the legal sense, including companies as well as individuals) to register and in doing so to declare the kinds of data they intend to store and the purposes for which they will keep data. They may not then use data other than for the declared purposes. Data subjects who are individuals are entitled to know details of entries concerning them, if need be upon payment of an appropriate fee. If the only registered purpose of keeping data is for preparing statistics and carrying out research and individuals will not be identified in any consequent publication, personal data may be exempted from subject access – another way of saying that in such cases data subjects have no right of access. (The Act finds terms that sound very positive and attractive to describe the denial of rights to individuals: it speaks of 'exemptions' to the 'subject access provisions'.) In addition to the exemptions relating to data kept for statistical and research purposes, data are exempted if they are kept for the purpose of detecting crime or are held under legal and professional privilege – a privilege which social researchers have not been allowed to claim. Curiously, a data user is not compelled to disclose data if the disclosure would involve self-incrimination and render the user subject to prosecution outside the terms of the Data Protection Act; and data lawfully disclosed cannot be used as evidence against the user in a prosecution brought under the Act. Further, a user need not disclose data that are held only as a reserve file from which to replace other data should they be lost. Since the Act was given its Royal Assent in 1984, statutory instruments have been introduced to extend this range of 'exemptions'; for example, health data and social work data need not be disclosed to subjects if they are likely to cause physical or mental harm, implicate other individuals or prejudice the conduct of social work. For the exact terms of all these provisions the reader is referred to 'Guideline 6' issued by the Data Protection Registrar (1989), whose authoritative guidelines are published periodically to clarify applications and set out modifications.

The Act affords some protection to individuals by regulating the disclosure of personal data but individuals have no general right against such disclosure. The requirement is that users may only disclose data to those persons described in the disclosures section of the data user's register entry. Even here, however, there are 'exemptions' which limit the rights of data subjects still further. Disclosures are permitted by employers to employees in order to allow them to perform their duties; personal data may be revealed for taxation purposes in emergencies, for national security and for certain legal purposes.

What is evident is that the Data Protection Act provides a number of controls, some but not all of which protect the interests of individuals. There are specified areas in which rights to prevent the circulation of personal data are not respected. Once the Data Protection Registrar authorises the registration of a data user according to the terms of the application, the interests of particular individuals are guaranteed only within the terms signified by the user. Those who place a high value on the protection of privacy may judge the Data Protection Act to be a weak and partial restraint upon the free flow of personal data.

In theory if not in practice the Act is supposed to support the development of a greater sense of professional responsibility among data users. One of the duties of the Data Protection Registrar is to encourage professional self-control in such forms as codes. Since the passing of the Act, however, there has been little response among social researchers, although the Committee of Directors of Polytechnics (n.d.) has issued guidance on implementation. It may well be, however, that the mood among social researchers is on balance to respect a greater degree of privacy than the Act requires.

In the immediate aftermath of the Data Protection Act there appeared an extensive literature that was more of an explanatory than of an analytical or critical kind. The *Guidelines* published by the Data Protection Registrar were supplemented by a number of books that were the products of legal minds such as Savage and Edwards (1984), Niblett (1984) and Gulleford (1986). These are straightforward presentations and elaborations of the Act and the analysis they offer is of a highly descriptive kind: for example Niblett (1984: 133–55) includes a 'Concordance to the Act' from which we learn that the word 'a' occurs in it 363 times and 'the' is used 1341 times:

> The total number of distinct words is 1,287 and the total number of words is 15,760 (Niblett, 1984: 133).

For the social researcher, however, the Act warrants a more critical attention.

3.3.2 Data protection outside the Act

The most obvious limitation of the Data Protection Act is that it only affects automatic forms of data use; researchers or any other users of data who seek freedom from legal control may do so by using manuscript or type-written records. To their credit, however, many social researchers have been less occupied with finding the loopholes that would allow them to take advantage of data subjects than with protecting their subjects by rendering them unidentifiable. Statistics are rounded to prevent identification of organisations and communities. Census officials are charged with the responsibility of concealing the identity of respondents: the case is told of a hospital gardener who tore up the census forms in front of the enumerator, who was the hospital's deputy secretary; the gardener was subsequently suspended from work, but the pertinent offence was that of the enumerator who communicated the information from himself in that role to himself as the hospital administrator (Bulmer, 1982c: 16).

Dalenius takes the view that manual systems are more culpable than computers and is critical of Swedish legislation for its preoccupation with automatic systems (Dalenius, 1982: 27). He advocates a method of protection by 'data transformation'. His idea is to enter data in the form of a code: a doctor may enter a diagnosis S as X and have a formula to translate one to the other to prevent the patient being treated for a false condition (Dalenius, 1982: 30). Where data are made available to more than one user the risk of ignorance of the mode of transformation is of course a serious one and there is a possibility of real data being lost. Where subjects' identities are necessary only for the purpose of relating files, the system of data transformation could have some value: subjects could be given code names, the key to which might be kept in manual form and therefore not subject to the non-disclosure exemptions defined in the Data Protection Act.

Another form of protection, hitherto respected on neither side of the Atlantic, is that of professional privilege. Patients communicate to their doctors, clients to their lawyers and penitents to their confessors on the understanding that these professionals will not be pressed to disclose the information they receive. As Reiss comments,

> in much social observation the only risk that ever exists is a risk arising from the failure of the society to grant legal protection for the information (Reiss, 1979: 175).

Similarly with Jorgensen (1971: 330) it is because American law does not accord privilege to anthropological data that the researcher is advised to use a secret and destructible index system to refer to subjects. Without such an escape, the question is what penalty a social researcher is prepared to accept rather than identify subjects or disclose sensitive data: a recent American book on ethical issues in social research carries advice on 'What to do before and after a subpoena on data arrives' (Knerr, 1982).

3.4 PROFESSIONAL GUIDELINES ON PRIVACY

There are several reasons for expecting the protection of privacy to be addressed in ethical guidelines operating in the professional associations or developed for the purposes of particular research projects.

First, privacy has in recent years been the subject of considerable concern in public debate and the invasion of it has been widely resisted and regulated in fields other than social research. The National Council for Civil Liberties has with other parties been vigilant of the incursions of state and various collectivities upon the domain of the individual. The Younger and Lindop committees have been concerned with aspects of privacy that have implications for social researchers as well as for the collection of data for administrative purposes and intrusions by commercial organisations and the media. Article 3 of the European Convention on Human Rights proclaims a right of personal privacy as a reaction against the depredations of fascism (Michael, 1984: 138). With such a measure of recognition of the right of privacy and concern that it be respected, professional bodies in the social sciences may be expected to endorse the principle and to indicate appropriate procedures.

Second, social research offers considerable opportunity for the invasion of privacy, implying that special care should be taken. Whether or not they first obtain the consent of subjects, those who deploy observational methods camouflage themselves in the research setting and often gain access to private transactions. Carlson (1967: 187) makes the point that interviewing is inevitably, if justifiably, invasive and recognises the principle of designing questionnaires to work from innocuous items which establish credibility to questions on more sensitive subjects (Carlson, 1967: 89 and see discussion following in 3.5). While survey methods based on closed questions to elicit quantitative data involve relatively little invasion, in-depth interviews with extensive supplementary questioning may lead to pursuits of subjects up whatever escape routes they try (Dale, Arber and Procter, 1988: 57). The scope for invasion of privacy in the name of social research is illustrated by a recent study in which children aged eleven upwards were asked how often they had sexual intercourse (Udry and Billy, 1987: 852).

A third reason for expecting privacy to feature prominently in attempts at professional control is that many of the classic offences against notional ethical principles have concerned invasions of privacy. Festinger's colleagues invaded the homes of their subjects; Humphreys and Douglas observed intimate sexual transactions; Kinsey and Hite inveigled respondents into reporting details about their own sexual behaviour: Kinsey's subjects were children and Hite used adult informants to report on the behaviour of their partners. It is not our purpose either in this section or in this book to condemn these apparent invasions. They are cited elsewhere because they illustrate what is possible by open methods and here because they have been the subject of public concern outside the social research community. Since the public image of social research is a palpable motive of the regulation of research by professional organisations the privacy of subjects might be expected to be featured prominently in codes and guidelines.

However, expectations of this kind are not realised: codes and guidelines have little to say about privacy which is barely mentioned, let alone elaborated. While the Data Protection Act has its limitations, it stands out against attempts at professional regulation as a brave attempt to operationalise and codify aspects of privacy for the protection of human subjects.

The statement of principles issued by the British Sociological Association (1982) is in this respect typical: it specifies procedures that relate in a tangential way to respecting privacy but offers no systematic strategy with privacy as a central concept. In the section concerned with 'the interests of subjects', it recognises the variable nature of confidentiality and urges researchers to honour whatever degree of protection they have offered their subjects; researchers should explain to subjects how they came to be included in the research sample, thus declaring sources such as address lists; and sociologists must satisfy themselves of the need to pursue the knowledge that makes claims upon the time of their subjects. In common with other professional organisations, the British Sociological Association invokes the principle of informed consent which assumes that subjects are competent to control their own privacy.

Codes for psychologists including that of the British Psychological Society are more occupied with the problem of physical and emotional harm than with the notion of privacy and protective measures are devoted to satisfying experimental conditions. In the other extreme there exist clear regulations to check intrusion and the disapproval that it is likely to engender: following Younger (1972: 115ff), which identified intrusions upon home life as a particular aspect of the invasion of privacy, the Market Research Society (1986: 13) sets out a clear rule:

> No calls in person or by telephone shall be made to a domestic household before 9.00 am weekdays, 10.00 am Sundays, or after 8.00 pm any day except by appointment.

As in so many cases, the counsel of the Social Research Association is among the most helpful available in code form; it is loosely worded, has the intention not of regulation but of raising awareness and it places the motivations of researchers in the context of other social values and interests:

> Social researchers should be aware of the intrusive potential of some of their work. They have no special entitlement to study all phenomena. The advancement of knowledge and the pursuit of information are not themselves sufficient justifications for overriding other social and cultural values.

What is generally missing from the codes – and what makes the example of the Market Research Society already quoted such a conspicuous exception – is a definition of the ranges of space and behaviour that are to be respected as private. The drawing of absolute boundaries would be difficult partly because these would vary according to other factors such as the type of data sought and the justifications of the pursuit and partly because transactions in relatively private domains have provided some of the most interesting data of social research, to the extent that professionals would not want to establish taboos of this kind.

Instead of operationalising the concept of privacy for the purposes of social research by giving clear – if inevitably problematic – definitions in the fashion of the Data Protection Act, the professional associations have preferred to endorse two kinds of measure which have the protection of privacy as a major purpose. These are the principles of informed consent and of anonymity and confidentiality: neither is satisfactorily effective and each of these strategies raises problems of its own which are discussed later in this book: the reader is referred to the next chapter for an exploration of the principle of consent and in particular to section 4.6 for a critical analysis and to section 6.4 for a discussion of issues of confidentiality. The practice of informed consent, it is argued, shifts from researcher to subject the moral responsibility for delineating the bounds of privacy and for refusing access to researchers: this is especially problematic in view of the relatively powerless role and unpractised negotiating skills of many human subjects and it renders their privacy the more vulnerable. Special difficulties attend the discrimination of whether subjects are private or public: if they are public, it is suggested, they need not or should not be offered anonymity or allowed the privilege of being informed or withholding consent. Without clear guidelines, social researchers may adopt criteria that suit themselves more than their subjects so the American Sociological Association has taken the bull by the horns:

> Individuals, families, households, kin and friendship groups that are subjects of research are entitled to rights of biographical anonymity. Organizations, large collectivities such as neighborhoods, ethnic groups or religious denominations, corporations, governments, public agencies, public officials, persons in the public eye, are not entitled automatically

to privacy and need not be extended routinely guarantees of privacy and confidentiality (Reynolds, 1982: 167).

Such a guideline is fraught with problems and it is perhaps for this reason that others have feared to make such recommendations. In the process of negotiating entry to a research field, privacy, anonymity and confidentiality are not seen as rights to which some parties are entitled and others not but as offers of conditions on the basis of which potential subjects may agree to cooperate; they have a variable quality which the ASA code does not recognise. No objective criteria are offered to help researchers determine how much media exposure is necessary before attention counts as 'the public eye'. Some researchers may interpret the code to signify that an individual who is in a professional capacity such as a public person surrenders rights to privacy in other aspects such as family life. Some religious denominations are so small and so local that the identity of individuals could not be protected if the denomination were named: this hazard has already been proven in the case of the Plainville study.

3.5 OPEN METHODS OF INVASION

The prevailing view is that open methods are more protective than closed methods of a range of subjects' interests, including their privacy. That assumption is explored in a general way in a later chapter (5.5). The purpose here is to assess the extent to which privacy is invaded by means of methods that are otherwise approved as ethical.

Open, unstructured and informal interview styles are said by those who use them to facilitate responses by interviewees who offer to the researcher data that they might otherwise have reserved. An interviewer can by a friendly self-presentation put the respondent at ease and encourage a considerable measure of disclosure. Those who adopt a relaxed mode present its merits in these positive terms and regard with disfavour the strenuous efforts of formal interviewers to establish something called 'rapport' (Finch, 1984: 70).

An early and influential use of the informal interview was by Zweig (1948) who recognised that it would be difficult by means of formal techniques to get intimate details of the spending habits of the poor people among whom he researched. He supposed that a questionnaire on such a subject 'would be indignantly turned down' (Zweig, 1948: 1). Those who might be prepared to record family budgets were not those who came within the field of his study. Instead, this professor of political economy at the University of Cracow and Doctor of Law claimed to have had 'casual talks with working-class men on an absolutely equal footing and in friendly intercourse' (Zweig, 1948: 1). Zweig judged the technique to be 'not unsuccessful'; respondents opened up and declared they had never before talked to anybody about such matters, regarding his interest as a sympathetic understanding (Zweig, 1948: 2).

This conclusion by Zweig is the sentiment featured in the title of Janet Finch's paper 'It's great to have someone to talk to' (Finch, 1984) in which she assesses the potential of the informal interview in the context of feminist research. Finch claims no special skills in easing responsiveness by interviewees but suggests that perceptions were disclosed to her by women which they would not have yielded to a man (Finch, 1984: 76–8). In the course of her doctoral research she interviewed the wives of clergymen – of which group she had been a member – and had the sense that respondents were placing some trust in her on the basis of her identity as a woman.

Neither Zweig nor Finch celebrate the possibilities of their interview techniques as the invasion of privacy but it has to be asked what is happening when a subject is enabled to 'open up'. If privacy is to be defined in subject terms as the space or range of behaviour which an individual asserts for self-protection, we may observe that this will vary according to the degree of charm or guile or the credentials of the interviewer. Having relaxed the respondent into disclosing intimate details that might have been withheld from another investigator, however, the friendly interviewer is free to publish interview transactions as Finch (1984) does and those are available for interpretation by less sympathetic researchers.

Observation has considerable potential as a strategy of invasion, even where the role of the researcher is explicit. The anthropologist Gilbert Herdt spent the night sitting in a New Guinea forest surrounded by newly initiated boys engaged freely in homosexual foreplay. Not surprisingly, he still had with him the odd hang-up from his western socialisation and he felt

> awkward and out of place, more like a voyeur than I ever did, peeping in on a private show (Herdt, 1987: 119).

This was indeed a private domain: it was the secret male society of the Sambia. The Sambia were pleased to have him there because it 'meant status, money, medical supplies and who knows what other riches to them' (Herdt, 1987: 3). Herdt's method involved no deceit. The anomaly of conventional ethical principles of social research is that it is excusable to buy one's way in to the privacy of subjects by making them offers they cannot refuse where as Laud Humphreys stands condemned for repaying his subjects by acting as a lookout and for not telling them that he was also researching.

The self-completed questionnaire and the formal interview are among the most explicit of all research methods and yet they are potentially as invasive as any. In theory there is a safeguard in that response is voluntary but in practice measures are taken to dispose the respondent favourably to the questioning procedure and to cooperate even with the most impertinent enquiries. Respect for privacy implies a recognition by the investigator that there are no-go areas and refusers must be respected even though they have an adverse effect upon the response rate which every researcher wants to boost. Lynda Measor adopts this view:

> If respondents have decided they do not want to tell you why they never married, failed to get promotion, or left their boyfriend last week, they have a right to privacy. It is unethical to poke around the issue, trying to pressure them for the data you want (Measor, 1985: 72).

Notwithstanding, many investigators do poke around and poking around is even regarded in the textbooks as an appropriate skill. Interviewers may establish a rapport and credibility in the initial stages of encounters with subjects and thereby weaken their subjects' defences of personal space. This practice, far from being accidental or irregular, is often commended as a fundamental principle in questionnaire and interview design (Richardson, *et al*. 1965: 43; Gardner, 1978: 47). Students are advised to slip in 'personal' questions at the end of an interview when respondents are worn down, lulled into a cooperative disposition and not likely to upset the whole of the interview by being offended (Stacey, 1959: 81). On the one hand refusal is regarded as a legitimate position and on the other everything possible is done to undermine it. Kinsey relaxed his eight-year-old respondents with games, puzzles and 'romping' before addressing questions about their sexual history (Kinsey, *et al*. 1948: 58).

Indeed, information sought through interviews and questionnaires is sometimes infinitely more private than that obtained through covert observation. Udry and Billy (1987: 852) asked children aged eleven upwards how often they had sexual intercourse. Interviewers walk in where covert observers fear to tread. Hite asked 'as many different kinds of women . . . as possible' in an age range from early teens to late seventies questions like 'could you describe what an orgasm feels like to you?' (Hite, 1977: 401) and 'How do you masturbate? Please explain with a drawing or detailed description' (Hite, 1977: 402). A favoured justification of open questions on such private matters is that subjects are supposedly free to refrain from answering if they so wish but this freedom is belied by the use of practised methods on the part of the professional which are designed to overcome subjects' defences.

The withholding of sensitive questions until late in an interview or questionnaire is widely practised. For example, the questionnaire designed for use in the national survey of 'the Educational and Vocational Experience of Young People' has 36 relatively innocuous items, after which come three questions about the countries in which subjects and their parents were born, how long they have been living in Britain and how much longer they expect to remain (Eggleston, *et al.* 1986: 304).

The survey undertaken by the Linguistic Minorities Project (1983) beats about the bush in a similar way before popping the same questions and provides a good example of the penetration of private spheres of behaviour by means of a professionally acceptable instrument of research. The self-completed questionnaire is used among children in the secondary school. The graphics are in the style of a comic strip and have the possible effect of wooing and softening reluctant respondents. On the last page of the questionnaire, after a sign which says 'Almost finished' come questions which 'seek basic personal information' (Linguistic Minorities Project, 1983: 62) including

What religion are you?
How long have you lived in Britain?
Which country were you born in?
(Linguistic Minorities Project, 1983: 75)

Though less dramatic than Kinsey's preparation of his subjects for private questions, the effect of the graphics is the same and the questions are also sensitive.

A second method of invasion through interviewing is the use of informants who have been unconscious invaders of the private domain. Such a strategy merely passes from the investigator to the subject responsibility for invasion and subsequent betrayal. Once again a startling example is provided by Shere Hite who asked women to report intimate details of their sexual partners, for example enquiring 'Did you ever see anyone else masturbating? How did they look?' (Hite, 1977: xiv).

There is some evidence that in these circumstances children are better able to look after themselves than adults. Here and there are cases of children entrusting to investigators confidences with which the researchers feel uncomfortable, but these are exceptional. Lynda Measor, Ian Birksted and Lynn Davies (Ball, 1985: 43–4) all attest the finding of Fine and Glassner (1979: 167) that children are well able to defend their privacy against the endeavours of plausible outsiders to be admitted. It appears that children have clear ideas of what can and what cannot be transmitted and the interviewer is unlikely within the time allowed to develop the sharing relationship which is the basic condition for disclosure.

A rather different opportunity for invasion is in the use of archive material for the purpose of social research. Archives are documents, usually typed or in manuscript form, which were originally intended for limited circulation which provide a record of part of the history of a family and its members, an organisation of any kind or a geographical area. Photographs, sound recordings, film and some printed materials are also included (Foster and Sheppard, 1980: 200). The authors and subjects of these materials rarely supposed that they would become sources for research. A letter between two persons may have been thought as private as a telephone conversation. In the case of administrative records – which in any case are confidential rather than private – the Public Record Act of 1958 requires that they be made available to the public after thirty years have elapsed. In the case of other materials stored in county record offices and other deposits, archives have often but not always been released by executors and other responsible custodians. Many but not all authors are dead but it is a difficult notion for some to understand that privacy should be honoured in one's lifetime but allowed to lapse at death or with the passage of time.

3.6 THE USE OF SURROGATES

The use of surrogates in research practice begs a number of ethical questions which are barely addressed in the literature.

The distinction is made between respondents and informants. In its general sense *respondents* refers to all participants who agree to be interviewed, surveyed or observed and distinguishes them from non-respondents. In the more confined sense, respondents are those participants who are used for data about themselves which may be personal and of a subjective kind. Respondents to a survey may provide information such as their ages, family circumstances, occupation, daily habits, preferences as consumers, beliefs and attitudes. Informants, by contrast, provide data of an ostensibly objective kind, often in respect of subjects other than themselves. Examples of informants include Russian exiles who give information about electioneering in the Soviet Union (Zaslavsky and Brym, 1978) and former Scientologists who talked to Wallis (1976, 1977) to the chagrin of Gaiman (1977). It is often possible to build up a sufficient picture of a situation from the testimony of a small number of informants especially if the data sought do not belong in the domain of opinion.

Of course, the distinction between respondent interviewing and informant interviewing is not hard and fast. In particular, an interview design can include questions that vary from one type to the other and the role of the interviewee will switch accordingly. It is, however, an instructive distinction in the discussion of ethical issues. In a number of different ways, the researcher may refrain from direct observation and the ethical obligations that attend that method and deploy interviewees as informants who are not compelled by the scruples about invasion and consent that are commended to professionals. On these terms, we may identify three broad categories of surrogate.

3.6.1 Informants from inaccessible fields

First, there are those whose participation implies the unwilling or unwitting participation of others whose behaviour is being registered with the researcher. Those implied in investigations which use surrogates may be for one reason or another inaccessible; the budget of the researcher may restrict travel, gatekeepers may refuse access or political or hierarchical regimes may threaten adverse consequences of participation. Again, they may have chosen to refuse to participate, leaving only the back door open for the persistent investigator. We may consider with these those who are willing but unable to participate, perhaps because of illness or inconvenience, and who authorise proxies to cooperate on their behalf; in their case, the question of consent is not begged but other problems concerning privacy persist.

The ethical problems attending research with subjects of these types is the more pronounced because the research is 'social'; that invariably means that the private world which a particular subject agrees to represent to a researcher involves other individuals who have not been approached. A compelling example already cited in this chapter is the work of Shere Hite who asked women to describe aspects of the sexual behaviour of their partners. That case is outstanding only because sex ranks high in the league of private behaviours but there are many other enquiries in which data provided by willing individuals relate to the behaviour of non-participating groups. Studies of marginally criminal behaviour such as that of adolescent gangs make frequent use of data from particular collaborators and from these represent a picture of norms that are general to the community studied. When Gary Fine (1980: 128) was unsuccessful in his attempts to accompany his young subjects on escapades of 'house egging' (throwing eggs at people's houses) and boy-girl parties where he could observe sexual pranks, he developed a rapport with 'key informants' who were able to give him the details.

One of the hazards of using particular respondents to report on behalf of peers is that it can unsettle relationships within the group or community and result in feelings of betrayal. Furthermore, concern has been expressed over the means by which individuals are persuaded to exceed the measure of cooperation which is granted by peers. Evidently, in the celebrated and controversial study of 'Plainville', 'James West' was prepared to pay some of his informants for their time; although only six of 200 interview subjects received payments, Plainvillers continued some time after the study to voice the criticism that 'West' had 'bought his information' (Gallaher, 1964: 293). Implicit in this criticism is the view common to other groups that a fair account cannot be derived from representative informants whom they do not authorise and Gaiman (1977: 168) makes the same criticism of Wallis for conducting extensive interviews with 'apostates'.

The complexity of this problem is illuminated by the case of Samuel Heilman, a sociologist who was offered a grant to write an ethnography of an Orthodox Jewish community to which, as a lifelong member, he had privileged access. He recognises the difficulty he faced as an 'emotional' one:

> Could I transform friends into informants and my life activity into research data? . . . There was also the question of whom I owed the greater allegiance, the academic or religious community (Heilman, 1980: 105).

The effect of conducting the research by participant observation was to marginalise Heilman within his own community and he reports feelings of insecurity, ambivalence and increased self-consciousness (Heilman, 1980: 106). What was still more painful was the review of his work by a rabbinic commentator which discredited him as an Orthodox Jew (Heilman, 1980: 105).

Whereas 'West' had made flat payments to his subjects at Plainville, the incentive to Heilman was appropriate to his professional aspirations. Its effects were similar in breaking down what might otherwise have been a determination to refuse, isolating the individual from the community and desegregating the sociological imagination and the religious inclination (Heilman, 1980: 104).

The Social Research Association is exceptional in recognising in its guidelines that ethical problems are not resolved by the use of informants:

> In cases where a proxy is utilised to answer questions on behalf of a subject, say because access to the subject is uneconomic or because the subject is too ill or too young to participate directly, care should be taken not to infringe the 'private space' of the subject or to disturb the relationship between subject and proxy. Where indications exist or emerge that the subject would object to certain information being disclosed, such information should not be sought by proxy (Social Research Association, n.d.: 16).

The distinction of this advice is that it relates to informants some of the ethical principles that researchers are encouraged to apply to their own conduct.

3.6.2 Retrospective observers

A second category of surrogacy is that of retrospective enquiry, usually by those who were at the time of the original observation already social scientists or have since become so. To the extent that Heilman was sponsored not merely because he could gain access to observe but also because he could call upon extensive previous experience, his case belongs here as well as in the first category. For the trained and practised sociologist or anthropologist, interpretation is an inevitable aspect of observation and observation itself a habit which cannot be broken. Bruno Bettelheim (1943) could not otherwise have survived his war-time experience in a concentration camp nor George Homans (1946) his time at sea in a small warship. Hospitalised sociologists likewise occupy time in bed by keeping field notes or else reflect upon their experiences in a disciplined way after the event (Davis and Horobin, 1977); the author of this book remembers the Easter of 1986 when all able patients in his ward were allowed home and the ward sister allowed him to have his typewriter in the day room (Homan 1986). Holdaway was initially a police officer in the force he later covertly researched and found himself drawn into the habit of observation as a result of a number of factors including marriage to a social science graduate and secondment to a university course (Holdaway, 1982: 59–61).

There is, then, a well-studied continuum of participant research from the covert and witting observer, to the unconscious observer and retrospective recorder, whose principal reason for not seeking consent was that he or she did not know at the time that observations would later be rendered as data. Retrospective observers include both those who present, interpret and take credit for their own findings – being subsequently, if not before, trained in the methods and sensibilities of social science – and those who present the data raw to investigators. Whether sociological sense is made of experience by those who were there at the time and have turned sociologist or by professional researchers to whom they present their memories does not alter the ethical implication that a situation that was closed or private may be opened and disclosed.

The practical problems of applying principles to guard against the invasion of privacy in these ways are such that they would not be respected. Oral history is too useful and too fashionable a method for a professional taboo to be placed upon it. Social science would have been so much the poorer had Goffman not been allowed to contribute the insights he developed by reflecting upon what he had seen in trains and on beaches. What the issue of retrospective research highlights, therefore, is the importance of *intention* in determining what initiatives can and cannot be regulated. Codes of principles operate only or mainly when a person in a potential field knows that he or she will be used in due course as a bearer of data, even though those data have been borne as innocently as a bird disseminates the seeds of plants.

3.6.3 Research workers

The third category of surrogate includes those untrained or half-trained assistants and collaborators who are involved in social research and undertake aspects of the work which senior colleagues for various reasons delegate. Projects which involve multiple interviewing can, of course, only be done with assistance. Others involve the playing of a number of roles by different kinds of people: it was for this reason that Festinger and his colleagues (1964) engaged others to penetrate a religious sect and Rosenhan (1973) sought recruits to be admitted to mental hospitals. Often participant research involves the playing of a role for which the principal researcher is either too well known or too old; for the second of these reasons, the author of this book could not undertake the kind of enquiry that is reported in *I Posed as a Teenager* (Tornabene, 1967).

Such individuals are surrogates both of the researcher for whom they stand proxy, and for subjects among whom they worked, in the sense that they can report back to the director or project team as informants of the observed situation. The danger against which a number of codes and guidelines guard is that individuals are engaged and sent into the field without due appraisal of the ethical standards which should be observed. The measure advised against this is the comprehensive training of all research staff to avoid dual standards and the use of research workers as sponsored informants.

3.6.4 Conclusion

Whether surrogates are informants from inaccessible fields or one-time unwitting observers now turning sociological evidence or employees or research students engaged to undertake work on a researcher's behalf, the moral problem that persists is that of passing to others the kinds of responsibility that are assigned to social researchers in the codes and guidelines. Social researchers are expected to make their purpose explicit and to proceed with the consent of their subjects. This leaves open the option of collecting data from various kinds of participant who are not constrained by professional scruples. The use of willing informants to investigate otherwise uncooperative communities has serious implications for the subsequent relationships of those individuals with their community; this affects not only interviewees but also those who are persuaded to exploit membership of a community for the purpose of their own social research.

Private domains invariably accommodate more than the single person who has agreed to be interviewed and others are implied in the information yielded. Inevitably, the researcher passes to the subject the responsibility for invading that privacy; the assumption made is that what invasions will not be acceptable to the interviewee will be the same as or include those that will not be acceptable to others within that domain. This assumption may be necessary for operational purposes and prior consent by others who are implied would not be practicable. But it is not a sound assumption, least of all when women are invited by a feminist researcher to answer questions about situations involving their male partners.

3.7 PROBLEMS WITH PRIVACY

The commonly observed principle that the bounds of privacy are to be defined by subjects and not by researchers gives rise to a number of problems, some of which also attend the procedure of informing and obtaining the consent of subjects and are discussed in the next chapter (4.6). The right of human subjects to privacy comes into conflict with other rights such as the right of the public to know. The social researcher will often encounter cases in which it is not possible to respect both the rights of subjects and the supposed public interest and ethical behaviour will involve balance and compromise. Indeed, there may be cases in which knowledge is the overriding consideration and it is not considered desirable that subjects should exercise defences against its pursuit. In practice, however, subjects who are aware that social research is in process – either because consent is sought or because it is conducted openly – hold the trump card in that they are seldom obliged to cooperate. This event is one of those in which researchers may consider the deployment of covert methods.

The right to public knowledge as recognised in social research is significantly different from such a right or interest as claimed in defence of invasions upon privacy made by or on behalf of the news media. In the case of private information disclosed by the press, it is invariably the case that interest is specific to identified persons or groups. It may be of public interest that a particular group of workers is in the habit of taking sleeping bags when on night shift: in industrial sociology this may illuminate strategies to occupy time but we do not need to know who they are or where they work; in the press, however, a photograph may be sought, location may be critical and the significance of the story may be attached to an industrial dispute in which the claims of the union are contradicted or embarrassed by the evidence of the report. Although some social research such as the study of Stevenage planning and politics by Mullan (1980) has attracted a particular form of interest by identifying its subjects, it is much more often the case that the data and interpretations presented in social research reports do not rely for their significance on the disclosure of names and addresses. To the extent that privacy may be distinguished from related concepts such as loneliness and solitude by the notion that it concerns a transfer of information, or the taboo upon such a transfer (Bulmer, 1979: 5), the identification of subjects is a critical factor. Researchers are inevitably witnesses to private behaviour, as are we all in the course of everyday life. Open settings such as bus stations offer a wide range of private behaviour to the casual observer: invasion may be accidental and innocuous and what has ethical implications is not so much the means by which an observer came to be there but what observations are brought away from the situation and presented as research (Lofland, 1972). Similarly, anybody can observe tearoom behaviour but it took Humphreys (1975) to develop it into a research programme and follow-up study which have been controversial not because he invaded tearooms but because he has informed the public on the tearoom scene. It is not who enters a particular sphere that threatens the right of privacy but what comes out of it.

A further problem with the right of privacy is that it is claimed for the purpose of self-protection by those who are not entitled to it and in order to conceal information which is the right of other parties. This again arises from the general understanding of privacy as that area around an individual in which he or she may desire to enjoy protection from outside interest. Those who may be considered unentitled to such a right and whose assertion of it may be regarded as an abuse include those in public office, those engaged in criminal activities and those whose behaviour may have such consequences as a public would want to pre-empt.

Each of these cases is problematic and, as ever, the ethical issue is hypothetical if the subject elects to refuse access. It is widely argued that persons holding public office have no right of privacy except in respect of aspects of their lives in which they are not publicly accountable. The simple form of the argument is that the public which pays them is entitled to know what they are doing. This may extend to others in the public eye who are not paid from public funds: it is argued that since public figures trade upon popular interest and enjoy the benefits of fame, their activities should be made available to the public. In a democracy, Galliher (1974: 139) argues, public officials surrender their claims to the right of privacy (see also Rainwater and Pittman, 1967; Sagarin, 1973). However, Spector (1980: 104) questions whether it is the business of sociologists to make public officials fulfil their public responsibilities and some would argue that this is the function of investigative journalists.

A similar ambivalence among commentators affects the claims to privacy asserted by subjects engaged in criminal activities and those whose behaviour is perceived to conflict with the interests of a wider public. Once again, the moral dilemma of the social researcher is faced less in negotiating access to the private domain than in deciding what can and should be transmitted afterwards. This dilemma is most acute where there is an established consensus against particular behaviours observed in research and where the reputation of research would suffer if witnesses to such behaviour were subsequently found not to have conveyed warnings. For example, there have in recent years been several cases of deaths of children following negligence and abuse by parents and guardians and public enquiries have underlined the responsibility of professionals to report and act upon findings with a view to prevention. The right of potential research subjects in this situation is compromised by the professional responsibility to monitor it not only for the long-term benefit of social and professional knowledge and insight but for the immediate purpose of preventing adverse outcomes in the particular case observed. Respect for privacy, whether by social researchers or by the public implies the acceptance of closed doors which in turn precludes preventive action. The same dilemma on whether to report observations in private behaviour arises where suicidal tendencies are recognised (Dale, Arber and Procter, 1988: 56) and it may well have been possible to predict and thereby to avert the mass suicide of the Jones sect had social researchers been willing and able to disregard that community's claim to privacy (Richardson, 1980; Levi, 1982). In such instances, the right to privacy may be subordinate to the right to know in that friends and family may desire to rescue those whom they judge to be victims of social movements or psychological disturbance and that policy makers are kept ignorant of essential information. It is in respect of such situations that Sudman and Bradburn (1982: 8) point out that the right of privacy is not an absolute right but is relative to the public right to know and Øyen is still more insistent that the protective shield around research subjects 'should not be allowed to introduce serious obstacles to the search for improved knowledge about social processes' (Øyen, 1976: 249).

A final concern about the subjective and discretionary definition of privacy is that subjects are often less aware of invasions than those who research them. A subject observed will be comfortable all the time he or she is oblivious of how penetrating are the skills of the researcher. Subjects do not necessarily feel the intrusion upon their space or know how much of their lives they are exposing. A respondent who unwittingly fiddles with a pen during an interview may be noticed by the interviewer to be exposing some kind of anxiety; one who uses a particular vocabulary may betray to an interviewer a prison or approved school background as readily as others signify a public school education or a career in the army. An ethic which relies upon the sensitivities of subjects to protect their own privacy thus exonerates the researcher who alone may be aware of how invasive an investigation has become.

CHAPTER 4

Informed consent

4.1 THE PRINCIPLE OF INFORMED CONSENT

The essence of the principle of informed consent is that the human subjects of research should be allowed to agree or refuse to participate in the light of comprehensive information concerning the nature and purpose of the research.

The principle has its origins in medical practice and research where it is said to have operated for more than a century (Schuler, 1982: 99); its elaboration, however, may be traced to the Nuremberg Code of 1946 which made provisions governing non-therapeutic investigation of human subjects and reflected concern over research on prisoners of war some of whom, for example, had been partly frozen in the course of an enquiry into the effects of frost-bite. The Nuremberg Code was unequivocal:

> The voluntary consent of the human subject is absolutely essential. This means that the person involved should have legal capacity to give consent, should be so situated as to be able to exercise free power of choice, without the intervention of any element of force, fraud, deceit, duress, over-reaching or any other ulterior form of constraint or coercion; and should have sufficient knowledge and comprehension of the elements of the subject matter involved as to enable him to make an understanding and enlightened decision (reprinted in Reynolds, 1982: 143).

That principle has been widely adopted and adapted in the professional codes governing medical practice and research and social research. In the United States it has the force of federal law which came into effect on 27 July 1981 (Sieber, 1982b: 34). According to this provision researchers must set out the nature and purposes of the research, the demands in time upon its subjects, the procedures to be adopted, any aspects of the research design that are experimental, information about likely risks and discomforts which the subject might suffer, a description of any probable benefits whether to the subject or to others, a statement of any alternative procedures or treatment that the subject might prefer, a statement of procedures to be adopted respecting the confidentiality of subjects and the maintenance of records, a statement of any compensations or treatments that are available should the risks be more than minimal, the name of a contact who may give further information or explain points relating to the rights of subjects and a statement clarifying the voluntariness of participation and assuring subjects that no penalty attaches to refusal. In the United States the regulation of research upon human subjects is the function of the Institutional Review Board within the Department of Health and Human Services and it is reckoned that the IRB devotes three-quarters of its time to issues of informed consent (Tanke and Tanke, 1982: 136).

Elsewhere, formulations of the principle of informed consent have been less specific and demanding and have not enjoyed the force of law. Professional associations of psychologists the world over endorse the respect for the dignity and rights of human subjects upon which the legal principle is based and they acknowledge the rights of subjects to know about likely risks, the voluntariness of participation and the magnitude of their commitment; however, there are circumstances in which information about the purpose of experiments can undermine their effectiveness, so that some experimenters prefer to brief subjects after rather than before the experiment; accordingly, the professional codes stop short of the obligations which are vested in professionals by American federal regulations (Schuler, 1982: 193–242).

Nor are psychologists the only professional researchers who are guarded in their enthusiasm for the principle of informed consent. The Social Research Association in Britain allows that the full version of the principle may not be always possible:

> Inquiries involving human subjects should be based as far as practicable on the freely given consent of subjects (Social Research Association, n.d.: 13).

The Market Research Society requires that information given by its members to human subjects should be accurate but does not specify that it should be comprehensive:

> Any statement made to secure co-operation and all assurances given to an informant, whether oral or written, shall be factually correct and honoured (Market Research Society, 1986: 9).

Such a formulation is a far cry from the rhetoric of human rights which prevails in American codes and regulations. Information here is seen as a means to the end of cooperation and there is an implication that it is variable according to what is required to secure consent. What is more important to recognise than the pragmatism of codified formulations, however, is their relativism. We notice that in professional guidelines the principle is seldom expressed in absolute terms: nevertheless, we find appeals to the principle as sufficient proof of the unethical character of, say, covert methods: Bulmer, for example, disapproves Homan's use of covert methods on the ground that they 'disregard the principle of informed consent' (Bulmer, 1980: 60).

While codes vary between professional contexts and from one country to another, there is a standard formulation of the principle in terms of four 'elements' (Bulmer, 1980: 60; Reynolds, 1982: 8 after Annas, Glantz and Katz, 1977; Beauchamp and Childress, 1983: 70). According to this more manageable formulation there are two elements implied in being 'informed' and two elements that constitute 'consent':

Informed =

1. that all pertinent aspects of what is to occur and what might occur are disclosed to the subject;
2. that the subject should be able to comprehend this information.

Consent =

3. that the subject is competent to make a rational and mature judgement;
4. that the agreement to participate should be voluntary, free from coercion and undue influence.

Simple and reasonable though this standard may seem, there are numerous cases which render it problematic. The expectation of a mature decision may exclude any research with children and the mentally ill. We have to ask whether payment for participation constitutes an improper influence, and where persuasion ends and coercion begins. Some research designs are too complicated for their intended subjects to understand. These and other complications are discussed below (4.2).

How much information is appropriate in any instance is a difficult judgement for those who brief subjects. Many commentators commend a measure of proportionality so that the greater the risk the more meticulous should be the operation of informing consent. This risk may be either that of harm to a subject during the course of an experiment (Schuler, 1982: 99) or a more self-defensive measure by researchers against the possibility of undesirable consequences following research on sensitive subjects. For example, when investigating the initiation of coitus in early adolescence, Udry and Billy (1987: 844) were most scrupulous in visiting the homes of potential subjects to explain their research plans and obtain the written consent of parents: as there were 1405 respondents this was a major undertaking.

Justification of the obligation for researchers to obtain the informed consent of their human subjects are wide ranging from those that emphasise the supposed rights of subjects to those that are prompted more by the professional interests of the researcher or the researching community.

First, it is argued, individuals have rights including the right to know what is happening to them. Article 12 of the Universal Declaration of Human Rights states that 'No one shall be subject to arbitrary interference with his privacy' and that 'Everyone has the right to the protection of the law against such interference'. In the spirit of the Universal Declaration, the American Hospital Association has produced 'A Patient's Bill of Rights' which grants patients rights over information about themselves so that they can give an informed consent to any treatment or procedure and the right to considerate and respectful care (Beauchamp and Childress, 1983: 336–8). When such rights are applied to the situation of social research, they are interpreted not merely as the right to know for its own sake but the right to self-determination and preservation. Some research projects, notably experimental research, carries the possibility that the behaviour of subjects will be seriously changed as a result of participation. The argument for the use of informed consent which develops from a statement of rights gives individuals the choice of whether they want to take that risk: it is a decision which they are entitled to make for themselves. The right that is established in consideration of potentially harmful research, however, may be less convincing where the research is innocuous; it does not follow that people in public places are entitled to give or withhold their consent to be discreetly observed. Further, the right to know must be set against the right not to know. A patient with a terminal illness may prefer not to know the prognosis. Similarly, Homan argued that pentecostals in prayer meetings were entitled to remain free of the inhibition that would be the effect of his declaration of himself as a sociological observer (Homan, 1980: 55). Of course, both in medical practice and in social research there is a danger of paternalism when the professional undertakes to judge what is in the best interests of the patient or subject and the disclosure of information may be the easy way out; this responsibility, however, can be shared if the doctor consults next of kin and the social researcher takes advice from a salient member of the researched community.

If we assert the rights of the individual as a basis for justifying the ethical procedure of informed consent, however, we may find ourselves without a case for requiring informed consent in the research of organisations. In practice, the right of organisations to give or withhold consent is often disregarded by investigators who are prepared to proceed without it (Mullan, 1980; Cohen and Taylor, 1981; Holdaway, 1982); but they do this at their peril and risk professional disapproval or litigation. In these cases, informed consent may be a means of protecting the researcher more than a recognition of the rights of research subjects.

Where professional codes do not commit themselves to more than a loose interpretation of the principle of informed consent – for example, the professional codes of psychologists in Canada and the United States, Germany and the Netherlands which are reprinted in Schuler (1982: 193–242) – they put in its place a commitment to respect of individuals and consideration for subjects. Informed consent is widely supposed to be the practical principle which expresses respect for persons and the implication is that procedures which do not include prior information and consent are disrespectful of human subjects. But informed consent must not be taken as the litmus test of respect for persons, it is argued below (5.5). Covert methods also have an ethical value.

Other arguments in justification of informed consent insist that it behoves professionals in the social sciences to be open and honest, that such a posture is the more likely to generate public respect and that researchers who trick their subjects get social research a bad name. These arguments all have a high moral tone but they ignore how widespread is the use of deception in public and professional life (Bok, 1978). Indeed, even those practitioners who claim to inform the consent of their subjects make some selection of content and to that extent tell only part of the whole truth. The issue is not between telling the truth and telling lies but about where one draws the line to decide how much information is sufficient. What is significant about these arguments is that they are developed not with a sense of the rights of subjects but from a more selfish interest in the public standing of the profession.

Lastly, it is argued that subjects who are not informed of the nature of an investigation before it is conducted will feel alienated or betrayed if and when they discover it afterwards. Or else it is suggested that researchers who do not elicit the consent of subjects render themselves liable for any damages that subjects may afterwards claim. Margaret Stacey reasons the utility of informing consent thus:

> It may be possible to persuade people to part with information for inadequately explained reasons or to mislead them once, but the respondents may discover that they have been duped and will react badly in the future to the same and to other research workers (Stacey, 1959: 72).

So better safe than sorry. We have now reached the point where researchers are operating the principle of informed consent not to protect their subjects but to protect themselves and to guard against the possibility that subjects will claim their rights through litigation. The argument against informed consent will be picked up below (4.6).

4.2 PROBLEMS AND ALTERNATIVES

Implementation of the principle of informed consent is easier said than done: the consequence of the practical problems encountered is that many investigators satisfy themselves with forms of consent that are less than wholehearted. Indeed, it has been observed that if the principle of informed consent were to be strictly applied 'entire classes of experimental and other investigations could no longer be carried out in a meaningful way' (Schuler, 1982: 99). Not only is the design of many experiments dependent on their subjects being unaware of their purpose, but also many designs are unintelligible even to colleagues, let alone subjects, Schuler suggests.

The requirement that subjects should understand the briefing presents difficulties with a variety of human subjects. An anthropologist may have great difficulty conveying the character and purpose of his enquiry to a community which has no concept of social research and will be inclined to resolve the problem with an explanation that is sufficient to justify the anthropologist's conspicuous presence. The offer of material benefits to subjects may also serve the purpose of allaying questions.

The reactivity of information provided for the purpose of consent is a problem not confined to experimental methods. We review below (Chapter 5) a number of observational studies which were conducted without the prior consent of those observed, though sometimes with the permission of appropriate authorities: these include long-term observations in mental hospitals, police work, in a bread factory and in public toilets. The purpose was to achieve a naturalistic view of normal behaviour, not selected by its subjects and not deliberately or inevitably responsive to the eye of the investigator. Not only the fact that research is being conducted but also the statement of hypotheses to be proven or falsified – which the more elaborated versions of the principle require – may affect the behaviour of subjects (Barnes, 1979: 105). Once subjects are led to expect a particular benefit from a course or treatment or clinical experience, they become more likely to report such an effect, not because of the experience itself but as a function of the expectation: this is known as the 'placebo effect' (Bok, 1974; Reynolds, 1982: 9).

The requirement of codes that investigators should indicate to subjects the consequences and hazards of participation is often impracticable because they are not always able to predict these. Stanley Milgram (1974: 193–4) has claimed that he could not have foreseen the severity of the stress suffered by the human subjects of his experiments on obedience. Morgan (1972) was not to know that the factory whose employees were anonymously reported in a paper he gave to an exclusive audience would be identified and publicised by popular newspapers. All that researchers can do is explain to subjects the probable consequences and they are urged also to take counsel from experienced colleagues so that these can be anticipated as realistically as possible: but at the end of the day it will be of little comfort to subjects to know that the harrassment or embarrassment or nervous strain they have suffered was not predicted by investigators.

It might be suggested that the briefing should not focus upon probable but upon possible effects so that subjects are appraised of the worst that might happen. Such a precaution, however, can have an adverse effect upon the response rate. Too much informing of consent can make subjects suspicious that something is not quite right (Sudman and Bradburn, 1982: 10). Eleanor Singer (1978) found that the very request for a signature to give consent affected the response rate and she suggests that if a signature is required it be sought at the end of an interview rather than before it.

Special problems relate to the requirement of consent when the research subject is a collectivity such as a school, hospital, business or small town. The ethics of proceeding on the basis of consent by authority figures without the consent of those to be observed is discussed below (4.4). The practical problem is in obtaining consent from individuals who may be recorded in photographs, on tape or film but may not easily be traced. Similarly, the observation of crowd behaviour, which is of potential benefit in the formulation of policies regarding the support of football matches, would be rendered impossible if individual consent were required from each of those observed. This is a matter of some concern to Reynolds (1982: 9) and the solution may be to waive the obligation to obtain informed consent for *post hoc* research, because there is no claim to privacy in public places or because the unit observed is a group rather than an individual. However sufficient or otherwise are these reasons, there are very few researchers who feel obliged to obtain the consent of crowds.

4.2.1 Alternatives

In some cases such as the census which is conducted in Britain during the second year of every decade (1981, 1991 and so on) the research is governed by statutory powers which deny to subjects the right to refuse. But the Social Research Association (n.d.: 13) counsels that 'even if participation is required by law, it should still be as informed as possible'.

What frequently happens is that researchers occupy the time set aside for informing potential subjects with a highly generalised and anodyne account which is couched in plausible terms and avoids any probabilities that might disincline intended subjects from participating. As Bulmer observes,

> In [open] participation, where the researcher's role is known to those whom he or she is studying, it is not unknown to play down, gloss over or be evasive about the ultimate purpose of the research and its outcome (Bulmer, 1980: 59–60).

Assurances given in connection with government surveys are bound to be vague because data are to be placed at public disposal and those conducting the surveys cannot say in advance to what purposes they will be put (Dale, Arber and Procter, 1988: 57).

Gardner sets out permissible ways in which the purpose of a social survey can be explained including:

> the survey will . . . give residents a chance to say what they think about certain important issues concerning the locality (Gardner, 1978: 36).

In other words the investigator ducks an explanation of what the research is really about and makes out that the survey is doing respondents a favour. Standard practice, counselled by the textbooks, is to use the informing of consent as an exercise in persuasion, presenting the research in its most credible form and avoiding those very aspects which might prompt refusal. So the Linguistic Minorities Project precedes a self-completion questionnaire for secondary children, in which respondents are asked their religion, their country of birth and how long they have lived in Britain with this information:

> This is a project about languages. We are trying to find out how people learn and use different languages and we hope you may be able to help us by answering our questions (Linguistic Minorities Project, 1983: 65).

What passes for information, then, is very often no more than a softening up of respondents and a selection of those facts most likely to facilitate access. This conception of the function of briefing is betrayed in the language used in the textbooks:

> having chosen what group or institution is to be studied, the researcher has to decide what their 'cover story' is going to be (McNeill, 1985: 61).

Another procedure directed towards confidence and willing cooperation – and one which is by no means intended in all the cases in which it is practised – is to honour the obligation of informed consent and then to cultivate a rapport with subjects to enable them to forget the definition of the situation as research. The investigator does the decent thing by fulfilling the letter of the law but the spirit in which the research is conducted is marked by a relative unawareness that behaviour is on the record. This is a legalistic interpretation of the principle of information and consent and investigators take the view that subjects have only to be warned once. The information is brought to bear on the moment of access but has little or no bearing on the subsequent research act. Rose Barbour, who is critical of covert methods, admits:

> Some of my most valuable data have been collected when my respondents have opened up on social occasions, having forgotten about my research involvement (Barbour, 1979: 9).

Two points are worth making: first, the distinction between open and covert methods is possibly no more than a snippet of information uttered at the outset of research and likely to be forgotten forthwith; second, those who take the principle of informed consent seriously must make it clear what situations are to be included for the purposes of observation.

In certain circumstances researchers may decline to give respondents the option of refusal because they trust their own judgement better than that of their subjects or believe that they know their subjects' best interests. This posture of 'paternalism' has been in the past widely adopted in medical practice where patients are prevented either by their condition or by medication from making rational and responsible decisions (Beauchamp and Childress, 1983: 168–9). In the literature of social research the word 'paternalism' is rather less current and the practice of it is much less fashionable but instances are to be found, particularly in research involving children. Children are seldom asked to give their consent and even that of parents is frequently given vicariously by headteachers. The ethics of consent by proxies is explored in more detail below (4.4).

That children are assumed to be incapable of understanding a research problem is only one reason for declining to inform their consent. Another is that the purpose of observation may not be known to the investigator at the time the data are collected. A common practice among action researchers, of whom Lee Enright is one example in many (Nixon, 1981: 37ff), is to write a diary on all that has transpired in the classroom during the day and only later to reflect upon this in search of a focus or problem.

The procedure of recording routine transactions for subsequent interpretation and without the declaration at the time of a research motive is well established in the social sciences and Erving Goffman is of course among its most celebrated exponents. However, the practice raises complex ethical issues. Is the avoidance of consent excusable merely because the intention has not been crystallised? Is any useful purpose served in refusing to admit data acquired accidentally or in innocence? Again, what assumptions are in operation here concerning the ownership of data and the teacher as their custodian?

Reynolds (1982: 34) and others suggest a procedure for situations in which the approval of subjects can be inferred without recourse to direct consultation. The community to be researched may be separated into two groups which are comparable in all essential characteristics but not necessarily of the same size. One of these groups is then treated as a control sample and is fully briefed on the nature, purpose and implications of the intended research. Its members are then asked individually whether they would participate. It is unlikely that the verdict would be unanimous and so the discussion turns to what constitutes a sufficient majority: Reynolds (1982: 34) suggests 80 per cent while Baumrind (1971: 894) insists on 95 per cent. We cannot be sure, however, that the control group will have a sufficient sense of the experience to be undergone by their matched peers; for example, since Milgram could not predict the degree of stress suffered by his subjects, he could not have estimated this realistically in briefing a group of peers, nor could they have understood at a distance what it would have felt like in the event.

There remains the possibility – which in some instances is the likelihood – that consent will be refused. Social researchers prepare for and react to this contingency in various ways. In the cases of large-scale surveys and extensive interviewing, refusals by individuals can be irritating and they can frustrate the aspiration of a high response rate but they are not terminal. Nevertheless, those who conduct research may be trained not to take 'No' for an answer. The refusal to participate is interpreted as a point of failure by the interviewer who is directed to revisit a household where a refusal has been given (McCrossan, 1985: 22–3). So while the principle of informed consent means nothing without the individual's right of refusal, the exercise of that right is likely to be more strenuously tested than the decision to participate. Refusal is perceived as a defensive position that a skilled investigator should be able to erode rather than a legitimate stand that should go unchallenged. Dicker and Gilbert evidence such an attitude toward refusers when reporting their experience of interviewing by telephone:

> only one person of the 27 selected refused to talk to the interviewer because that person said his time was too valuable to spend talking to a researcher. Even this person, with tactful responses by the interviewer, provided a small amount of information relevant to the study before the call was terminated (Dicker and Gilbert, 1988: 70).

One forms the impression that some interviewers have the tenacity of Jehovah's Witnesses.

Organisations may find it as difficult to refuse to participate as individuals. It must not be supposed that long-term observational studies are always conducted with the consent of the management. Simon Holdaway was convinced that if he sought consent to study the police force of which he was a member, it would not be granted: so he proceeded without asking (Holdaway, 1982: 63). In his study of Bishop McGregor school, Burgess was advised that relations with parents were not good and that it would be foolish to seek their consent:

> Mr Goddard (the Headmaster) indicated that if I was to contact the families it was unlikely that I would get their full co-operation. Indeed, he indicated that because many of their children had behavioral problems,

members of the school had often written to them. The product of these contacts was considerable hostility (Burgess, 1984: 196).

Cohen and Taylor, on the other hand, sought consent, acted as though it had been granted, and then had it refused. They had taken up the role of adult education tutors in Durham prison and from that vantage point proposed a study of the experience of long-term imprisonment. This proposal went through all the proper channels and was eventually turned down by the Home Office:

> Fortunately we were able to reply that most of the work had already been done. We are, however, now frustrated by the Home Office's rejection of our repeated requests to visit ex-members of class who are now in other prisons and by their censorship of our letters (Cohen and Taylor, 1981: 49).

Official refusal came too late: the book saw the light of day.

In many of the examples cited so far, the principle of consent has been dishonoured by researchers, either because they have manipulated its conditions or because they have proceeded without it. In contrast, a number of researchers have operated more 'democratic' procedures which we may now examine.

4.3 DEMOCRATIC PROCEDURES

The adoption of democratic procedures and, in particular, the practice of 'democratic evaluation' in educational research may be seen as an extension of the right sometimes allowed to subjects to be informed of the nature and purpose of research and to give or withhold consent. However, a democratic relationship goes far beyond the initial stage of negotiation and has implications for collaboration in the process of interpreting data and for further negotiation up to the event of publication. Consent is perceived not as a one-word and irrevocable utterance at the outset of a project but as a continuous process of review. Democratic procedures accord to subjects rights over data collected from them. This means that their consent is sought not only to allow the collection of data but also to see the data that have been collected and to give clearance for their release. This overcomes one of the problems of the principle of informed consent as customarily practised, whereby subjects may have little idea of what data will catch the eye of a trained observer.

Democratic procedures assume one of their purest forms in the practice of some educational researchers. Their interest is in evaluation, which is concerned with the quality of the educational service including the performance of teachers. Evaluation is distinguished from 'assessment', which is the measurement of pupil performance, although of course this may be taken into account (MacDonald, 1976: 87). In a changing social and political climate in which teachers, like other professionals, are made more accountable to the public and in which parents are entitled by law to choose schools on the basis of available evidence, evaluation of the activities of a school and of the teachers within it is a sensitive matter and methods and manner of publication must be considered with special care. As in other fields, the greater the potential harm to subjects whose behaviour might be adversely reported, the more scrupulous must be the process of negotiation.

The notion of 'democratic evaluation' is attributed to Barry MacDonald who distinguishes it from other types. 'Bureaucratic evaluation' is a process in which the evaluator adopts the values of the government agencies which have control over the allocation of resources. The key concepts of bureaucratic evaluation are 'utility', 'service' and 'efficiency' and its justificatory concept is 'the reality of power'. 'Autocratic evaluation' assumes the expertise of the evaluator whose contractual arrangements guarantee non-interference and who retains ownership of the study. Both forms are likely to be seen as threatening by their subjects who have no part in the vital functions of gate-keeping and interpretation. Although MacDonald does not say so in as many words, aspects of bureaucratic and autocratic evaluation will be recognised in the practice of Her Majesty's Inspectorate. The 'democratic' evaluator, in MacDonald's analysis, is relatively independent of sponsors and aims to provide an information service to the whole community, although informants have control over the information they provide and are offered confidentiality. The key concepts of democratic evaluation are 'confidentiality', 'negotiation' and – because it aspires to address as wide an audience as possible – 'accessibility' (MacDonald and Walker, 1974: 17–18; MacDonald, 1976: Walker, 1985: 86–7).

The principles of the democratic approach are operationalised nowhere more systematically than in the work of Helen Simons (1979). Her contribution is something of a time-piece and issues from the situation in schools in the late 1970s when, in the wake of the Ruskin College speech, teachers feared a loss of professional autonomy and the threatening prospect of accountability. Her response holds good in the 1990s as teachers come to terms with the burgeoning of parent power, the notion of appraisal and the legal obligation upon schools to make public various information about their performance.

Her principal concern is that evaluation should be controlled not by an agency outside the school but by the teachers within it. To that extent, the principles she develops are represented as democratic rather than as ethical but they happen to constitute the same safeguards that are enshrined in ethical guidelines elsewhere in the social sciences. She guards against the intrusion of privacy by insisting upon confidentiality and giving teachers control over the release of data. One of the difficulties in introducing a safeguard in these terms in the present climate, however, is that the right of teachers to withhold information – if it ever existed – has been eroded by the provisions of 1980, 1986 and 1988 Education Acts. When Simons wrote, HMI reports on schools could be treated as confidential but they are now public documents. In her words,

> Negotiation helps to ensure that a balance is maintained between the 'public's right to know' and the individual's 'right to be discreet' (Simons, 1979: 51).

Subsequent government policy in education has profoundly affected that balance in favour of the public's right to know.

Simons is always scrupulous to a fault in matters of ethical principle but in a later paper confesses some of the practical problems that attend such conscientious practice. Negotiations over the release of data frustrate the aspiration to complete a project quickly because each consultation takes time. In the course of an interview, an investigator was prevented from using information which could break the rhetoric or accelerate the interview because it was locked in confidence. Participant control meant that respondents might change their minds at a late stage on what data could be used (Simons, 1981: 46–7).

The extension of the subject's right to give or withhold consent to a point where it constitutes a more far-reaching control of the research is taken on board and implemented by the SAFARI Project and challenged by David Jenkins (1980). Whereas SAFARI takes the view that the obligation of the researcher to the subject is paramount, Jenkins takes the contrary position and gives priority to obligations to the audience, notions of accountability and the public right to know. To the extent that teachers are paid from public funds and have the education of children as their professional responsibility, it is arguable that they should not be given the right to conceal themselves from public scrutiny or be so shielded by fellow professionals who act as researchers.

However, researchers as well as subjects may be held accountable and one of the effects of involving subjects so closely is to render the researcher accountable to them for the data that are selected and the way in which these are represented. That notion of the accountability of the researcher, attended by hazards though it may be, deserves to be considered for application more widely in social research.

4.4 CONSENT BY GATEKEEPERS

4.4.1 Types of gatekeeper

Gatekeepers are those who control access to data and to human subjects. Whether or not the granting of access implies consent to conduct research varies according to the gatekeeper and situation. We may distinguish four types.

First, there are those gatekeepers who control spatial access and perhaps have some kind of right or legal responsibility which obliges the social researcher to approach them in a formal way. The gate is that which opens up the field. In this type belong factory owners, employers and managers, headteachers of schools and hospital administrators. There are also gatekeepers whose position is not empowered in any legal sense but whom it is normal or courteous to approach for clearance: for example, clergy believe they have a right to be consulted in connection with proposed research in their congregations. And there are those whom the social researcher has to approach if only because they hold the keys, in the form of information without which it is impossible to proceed: among this kind are the officers of organisations who have lists of members or address lists or other data which are necessary for the selection of a sample or for the pursuit of subjects. The sampling of subjects may even be a role assigned to the gatekeeper: the Linguistic Minorities Project (1983) involved a self-completion questionnaire administered to children in secondary schools selected for the purpose by their teachers.

From a methodological point of view, the use of gatekeepers in this way has the advantage of being a non-reactive strategy. The researcher fulfils the obligation to obtain consent but it is not the consent of the research subjects, so that the investigation is conducted with the advantage more often associated with covert methods. With adult subjects, there is sometimes but not always a request for direct consent, but this is seldom regarded as an obligation when the subjects are children. Research in schools normally proceeds on the basis of consent by headteachers and sometimes by class teachers but 'No one consults the pupils' (Ball, 1985: 39). Teachers readily volunteer the cooperation of children or invite researchers into the classroom without introducing them to the children in an explanatory way. However conspicuous the presence, the purpose and nature of the research are allowed to remain mysterious. Ball quotes the report of Lynda Measor:

> I asked that no introduction be made about me, I didn't want teachers telling kids what I was . . . What I used to do, I'd sit in the back of the

class and kids would turn round and look at me, girls, almost exclusively girls, certainly at first, and I would make a point of smiling and being friendly (Ball, 1985: 40).

A second type of gatekeeper includes all individuals and collectives who hold raw data sought for social research purposes, whether collected for that or for another reason. Where the information is personal, identifiable and retrievable by automatic means, the Data Protection Act refers to such a gatekeeper as a 'data user'. Special ethical problems relate to the release of data by those who hold them and these are treated in the discussion on secondary analysis (4.5).

Third, there are gatekeepers who are in a position – whether objectively or subjectively defined – to give vicarious consent for subjects deemed not able or entitled to judge for themselves. The standard example of vicarious consent is that which is given on behalf of children by parents or guardians or teachers acting *in loco parentis*.

We noted above (4.2.2) the case of Robert Burgess who conducted research in a school and was given clearance by the headmaster who advised him not to approach parents as there was a risk that they would not grant consent for Burgess to research among their children. This instance highlights two aspects of a more general problem. If consent by parents or subjects is likely to be unforthcoming, the role of the gatekeeper provides an alternative basis for clearance; still more seriously, the gatekeeper's function withholds from subject and parent the right to refuse. The headmaster in Burgess's account did not exercise his judgement as he believed the parents would have exercised theirs had they been invited: he was not honouring their supposed right but advising Burgess on how to prevent them from obstructing his research. A second aspect is that the head gave Burgess not only spatial access to the school but consent to observe teaching colleagues whose own views were pre-empted by the decision of the headmaster. Witness to gatekeepers' pre-emption of subjects' consent is not peculiar to the experience of Burgess. Reflecting upon his research of health visitor training, Dingwall observes that in hierarchical institutions consent is often given by senior personnel and subordinates cannot withhold their own consent without incurring the disfavour of seniors (Dingwall, 1980: 878). Dingwall takes the view that 'only senior personnel can be genuinely said to be in a position to give free consent' and reports,

Several students told me later that they realised on the first day that they were not free to say 'no' and that it would probably not make much difference if they did (Payne, *et al.*, 1981: 248).

While it could be thought that employers and managers act as gatekeepers only in the sense of giving spatial access and not in giving the consent of employees to be observed or interviewed, therefore, this assumed principle may not prevail in practice.

A fourth type of intermediary between researcher and subjects is the associate who is engaged to introduce the research task and purpose either to those who exercise the right to give clearance or to the subjects themselves. Warwick proposes such a role in order that subjects who are illiterate or who cannot understand the nature or purpose of proposed research should have it expressed in intelligible terms and he designates such an associate as 'cultural interpreter' (Warwick, 1983: 327). The function is particularly useful in cross-cultural studies. As an agent in the acquisition of consent, we may distinguish the cultural interpreter from other gatekeepers in that his or her influence emanates – in Weber's terms – not from traditional but from charismatic authority. The person may be bilingual or may be peculiarly competent for the task of persuasion by sharing both in the value system of the subject community and in the aims and purposes of social research. For example, a school teacher taking a degree course in a university or polytechnic may be asked by a tutor on the course whether that teacher's school would cooperate in a proposed research project and the teacher agrees to ask colleagues in the school. Bearing upon this are the aspects of favour and authority which haunt consent at many levels and perhaps belie the notion of its voluntariness. Colleagues in the school may for personal reasons want to be helpful to the teacher involved and as a favour to their colleague agree to respond to the research project. The likelihood is that intermediaries of this kind will be chosen not only because they can present the proposed research in an intelligible way but because they will do so sympathetically and assure subjects of its good intentions and relative harmlessness.

4.4.2 Ethics of gatekeeping

The use of gatekeepers is barely countenanced in professional codes and guidelines, except for the purpose of research with children and with subjects whose capacities of judgement are diminished. The ethical principles of the British Sociological Association (1982: 2) provide for the explanation of research to facilitators and subjects, so that consent by one party does not remove the obligation to consult the other. In the same way the British Psychological Society (1985: 41) requires the valid consent of 'participants'. Special provision is made in respect of subjects whose capacities to give valid consent are impaired, including the young, the mentally handicapped, the elderly, those in the care of an institution and those detained under the provision of the law: in their cases, psychologists must respect their rights, take proper advice on who has the authority to give their consent and obtain this before proceeding (British Psychological Society, 1985: 42). The *Code of Conduct* of the Market Research

Society (1986: 13–14) treats of the particular case of children under fourteen years and sets out the information that must be made available before consent is given on their behalf; but it leaves the researcher free to obtain consent from either a parent, guardian or other responsible person and we have seen above (4.4.1) from the experience of Burgess the danger of such flexibility.

The possibilities of playing off gatekeepers against each other and of gatekeepers acting in their own interests rather than of subjects raise serious questions over the ethics of obtaining consent from second parties. In the debate about biomedical ethics, Paul Ramsey has argued that irrespective of considerations of benefit and harm, we should never allow children to be used in non-therapeutic research because they cannot give valid consent for themselves. For Ramsey, respect for persons is the over-riding consideration (Beauchamp and Childress, 1983: 7). The forms of social research in which Ramsey's view has most force are those in which the subject may endure pain or discomfort or be visited by adverse after-effects or may have a deserved rest disturbed and privacy invaded by an interviewer at the side of a deathbed. Some educational research which involves unobtrusive observation and anonymous recording or the testing of aptitudes and achievements would cause less anxiety among parents and the researching community. There may therefore be a case not for blanket guidelines on second-party consent but on determining what kinds of research are appropriate for clearance by professionals and other parties.

Much of what we have discussed so far has been about the excessive powers of various kinds of gatekeeper and the arguments made have suggested that those powers should be checked. However, what has caused the greater excitement among researchers as well as those in authority has been the by-passing of gatekeeper consent. The prison research of Cohen and Taylor was subject to a long period of negotiation with the Home Office with various strategies being assayed to prevent the research being conducted and published. Cohen and Taylor (1977) present their gatekeepers as the nasties in their story. These arose from a disapproval of social science as the method of research and included an attempt to discredit findings which Cohen and Taylor (1977: 79) refer to as 'anticipatory censorship'. The Home Office issued advice that 'this is not proper research' and tried to pre-empt findings with the assurance that 'things are changing anyway'. Later, it took a different tack by expressing anxieties for the investigators' safety (Cohen and Taylor, 1977: 80). When their book appeared in paperback, the *Times Literary Supplement* reviewer commented,

> It is possible that there are some in the Prison Department who may cherish the hope that this little Penguin will waddle off into obscurity (Cohen and Taylor, 1977: 81).

Others have heeded the obstructiveness of gatekeepers and decided to get by without it. Holdaway did not ask for official approval by the police among whom he researched because he was convinced that it would not be given if the nature of his research was declared (Holdaway, 1982: 63).

Mullan (1980) went still further in by-passing the custodians of confidential records. He found that the principle of confidentiality was used to block the access of a researcher to sources of information which he judged in his case to be indispensable. His study of local planning and politics over the first thirty years of Stevenage New Town was of a public organisation and his subjects were public servants. To that extent the public right to know might have been more cogently argued in such a study as Mullan's than in a study of a spiritualist sect or a bread factory. For eighteen months Mullan made use of overt interviews, official statistics and other materials on public access but he believed that he needed to get beyond the surface of things (Mullan, 1980: xiv). In particular he wanted access to minutes which were of two kinds, confidential and very confidential: from its earliest days the Corporation Board of Stevenage had kept a 'private minute book' for the purpose of recording 'particularly confidential matters' (Mullan, 1980: 335). Mullan's applications to see these minutes were refused within Stevenage so he appealed to the Department of the Environment; this appeal was both unsuccessful and resented by the corporation's General Manager who reminded Mullan that he had been given a great deal of help – which Mullan acknowledges – and this appeal over the heads of local officers was 'a rather poor way of saying thank you' (Mullan, 1980: xv).

A number of ethical questions arise at this stage of research. It is widely recognised that powerful groups can use the principle of confidentiality to protect themselves. Arguably the public right to know is more compelling than the right of public servants to conceal. If minutes are made private in order to exclude those who might want to scrutinise a committee's motives and interest, the case for public access becomes more persuasive; if, however, they are private because they contain details of individuals' income, health and family history which a committee might need to consider when allocating housing, it is right that information obtained by the committee under the cover of confidentiality should not then be disclosed. Unless and until we know the content of minutes and the reasons for their being locked into confidentiality, we cannot judge how just is the refusal of access. It is still more difficult for a researcher with eighteen months of fieldwork behind him to find the development of his project stymied by a decision of this kind.

In the absence of permission Mullan decided to obtain a view of the confidential minutes and through a number of sources he was able to see the Corporation's full set of minutes, though not the 'private minute book' (Mullan, 1980: xiv, 335). For Mullan, it was the value of the data he sought that justified the course he took:

It is my opinion that the nature of the information contained in the minutes is of such value, particularly in relation to the central factor of the housing allocation process, that the use of it outweighs any other considerations (Mullan, 1980: xv).

4.5 SECONDARY ANALYSIS

4.5.1 Sources of secondary data

Special considerations are necessary in the case of data which are collected and stored for certain purposes and by particular parties and are then put at the disposal of others, whose interest may not be anticipated either by investigators or by respondents at the time of the original enquiry.

There are various kinds of data available for secondary analysis. In Britain there are two principal sources of data which are collected under statutory powers which give respondents no option of consent and are widely used in the course of social research. One of these is the official census which is conducted once every ten years and includes a battery of questions about personal circumstances; data are sought for administrative purposes and are used to inform government policy, so that the questions asked change from one census to another. The other is the electoral register compiled for the purpose of the franchise but made publicly available and widely used as well by marketing agencies as for social research. Archives held in public and county record offices provide a rich source of raw data; personal correspondence, minute books, account books and wills find their way into record offices, more often by consent of a custodian of papers than by consent of the individuals whose personal data are recorded in them. Further, raw data are collected, stored and sometimes published in the course of one research project and made available to subsequent researchers who may wish to extend the analysis or offer a reinterpretation; this practice is in part an aspect of the accountability of researchers since it exposes them to scrutiny and is a safeguard against the possibility of subjects considering that they have been unfairly represented. Had not access been given to his original data, Sir Cyril Burt might never have been discredited (Wade, 1976).

Discussion of ethical issues in secondary analysis must take account also of types of data which are not currently available but which, according to some points of view, should be. As is so often the case, the challenge to conventional ethical principles begins with an example from medical practice: while consultations between patients and medical practitioners must be regarded as utterly confidential, it was only by the willingness of some doctors to represent their findings in statistical form to medical researchers that a connection between cigarette smoking and lung cancer was discovered. Hartley (1982: 179) observes that in the United States there are over 1000 million medical consultations per annum which are recorded confidentially and for other purposes than research; these constitute an enormous source of potential public benefit to show, for example, the social and geographical distribution of particular disorders. The magnitude of such a benefit puts to a severe test scruples about privacy and consent, especially if it is possible to represent data in statistical form without divulging the identities of subjects. The case for greater access to health records may by the same arguments be extended to apply to other kinds of information such as records of educational achievement, and records of law courts, probation services, welfare agencies and so on.

Although procedures for access to records are often complicated and there are senses in which secondary analysis may be less satisfying than research with live subjects and procedures in which the researcher may take credit as well for the collection of data as for their interpretation, there are several methodological attractions. A major advantage is that the costs of data collection will in most cases already have been borne; if this has necessitated fieldwork, it will constitute a considerable saving. It happens that those able to afford to commission pollsters do not necessarily want or need to make the fullest use of their data; national newspapers, for example, select newsworthy items from opinion surveys for immediate publication and may be prepared to place the full computer print-out at the disposal of research students. What is saved in financial terms is matched by a saving in time; as well as enabling the investigator to proceed straight to stage two or three, subjects are spared having to give further interviews. Another advantage recognised by Reynolds (1979: 215) is that data are not disturbed by the process of collection: there is nothing reactive, for example, in the consultation of birth registrations or marriage licence records.

These attractions notwithstanding, many researchers have been seriously concerned about the existence of stores of data and the regulation of access to these: their minds have been concentrated by the alarming capacities of computers to store and release data and the particular issue of data protection, which has a direct bearing on the ethics of secondary analysis, has been discussed above (3.3). The British Association Study Group (1974) articulated a number of concerns about secondary analysis on ethical grounds. They noted a general increase in the compulsory collection of data; to their example of the use of censuses we may add the greater recent use of the findings of Her Majesty's Inspectors of schools who do not require voluntary consent to their observations and questions. The Study Group was further concerned with the building of stores of data which might be tapped by police, employers and others to whom subjects might not have given consent voluntarily. It feared also that policies would be increasingly based on profiles from stored data rather than contact with real people made for the specific purpose of policy formulation: the implication here is that data may be used as an adequate available source but they are not the ideal that is achievable by research procedures designed for the purpose.

Roger Jowell, whose concern is less with the quality of data available for secondary analysis than with issues relating to the protection of their subjects, reserves opprobrium for the electoral register which, on the pretext of ensuring the enfranchisement of all adult subjects, provides an annual published record of names and addresses which serves as a much sought after 'hit list' (Jowell, 1982: 43) for market researchers and the senders of junk mail. By contrast, census data have since 1966 been subject to a 100 years closure before being deposited in the Public Record Office. As Jowell sealed the envelope of his 1981 census return he wondered why such protection was necessary on data that in any case were casually observable. In his judgement and in that of Hakim (1979: 141–2) the census is a relatively innocuous source of secondary data and one which is scrupulously regulated.

4.5.2 Ethical issues

For a number of reasons those who process data that have been collected elsewhere and at an earlier stage in the research may feel remote from the situation in which ethical principles should be applied and assume that they have been spared the moral dilemmas attending work in the field. It is the interviewer on the doorstep who stands at the frontier of private space, who must judge the acceptable limits of intrusion, who must face, evade or respond to the emotional needs or requests for advice being made by informants, who must appraise subjects of the nature and purpose of the enquiry. By the time they become available for secondary analysis, data have normally been anonymised, broad-banded or represented in statistical form to render identification impossible. The sense that the secondary analyst has is that all moral obligations have already been satisfied. Indeed, there is a sense in which secondary analysis is a more considerate and therefore more moral procedure than the primary phases of data collection which invariably make demands upon the time and tolerance of subjects. In consideration of the need to minimise the intrusiveness of social research, the ethical guidelines of the Social Research Association (n.d.: 12–13) suggest:

> One way of avoiding inconvenience to potential subjects is to make more use of available data instead of embarking on a new inquiry. For instance, by making greater statistical use of administrative records, by linking records, information about society may be produced that would otherwise have to be collected afresh.

While secondary analysis may have the virtue of avoiding demands upon subjects there is an inherent problem in that secondary analysts may not be bound by the conditions upon which subjects gave their consent in the first instance. Data may be collected for an initial purpose which subjects regarded as worthy, translated into statistical form and so stored and then used for another purpose by a secondary analyst. The trust which respondents place in researchers is often personal: so it is that some feminist researchers find that female respondents confide in women researchers what they would not disclose to men, believing that the data will be sensitively and responsibly interpreted. Some disadvantaged groups may be inclined to grant consent to be interviewed or observed only because they believe a researcher to be committed to their own interests.

That data should be placed at the disposal of fellow professionals is a principle of intellectual honesty. It allows for the re-interpretation of findings and for the conduct of a debate which is valued as healthy and desirable in an intellectual community. On the other hand, subjects might have yielded data on the implicit assurance that they would not be presented in a contrary form. The implication is that researchers who are collecting data which may be made available at a later stage for critical re-examination by their peers must be both modest and realistic in the assurances they give their subjects when informing consent. So too must those who are employed to gather data by interviews and other means, subsequently to be turned over for processing and interpretation by the project directors:

> Although they can pass on the official message from their employing organization, they cannot, for example, assure pensioners that the income information that they give will not be used to justify cuts in pensions, or promise mothers that a change to means-tested child benefits will not be introduced as a result of research using the [General Household Survey] (Dale, Arber and Procter, 1988: 58).

Attempts have been made to develop principles for secondary analysts that come as near as possible to that of informed consent, the pure forms of which are hardly operable in retrospect. Subjects may have died or moved away or may have been rendered unidentifiable; they may never have been identified; or else they may be so numerous as to render contact and consultation a formidable and expensive operation. In any case, to be pursued two or three years after giving an interview only to be asked whether data now compiled in a statistical form could be re-interpreted or applied to some other purpose is an entitlement that not all respondents would value, let alone claim. For most practitioners, the critical ethical responsibility is to ensure that stored data do not allow the identification of their subjects. The British Association Study Group (1974) concluded its enquiry with the rule that,

> The researcher must never collect identifiable information without the explicit informed consent of the subject, and that he or she must never pass that information to anyone else without explicit informed consent.

Between the extremes of allowing free access to all who knock on the door and absolute exclusion there are two happy media. In both strategies the researcher asks the custodian of data to select appropriate cases. Either the data holder asks subjects for permission to give their names and addresses to the investigator or else passes to subjects a letter from the researcher detailing interest and purpose with a covering note to stress that the researcher does not know who is receiving the letter (Hartley, 1982: 180). As we suggest above, the risk is that the pursuit of subjects to honour their rights may be thought more a nuisance than a prerogative; we may soon reach the point when nobody wants to give an interview for fear that they will never hear the end of it.

4.6 CRITIQUE OF INFORMED CONSENT

There have emerged in the above account several implicit criticisms of the principle of informed consent and in this section we elaborate and supplement these. In particular, we have been concerned with problems of practicability, such as the degree to which the ideal of informing consent which is commended in the codes can be implemented in the event (4.1 and 4.2). We have also glimpsed (in 4.2) the tension between the recognition of a subject's right to refuse and the motivation of the researcher to secure a high rate of response; the effect of this professional motivation is to incline investigators to fulfil informed consent as an ethical obligation and then to encourage the subject to forget such aspects of the information as might at any stage prompt withdrawal. Another strategy is to introduce or trade upon legitimate pressures which disincline the potential participant to refuse, such as peer group pressure or material incentives. In this section we are concerned with the ethical and moral implications of such practices and with relating the principle of informed consent to issues of rights and responsibilities. The principal moral objection to informed consent is that it provides less of a protection for the subject than for the researcher: in the act of consent, responsibility for such aspects as the safety of the subject transfers from the investigator to the subject.

4.6.1 Some assumptions questioned

A first assumption of the principle of informed consent as it is commonly formulated is that individuals have the right to refuse. Researchers acting under statutory provision to collect census data or to compile electoral registers tend to offer the usual briefing but the options of consent or refusal are not allowed. The right to refuse is established primarily in respect of the protection of privacy but in professional practice it has been accorded more generally to public and notionally accountable aspects of individuals' lives. In consequence, those from whom consent is sought may refuse it in order to withhold from scrutiny a practice or system in which there is legitimate public interest and which may be widely disapproved. For example, a religious sect in which there is a high level of psychological disturbance attributable to its methods and teachings or a department of local government among whose employees certain privileges or material benefits are unofficially regarded as legitimate, might be considered in some measure accountable to the public whose relatives have been recruited by the sect and whose money sustains public employees; in the option of refusal, they are granted a right to which many would not regard them as entitled. When the headteacher of a school or the manager of a business is approached for consent, the implication is that the right to grant or withhold is personal and that individual rights obtain; however, the individual may in that role be accountable to the public, as may the school or the business. In these events the person approached is enabled to conceal possibly shady practices from the view to which the public may be entitled. For some social scientists, the pursuit of knowledge is so desirable a venture that the withholding of consent should not be allowed to stand in its way (Denzin, in Bulmer, 1982a: 143).

A second assumption is that consenting subjects have a sufficient awareness of what they are disclosing. We have referred above to ways in which consent may be only partially informed when it is secured and to the methods by which resistance is eroded or the consciousness of the research act is enabled to lapse. The point we make here refers rather to the differential vision of the social researcher and participants. The subject may have control over the release of raw data but the researcher attaches a significance to these that untrained subjects may not apprehend. For example, in a recent educational research project an undergraduate student who was interested in children's perceptions of other countries showed pictures of tents, boats, houses and other dwellings. Children were then asked to imagine that following an air accident they had arrived by parachute outside the dwelling shown and to tell the story from there. They had consented to this task and would have understood that the student, being a teacher-type, was interested in handwriting, spelling, word power and imagination. Lacking psychological insight, they did not know how much more they were betraying in terms of prejudices and stereotypes. This differential intellectual capacity is not confined to the use of children as subjects: teachers may be equally unaware of how much they are giving away:

Teacher: Don't expect me to tell you anything about the Head.
MacDonald: You just have. (Walker, 1985: 84).

4.6.2 Rights and responsibilities

The principle of informed consent serves the subject's supposed right to know that he or she is involved in an act of research; in operation, the right to know becomes the obligation to be told and is therefore exclusive of the right not to know. The notion of the right not to know is already established in medical ethics where it has clear applications in cases of terminal illness: Fletcher (1978: 149) tells of a cheerful patient who never smiled again after he had been told that his condition was cancer. A comparable negative effect can attend the informed subjects of social research. Participants in the prayer meetings of a religious sect, for example, may have no reason or wish to refuse access to an observer prepared to adopt the guise of a participant but may prefer not to know since the consciousness of being observed may be inhibitive. Both in medical practice and in social research, there is a procedural problem in ascertaining whether individuals would prefer to be ignorant without signifying the critical information that would be revealed if it were desired. The social researcher may sometimes resolve this problem to some extent by seeking the counsel of peers or leading members of the community being studied.

What matters much more than the awareness that social research is taking place, however, is the knowledge or assessment of risks and consequences on the basis of which consent is granted or withheld. The moral responsibility for the safety of participants in research is widely recognised to rest with the researcher. In the informing of consent, the decision on whether or not to proceed is passed from the researcher to the participant. The right to refuse is bound up with a responsibility for consequences. There is a considerable element of self-interest in the briefing of research subjects and when the indemnity principle is thinly disguised – for example, when a signature is sought – subjects are rather less willing to commit themselves (Singer, 1978). Diener and Crandall warn that the researcher might use informed consent to justify studies without maximum safeguards, reasoning that the subject can choose not to participate. This *caveat emptor* has been rejected as irresponsible in other areas of life such as business, and it cannot be allowed in research. Thus, informed consent is a necessary *but not sufficient* ethical precaution in risky studies (Diener and Crandall, 1978: 50).

The recognition of a subject's rights and interests, then, is only one aspect of the central professional ethic of informed consent, another being the protection of the researcher. Whatever consequences ensue, it is important that participants cannot say that they had not been warned. As Schuler (1982: 102) recognises, it is in the informing of consent that researchers can assure themselves that they are following prescribed principles and relieve themselves of certain responsibilities toward participants. The moral responsibilities which pass to subjects when researchers indemnify themselves include the invasion of privacy of participants as well as of those who are implied in the interviewing of surrogates, the risk of harm to participants and the moral obligation to pursue truth. The acquisition of consent allows the abdication of all these responsibilities.

The invasion of the privacy of third parties by use of surrogates has been discussed above (3.6): the point to be made at this stage is that consent is given not by individuals but by third parties who may little appreciate the moral implications of their willingness to participate. The informing of subjects about the possibility of certain kinds of harmful effect is standard practice in psychological research; it is also a necessary precaution in some types of sociological research in which research workers and other participants are asked to enter dangerous situations and investigate sensitive issues likely to attract publicity. The point here is made by Schuler (1982: 101): too often, those who conduct intrepid research have little idea of the risks involved and yet they feel relieved of the responsibility by having forewarned their subjects. Further, the moral obligation to pursue truth is compromised when the option of giving or withholding consent legitimises the obstruction of that pursuit. The very integrity of social science is at stake if its ethics commit researchers to work only with willing subjects.

A further concern is that in practice researchers regard the consent of participants as a license or clearance to engage in conduct contrary to the principle of subject control which is the spirit of the requirement of informed consent. For example, social researchers will encourage participants to forget that they are being observed or interviewed; this means that consent belongs to a particular moment in the encounter and is given on the basis of selected information, but the researcher is careful to close the issue there and not to give subjects the opportunity to withdraw from the research act as its reality unfolds.

It is not only in the sense that there is no turning back for the consenting subject that field relations bear a resemblance to sales practice. Indeed, the conditions in which consent is sought belie the principle that it should be voluntary. The relationship of the researcher to the potential subject is a powerful one and the researcher is trained in securing a disposition to cooperate. In some cases non-participation may be thought to incur the disfavour of senior colleagues; even where no penalty applies, there may be other subtle sanctions against refusers such as the embarrassment of having to leave the room alone (Sherif, 1980: 412). Interviewers are humane and friendly for the pragmatic reason that potential respondents are more likely to consent to participation (Oakley, 1981: 33). In the context of non-therapeutic experimentation in medicine, Häring is mindful of the power that a practised researcher can exert in the process of negotiation:

> There is a vast difference between extorting consent by overwhelming psychological suggestion through cleverly chosen information and gaining consent through completely objective information presented in such a way as to invite the full exercise of judgment and freedom (Häring, 1972: 215).

The exercise of reason is crucial. If it is impaired by the manner in which the researcher approaches potential subjects, the right to give consent voluntarily is not being honoured. Some commentators like Carlson are concerned that the educated, literate and aware know that they can refuse and they know how to, while the less educated defer to and comply with the social researchers who approach them; he believes that we do not have adequate answers to those who say we exploit vulnerable groups (Carlson, 1967: 88).

CHAPTER 5

Covert methods

5.1 CASE STUDIES

5.1.1 Hiding under people's beds

Most of the cases of social research which in recent years have prompted debate about the ethics of covert methods have involved the concealment or disguise of the researcher within an otherwise acceptable social role. The method has been that of participant observation and the question is whether the real purpose and identity of the investigator should be declared to participants.

More rarely, covertness has taken the form of the concealment of the means of recording. With the availability of new technology including bugging devices and hidden cameras the scope for this is considerable. In earlier days it implied the physical presence of the investigator being so placed as to avoid the notice of unwitting human subjects. So we have the bizarre spectacle of Henle and Hubble (1938) who stowed themselves under beds in student dormitories on Sunday afternoons so that they could write on their clip-boards the conversations of students sitting on or otherwise occupying the beds. Such a method is nowadays as unnecessary as it is unfashionable. Most commentators – and certainly most students – would regard such a placement of researchers as an intrusion of private space. The quest for and informing of consent would, one assumes, have an inhibiting effect upon the conversations to be monitored. On these grounds, a research proposal along these lines would today be thrown out by the Institutional Review Board. In their defence, however, Henle and Hubble were not interested in personal aspects of their subjects' behaviour, only in the phenomenon of 'egocentricity' in adult conversation. Notwithstanding, social researchers today tend to regard this as too transparent a case of sublimated voyeurism and are uncomfortable about the inclusion of such enterprising field methods in the work of their profession.

5.1.2 Pseudo-patient studies

In 1971 a number of Mexican-American women asked at a family planning clinic for contraceptives. Professionals at the clinic took the opportunity to engage in a piece of non-therapeutic research.

Without telling the women, they decided to monitor side-effects by giving some women genuine contraceptives and others placebos (that is, tablets that looked similar). Those who were given placebos showed more dramatic side-effects than those who were given contraceptives: 'they became pregnant' (Bok, 1978: 71). If this was to have been the finding, it hardly justified the choice of unwitting subjects and consequent human distress.

For their part, social researchers have turned the tables on the medical profession by seeking treatment for symptoms which they fabricated. One of the earliest instances of a social researcher masquerading as a patient in need was that of William Caudill (1958): he was a research anthropologist who entered a psychiatric hospital with his true identity known only to two of the senior medical staff. He stayed there as a patient for two months, after one week of which he was allowed out in the afternoons, which he took as the opportunity to write up his notes. Later Caudill returned to the hospital, this time making his identify and research purpose clear to the patients and staff (Caudill, 1958: 22). Having conducted research in the same place by both covert and overt methods, Caudill was in a good position to appreciate the complementarity of the two approaches. In the role of a patient he discovered less about 'facts' and more about 'feelings'. The patient perspective afforded him some insight of the organisation of life on the wards but little about the operation of the hospital at staff level. The concealed study had been one-sided and the overt study gave Caudill the chance to correct the imbalance. On reflection he saw the concealed study as a vital contribution to the research overall:

> if, in reporting on the second study in this book, I have convincingly portrayed some aspects of the life of patients, it is in part because of the earlier study when I was, for a time, in the situation myself (Caudill, 1958: xv).

Later, Rosenhan (1973 reprinted in Bulmer, 1982a) was one of eight investigators (three women and five men) who presented themselves at hospitals in different states on the American east and west coasts and reported, dishonestly, that they had been hearing voices saying 'hollow', 'empty' and 'thud'. Seven were successful in gaining admission. They used false names so that no connection would be made with the authentic medical records and they declared false occupations, not least because some of them were mental health professionals and it was feared that these might be treated differently. They had been told that they would have to gain discharge from the hospital by their own means and by convincing the hospital staff that they were sane. All but one of them applied for such discharge almost immediately after admission but the average period of detention was 19 days and one of the pseudo-patients was not released for 52 days. During this time a total of 2100 tablets were given to the eight investigators, although most of these were either pocketed or flushed down the toilet, as were the tablets given to other patients. The study was conducted at a time when medical opinion was confident that sanity and insanity could be distinguished on the basis of presented symptoms: of course, it had the effect of challenging such confidence. It also provided valuable professional insight for mental health professionals, especially those who took part: Rosenhan wrote, 'Too few psychiatrists and psychologists, even those who have worked in such hospitals, know what the experience is like' (Rosenhan, in Bulmer, 1982a: 17).

The case of 'David Kent' is that of a piece of participant research by a pseudo-patient seeking the experience of suicidal depression. It was under this pseudonym that David K. Reynolds presented himself at an American hospital with a fabricated story that he had recently attempted to take his own life. He was duly admitted and while in hospital attempted a pseudo-suicide having taken the precaution of cutting the rope before making the noose. He tells of his feelings as he tied the knot in the view of other suicidal patients. It is of course questionable whether these were the feelings of genuinely suicidal patients or merely those that Reynolds supposed they would experience. During his research Reynolds became constipated and he attributed this to the psychological holding back or in of depression (Reynolds and Farkerow, 1976).

A number of social scientists who have been hospitalised by accident rather than by design, as it were, have taken their opportunities to collect data with various degrees of covertness. The collection of reports edited by Davis and Horobin (1977) includes accounts of experiences of a chronic dermatological illness, an orthopaedic ward, a tropical diseases hospital and staying on a children's ward.

In such situations, social research is as much as anything a way of occupying the time. In 1986 I found myself in a neurological hospital with a condition called myelitis which had the effect of paralysing me from the chest down and restraining me from entering other social fields than the men's medical ward to which I was committed. Being also (registered) blind, I had only the radio and conversations to occupy me through a period of two months. I did not make a conscious decision to research the situation: rather, observation and reflection had already become habits that I could not suppress. I shared my reflections with the hospital registrar, house doctor and senior physiotherapist whenever they had the time to listen and respond, usually amid periodic tests and treatment. When at last I was able to sit up I was allowed to have my typewriter in the hospital and I wrote a paper which I circulated to the matron, the medical and nursing staff and the physiotherapy unit. At their suggestion I approached the *British Medical Journal* in which it appeared as 'Observations on the management of mood in a neurological hospital' (Homan, 1986). For a mind disciplined by practice in the social sciences, it is often difficult to register the point at which incidental observations become purposeful research.

5.1.3 Becoming black

One of the most remarkable examples of the use of disguise and a case in which the risks were particularly serious is that of John Howard Griffin (1977) who in the late 1950s took medication to change the colour of his skin and present himself as a Negro in the southern states of America. The experiment began as a 'scientific research study of the Negro in the South' with careful compilation of data for analysis' (Griffin, 1977: i) but Griffin ended up filing his notes and presenting his account in journal form. He sought medical advice from dermatologists who prescribed tablets to be followed by exposure to ultraviolet light. By his request the treatment was accelerated: he was apprised by doctors of medical risks such as damage to the liver and also of social risks when penetrating a black community. After some weeks,

> The transformation was total and shocking. I had expected to see myself disguised, but this was something else. I was imprisoned in the flesh of an utter stranger, an unsympathetic one with whom I felt no kinship. All traces of the John Griffin I had been were wiped from existence. Even the senses underwent a change so profound it filled me with distress (Griffin, 1977: 11).

In the weeks that followed he experienced what he called the 'wearying rejection' (Griffin, 1977: 47) of the American Negro. Television appearances and press coverage of his experiment prompted a hostile response to him and his family, under the pressure of which his parents sold their home and removed to Mexico (Griffin, 1977: 60). When eventually he recovered a white pigmentation, he had to leave a black neighbourhood quickly and was fearful in leaving a black home in a white skin (Griffin, 1977: 129).

5.1.4 Getting baptised

The work of Ken Pryce (1979) illustrates some of the complexities of the role of covert researcher as well as the problem of proceeding on the basis of a vicarious consent. Pryce was a sociology student who settled in the St Paul's area of Bristol with the purpose of investigating a range of West Indian lifestyles there. His being Jamaican helped him establish a rapport with those who were to become his subjects, sometimes before he had the opportunity to explain his motives. On the one hand he developed and sustained research relationships with hustlers and prostitutes. On the other, he frequented and eventually became a member of a West Indian pentecostal church.

The circumstances in which Pryce took up membership and became baptised are curious as these initiatives were less of his own design than they were that of his subjects. At first he tried floating between two congregations but this strategy only invited the suspicion in one that he was spying for the other. So he became regularly involved with one of the churches and took the opportunity to explain to its pastor the background of his research. The pastor accepted the nature and purpose of the research and agreed to help but it soon became clear to Pryce that 'he wanted something in return – my baptism and permanent membership of the church' (Pryce, 1989: 284). The pastor told the congregation that Pryce had been sent there by God and members gave him generous gifts such as shirts. The pastor pressed Pryce to be baptised and he realised that it was only through baptism that he could be recognised by other members as 'saved' and have the opportunity of seeing things from the inside:

> I had no choice therefore but to give in one Sunday morning when I and other unsaved persons like myself were called to the altar and asked if we were ready to be baptized. With hands laid on our heads, we were prayed for and cajoled into accepting baptism, which we all did (Pryce, 1979: 285).

There are several distinctive features in the manner of Pryce's adoption of the covert participant role. First, although his purpose was not known to the greater number of his subjects, it was at least confided to the principal of them. Second, Pryce's account illuminates the reciprocity of the relationship between researcher and researched: they got something out of him in exchange for what he got out of them. Third, Pryce's absorption into the body of the faithful was as much the initiative of its pastor as it was a determined strategy by the researcher: once the mechanism of induction had been activated, Pryce's part was markedly passive. Pryce did not so much penetrate the community of his subjects as allow them to draw him into it.

5.1.5 Baking bread

Jason Ditton's covert research in the field of industrial sociology involved the exploitation of the roles of plant worker in a bread factory and later of despatch operative, the first of which he had previously occupied as a vacation job during his undergraduate years. He returned to the factory at the commencement of his doctoral research as a covert participant observer; at that time his principal research interest was to determine whether workers paid by the hour operated a kind of 'output restriction' unlike workers paid by the piece.

Ditton worked twelve-hour shifts and could not hold in his memory all the data he collected. His habit was to retreat to a lavatory cubicle and write up notes after every interesting conversation. This practice by covert researchers is sometimes known as the condition of, 'ethnographer's bladder'. 'Looking back,' says Ditton (1977: 5), 'all my notes for that third summer were on Bronco toilet paper!' When his workmates showed a concerned interest in his frequent need to retire to the loo, he took to writing his notes more openly, saying that he was jotting down some thoughts that had occurred to him relating to his studies.

The eventual foci of Ditton's research and the theme of his published writings concerned aspects of the workers' behaviour which many would disapprove and regard as criminal. He was concerned with how factory workers coped with the monotony of their work; the strategies he illuminated included five schemes for 'manipulating time' (Ditton, 1979) and the practice of 'fiddling' (Ditton, 1974). The book which is substantially his doctoral thesis appears under the title *Part-time Crime: An Ethnography of Fiddling and Pilferage* (Ditton, 1977).

5.1.6 Paddington station

The work of Mary Sissons (1971) incorporates both covert and explicit components. Behaviour was recorded without the consent of subjects but the research purpose was explained in the course of gathering further demographic data about subjects for the purpose of interpretation. She engaged a professional actor to stop travellers on Paddington station and ask for directions to Hyde Park; a concealed camera was used to record this part of the operation. When the actor's supposed enquiry was concluded subjects were then approached by a self-confessed social researcher; only one of the 80 subjects showed hostility to the study once it was explained. They were then asked questions that enabled the researcher to relate such variables as social class to certain features of their non-verbal communication. As Barnes (1977: 13) puts it, 'the object of the experiment was not to discover the best way to Hyde Park'.

5.1.7 Tearoom Trade

The work of Laud Humphreys is one of the most noticed and controversial cases of arguably unethical methodology in the history of social research. It is hardly typical but it compels attention for the number of problems it raises in respect of deception and invasion. His critic Donald P. Warwick comments, 'The concentration of misrepresentation and disguises in this effort must surely hold the world record for field research' (Warwick, 1982: 46).

The 'tearooms' in which *Tearoom Trade* (Humphreys, 1975) was researched were men's public toilets in the United States; the 'trade' consisted of casual homosexual encounters, of which Humphreys observed and reported in some detail a great variety. Humphreys assumed the role of lookout voyeur or 'watchqueen', whose responsibility was to cough at the approach of strangers while Humphreys' subjects enjoyed various kinds of physical interaction, which he observed and later noted. Humphreys kept records also of the age, dress and car registration numbers of his subjects, by means of which he was able to trace them to their home addresses. At the same time, Humphreys was involved with a health survey and he was able to include some 50 of his own subjects in this survey. He waited a year, changed his dress and hairstyle and visited at home those whom he had for some time previously observed in the tearoom. He was satisfied that the former 'watchqueen' was not recognised by respondents to the supposed health survey.

5.1.8 When Prophecy Fails

The research undertaken by Festinger, Riecken and Schachter (1964) and reported in the book *When Prophecy Fails* (first published in 1956) is a remarkable case of deceit and invasion, although the authors' methodological account (1964: 234–49) addresses pragmatic issues rather than ethical ones and shows little awareness of the implications for the profession of social research.

The purpose was to penetrate a religious sect whose distinctive belief was that the end of the world was imminent and that its destruction was to take the form of a flood. Believing that sect members would be unreceptive of non-believers, the research team elected to proceed with neither the knowledge nor the consent of their subjects. Their problem at the practical level was to inject enough 'believers' to monitor the activities, beliefs and commitments of all existing members without incurring a reactive effect. To the extent that some of the psychology and sociology students and staff who contacted the sect to observe were identified as emissaries – not from Festinger but from outer space – the researchers failed: the appearance of emissaries served to confirm the sect belief in Guardians upon which the researchers aspired to have no effect. For example, a young woman whom they hired and trained was armed with a 'psychic experience' to report to sect leaders. This achieved the immediate objective of gaining an entrée but it also had the effect of reinforcing belief. Females were used to good effect in gaining access to households and some of them lived part-time in the homes of sect leaders. Eventually, when a male observer turned up at the home of a sect member on Christmas Day he was readily admitted as a spaceman (Festinger, Riecken and Schachter, 1964: 234–8).

Although it was no part of the initial research design, the encouragement of beliefs and hopes well suited the ultimate purpose of observing the management of disconfirmation. Festinger's well-known theory of 'cognitive dissonance' regards the behaviour shown by individuals and groups whose expectations are not fulfilled; in particular, they react not by relinquishing beliefs but by affirming them with greater zeal and even recruiting more energetically. This could hardly have been observed had the subjects of *When Prophecy Fails* known throughout that those who joined them in the month or so leading to the expected cataclysm were not emissaries from outer space but psychology students doing fieldwork.

Discussion of the ethics of such methods as those of Festinger and his colleagues has not been confined to the literature of social science but has been brought to wider attention by Alison Lurie (1978). Her novel *Imaginary Friends* involves a beautiful prophetess Verena through whom a religious cult, the Truth Seekers, communicates with beings on another planet.

5.1.9 Infiltrating the National Front

Nigel Fielding (1981) used a mixture of covert and overt methods in his investigation of the National Front. He approached the Front's headquarters with requests to interview officers at national level and these were granted. At the level of local branch, however, he conducted observations without announcement or the acquisition of general consent. It is normal for meetings of the National Front to be attended by interested non-members and it was in such a peripheral role that the researcher was able to find a place (Fielding, 1982: 85). However, Front members are always vigilant of infiltrators and *agents provocateurs* and were known to be suspicious of all 'outsiders', particularly writers (Fielding, 1981: 8). Indeed, in 1974 when the journalist Martin Walker was researching his book, the National Front issued this bulletin to its members:

> No co-operation, assistance, advice, information or comment – no matter what the subject or issue – may be given by any member of the National Front to Mr Martin Walker or to any other journalist suspected by members to be working for or on behalf of Mr Walker. Any questions from him must be replied to by use of the simple statement 'No

comment'. This ruling applies to all forms of attempted interviews by Mr Walker, be they 'on or off the record', 'informal', 'social' or whatever (Walker, 1977: 13).

Fielding found that when political issues were being disputed it was expedient to make a contribution in order to avert suspicion that his attendance and interest might have been based on some ulterior motive (Fielding, 1981: 139). To this end Fielding adopted a visibly sympathetic attitude in his enquiry which ran against the grain of his predisposition: it was also contrary to the messages expressed by his physical appearance which was regarded by one National Front member as that of 'a typical long-haired student' (Fielding, 1981: 232). He signalled a general assent to National Front beliefs and offered to help at its headquarters during an election campaign; in the event the offer was not accepted as it would have entailed his being present at some confidential discussions (Fielding, 1982: 87).

5.1.10 Telephone tapping

A study which involved the recording of telephone calls was conducted in 1974 by Barnard; his unpublished corpus of over 700 conversations was picked up and analysed by Beattie (1983: 88–100). The calls from which Barnard took transcripts were recorded in a trunk telephone exchange in the cognizance of telephone operators who were assured that the material was to be used for research purposes only and that their performance was not being assessed. The conversations monitored were directory enquiries. The operators, whose identities were not preserved in the transcripts, were so fully apprised of the research that the data collection was overt as far as they were concerned (Beattie, 1983: 89). However callers were neither identified nor informed. Nor indeed was any remotely 'personal' use made of the data. The context in which Beattie draws on the Barnard transcripts is a study of talk with particular reference to turn-taking in conversation.

5.2 TYPES OF COVERTNESS

The field method most widely used in a covert way is that of participant observation but other methods may also be deployed covertly. What is often represented in the literature as 'informal interviewing' is informal in the sense that there is no contemporaneous note-taking and that any cautions and information concerning the nature of the research, in the context of which the conversation is conducted, were given on an earlier occasion. The significant factor in both observation and interviewing is that the investigator is perceived by subjects in a role and with a purpose other than those of research. The definition of the situation as a research act may prevail with the investigator but it is not dominant in the perceptions of subjects.

Technological advances in this century have made it possible for social scientists and others to collect data without being present themselves. Telephone tapping, the use of bugs, hidden cameras and tape-recorders are all at the disposal of investigators although their use is of course inhibited by public disapproval as well as professional and ethical scruples.

The same disapproval applies to the acquisition by guile of confidential documents or computer data. It is felt that what was wrong at Watergate cannot be right in social research. Nevertheless, Laud Humphreys persuaded the police to let him have the private addresses of subjects whose vehicle registration marks he collected and Bob Mullan (1980) acquired confidential documents in his local government study of Stevenage.

A principal justification of these strategies is that they are unobtrusive and yield naturalistic data: this is a pragmatic argument which has an ethical dimension in that it is also suggested that subjects are entitled to be disrupted by the conduct of research. However, the notion of a public right to know has to be invoked to justify the acquisition of private documents by dishonest means or the infiltration by Angela Calomiris (1950) of the American communist party, of which she remained a member for seven years becoming Financial Secretary of the West Midtown branch in New York and finally breaking cover to testify for the government in the trial of the 11 'Red leaders'. The more recent work of Nigel Fielding who penetrated the National Front in Britain belongs in this tradition.

Now we may distinguish four principles of covertness.

5.2.1 Concealment

Half a century after Henle and Hubble (see 5.1.1), the prospect of sociology or psychology tutors lurking under their students' beds on a Sunday afternoon seems absurd. However, the bugging of private space still takes place. A method used in the Bristol Language Development Study to monitor the speech of children before school age involved the inclusion of a harness and microphone on which children's sounds (as well as other speech in the area) were recorded (Wells, 1981: 6). Walker and Atherton (1971), found that the tape-recorder had an institutionalised role in the pentecostal convention where it was used as a means of conveying the 'blessing': it was therefore inconspicuous when they used it to record transactions for the purpose of their research.

The use of a video camera concealed in a hold-all and carried by two journalists, one black and one white, was in 1989 a feature of the BBC television programme 'Black and white'. Each of the journalists responded to advertisements of accommodation and situations vacant. The film they made and broadcast illustrated the different kinds of reception that were accorded to black and white applicants. Even within the world of the media, where sanctions and scruples are quite different from those that obtain in social research, there was a reaction against this technique and it was not readily accepted that the aim of exposing racism justified the method of concealment.

The tapping of telephone calls is vigorously disapproved and its use under warrant from the Home Secretary and by authorised persons only is reserved as a measure to combat terrorism and violent crime. The statement in the House of Commons by the Home Secretary William Whitelaw on 1 April 1980 makes no exceptions for social researchers:

> The interception of communication, whether by the opening and reading of letters, or by the recording and listening to telephone communications, is an interference with the freedom of the individual in a democratic society. Nonetheless, when carried out by the properly constituted authorities, it is justified if its aims and consequences help to protect the law-abiding citizen from threats of crime and violence and the fabric of democracy from the menaces of espionage, terrorism and subversion.

So absolute a prohibition may be a little hard on those who only wanted to study the grammatical structure of sentences but if it is in the national interest they will no doubt be prepared to find other methods.

5.2.2 Misrepresentation

Disraeli is supposed to have defined a gentleman as one who knows when to tell the truth and when not. While members of some other professions have to make that judgement for themselves, social researchers are firmly guided by their professional associations to avoid all kinds of deception and dishonesty.

When Wallis took up his research in the Church of Scientology he did not permit himself to lie outright over his identity or intentions (Wallis, 1977: 154). Others have examined their consciences and imposed similar restrictions but there is also a tradition of lying, giving false names, inventing a medical history and claiming false symptoms (Caudill, 1958; Sullivan, *et al.*, 1958; Lofland and Lejeune, 1960; Rosenhan, 1973). Between the declaration of falsity and the declaration of the whole truth there is an intermediate position in which investigators avoid having to reveal information that might make the research relationship difficult (Wallis, 1977) or gloss over the nature of their research in such general terms as are either misleading or else are designed to avert alarm: Whyte told his subjects in street-corner society that he was interested in the social history of an urban area when he was really investigating the sociology of the slum (Whyte, 1951: 494).

There is more to misrepresentation than lying, however. Sometimes, practised role behaviour signifies experience or membership of a particular group: the posture of Humphreys in the tearoom and of Homan as he arrived at pentecostal meetings signified – misleadingly – that they were already established in the communities they were observing.

5.2.3 Camouflage

Some researchers emulate the chameleon. Their aim is to become invisible in the field in which they are working. For some, the disguised role is already achieved before the intention to research is formulated; Holdaway (1982) was a policeman before he used that role as the cover of his research and the contributors to the collection of Davis and Horobin (1977) were *bona fide* patients who after admission decided to use the cover for research purposes. While some of these knew at the time that they were collecting data, others did not and a special case is made in this chapter of those whose research is a reflection upon experience innocently acquired.

The more dramatic cases and those which exercise professionals in respect of ethical principles are those in which the researcher trains for and practises a role in order to deceive subjects; among these are the investigations of 'pseudo-patients' collected and discussed by Bulmer (1982b) and the famous adventures of Laud Humphreys.

5.2.4 Acquisition of confidential documents

Humphreys extracted from the police the addresses of those he wanted to contact: the judgement of professionals is that this offends established principles and that the police were also at fault in releasing such data. Wallis (1977: 152) came by a contact list which he sensed should not have been in his hands although the means by which he acquired it were perfectly honest. In this chapter the ethical problems of using guile to obtain written sources are explored as the same problems attending the use of guile in observing and interviewing subjects and issues of confidentiality are treated in Chapter 6 (6.4).

While Wallis was not at fault in receiving what might have been a confidential address list, it must have some point in the chain been removed from confidential cover. Researchers commonly allow others to collect data on their behalf and to report it to them. The use of surrogates and lapsed members as interviewees is, like bugging, a means of researching a field by remote means. The question of whether such methods are open, as is commonly assumed, is addressed in the discussions that follow.

5.3 THE CASE AGAINST COVERT METHODS

5.3.1 A professional consensus?

The guidance on the matter of covert methods which the professional associations offer their members amounts in simple terms to a counsel against their use: this is tied in with the principle of informed consent which they unanimously endorse and a concern about the public image and reputation of professional social researchers. However, there is here and there a recognition that informed consent is not always achievable in its absolute form and that special circumstances might render appropriate a less than honest negotiation with subjects. In such an event there are various measures that can be taken such as consultation with experienced colleagues on the necessity for any element of covertness and the explicit debriefing of subjects, so that at least they know that research has been taking place even if they did not know it beforehand.

The 'Statement of ethical principles and their application to sociological practice' which is issued by the British Sociological Association (1982) provides that researchers

> should explain their work as fully as possible to sponsors, facilitators and subjects in ways that are likely to be meaningful to them.

That wording allows that in some cases such an explanation may not be possible. In any particular case there will be a tension between the degree to which subjects are entitled to be consulted and apprised and the desirability of collecting data in as natural a form as possible. As the discussions in this chapter illustrate, the possibility of being open is variably problematic and negotiable. Researchers who suppose that openness was not possible find their assumptions debated vigorously within the profession when their work is published.

The *Code of Conduct* of the Market Research Society (1986) relates principally to survey and interview methods and provides that subjects should be informed of the identity of interviewers and the organisation for which they are working, with more explicit details of the research available on request, possibly in leaflet form. Covert methods are not entertained as appropriate in market research.

The ethical principles of the British Psychological Society (1978) go further than others in specifying the circumstances in which covert methods might be allowed and the appropriate precautions which the researcher should adopt. Psychologists are urged to consult experienced and disinterested colleagues before perpetrating any deception of the subjects of their research:

> Deception of subjects, or withholding of relevant information from them, should only occur when the investigator is satisfied that the aims and objects of his research or the welfare of his subjects cannot be achieved by other means. Where deception has been necessary, revelation should normally follow participation as a matter of course. Where the subject's behaviour makes it appear that revelation could be stressful or, when to reveal the objectives or the basis of subject selection would be distressing, the extent and timing of such revelation should be influenced by consideration for the subject's psychological welfare. Where deception has been substantial, the subject should be offered the option of withholding his data in accordance with the principle of participation by informed consent.

The principle of seeking the counsel of experienced colleagues and the possibility of retrospectively informed consent are reaffirmed in the general 'Code of Conduct for Psychologists' issued by the British Psychological Society (1985).

The Department of Behavioural Sciences at Huddersfield Polytechnic adds a useful gloss that could be taken on board in other codes and guidelines: it recognises the necessity of an element of deception in some investigations but rules that this should never involve matters of risk and safety on which subjects have the invariable right to be comprehensively apprised.

5.3.2 Objections to covertness

Objections to the use of covert research methods range from those expressed in terms of moral indignation (to concerns on behalf of the profession of research) to misgivings of a more pragmatic kind. It is in terms of such a continuum that they are ordered below although seldom is an argument expressed purely in terms of ethics or of professional standards or of appropriate methodology. It is possible to express the case against covert methods in terms of 13 contentions:

1. *Covert procedures flout the principle of informed consent.* So argues Bulmer (1980: 60), as though the principle of informed consent were sacred. As we have seen above (4.6) and will see below (5.5) it is a principle as much dishonoured in the practice of those who subscribe to it as in the use of covert methods. We can perhaps respect the spirit of the principle of informed consent as it applies to the use of covert methods by saying that these deprive subjects of the control of data that are arguably theirs. Covert methods are then seen as the theft of data from subjects and the debate is about the circumstances that warrant such a theft

in the cause of a greater good and about how we identify situations in which subjects should not be entitled to withhold data.

2. *Covert methods help erode personal liberty*. This is one of a number of arguments that recognise that social research contributes to a wider sphere of human relations and that its practitioners have a responsibility of leadership in the process of those relations. In Warwick's critique of Laud Humphreys' methods he quotes with approval Nicholas von Hoffman of the *Washington Post*:

> No information is valuable enough to obtain by nipping away at personal liberty, and that is true no matter who is doing the gnawing (Warwick, 1982: 44).

3. *Covert methods betray trust*. The term betrayal has moral overtones and these are intended in the argument and quite appropriate but the argument also has a utilitarian value. Trust is a desirable relationship when research depends upon any kind of cooperation. To damage or destroy relationships is foolish not least in respect of self-interest. Bulmer (1982b: 632) makes the point in respect of the methods of pseudo-patients such as Caudill and Rosenhan and he notices with disapproval the breach of the confidential relationships which they developed with their doctors. The objection that professional attention and care has been fraudulently obtained applies, of course, rather less to other studies and not at all to those in the collection by Davis and Horobin (1977) who had genuine reasons for occupying hospital beds.

4. *Covert methods pollute the research environment*. This is the aspect of the previous argument which stresses professional self-interest. After the publication of a covertly researched paper on pentecostal worship, by Homan (1978), Dingwall asked,

> How are the next legitimate researchers into Pentecostalism going to be received when the deceit of one of their colleagues becomes known (Dingwall, 1979).

5. *Covert methods are bad for the reputation of social research*. Whereas the previous argument assesses the effect of covert methods upon particular groups of potential subject, it is now argued that the activity of research has a certain status and salience in a society and this should be upheld by all who practise it. It is further submitted that covert methods jeopardise that reputation in a way that open methods do not. One of Warwick's concerns about the work of Laud Humphreys is that it is likely to reinforce the view that social researchers are sly tricksters (Warwick, 1982: 58). Erikson elaborates such a concern thus:

> We are increasingly reaching audiences whose confidence we cannot afford to jeopardise, and we have every right to be afraid that such people may close their doors to sociological research if they learn to

become too suspicious of our methods and intentions . . . Any research tactic which attracts unfavourable notice may help to diminish the general climate of trust toward sociology in the community as a whole (Erikson, 1967: 369).

6. *Covert methods discriminate against the defenceless and powerless*. It is submitted that relatively powerful groups have their affairs protected either by law, such as the Official Secrets Act, or by recourse to litigation against those who have infringed their liberties and damaged their interests. This is the basis of one of Warwick's objections to Laud Humphreys:

Had Humphreys passed as a voyeuristic gardener or chauffeur for a prominent family he would have been subject to legal and other kinds of retaliation. The man in the tearoom could not fight back (Warwick, 1982: 57).

The point may be made of other uses of covert methods than that of Humphreys but it is not universally true; Caudill and Rosenhan can hardly be criticised on this basis; still less can Holdaway who researched the police in the role of a policeman.

7. *Covert methods may damage the behaviour or interests of subjects*. Jason Ditton (1977: vii) recognises that his findings are likely to have an adverse effect upon the real wages of those who were found to be indulging in fiddling and pilfering. Humphreys drew attention to a world that would have been preferred by its inhabitants to remain unnoticed. In the long term, the interests of both groups may have been favourably served and the election of Humphreys to the National Committee for Sexual Civil Liberties suggests that there were sections of the community in which he was well received. Whether the effect of research is favourable to its subjects or unfavourable, the implications of publication are such that subjects are arguably entitled to have a control of which covert methods deprive them.

Another aspect of harm to subjects is the abuse or devaluation of their behaviour which is sometimes implied in the assumption by a researcher of a fully participant role. In the observation of religious groups there are rituals and sacraments which are not intended to be taken lightly. Albeit in the knowledge of the pastor, Pryce (1979: 285) allowed himself to be baptised and Homan (1980: 53) took part, with some misgivings, in the 'breaking of bread'.

8. *Covert methods may become habitual in the everyday life of the person doing the research*. We come now to concerns about the effects of covert research upon the researcher and the community. First, it is suggested that deception becomes a way of life. There is an extent to which any discipline invades the lives of its students outside the hours that are formally assigned to it. This is true of social research. When those who have trained in research

find themselves as hospital patients, they cannot stop themselves observing and note-taking, as the anthropologist Rosemary Firth found (Davis and Horobin, 1977: 143). In taking up a participant role in a community, one's subjects gradually become one's friends; the danger is that outside the context of the research one's friends become one's subjects (Homan, 1982: 117). The anthropologist Margaret Mead could see that training in the habit of lying to other human beings when doing research

> tends to establish a corps of professionally calloused individuals, insulated from self-criticism and increasingly available for clients who can become outspokenly cynical in their manipulation of other human beings, individually and in the mass (Mead, 1969: 376).

9. *The habit of deception may spread to other spheres of human interaction*. What the practice of covertness can do in the individual it might also do in a society as a whole. Warwick expresses this fear as his strongest objection:

> A democratic nation is ultimately built upon respect of constitutional processes and restraint in the use of means. If one group arrogates to itself the right to use non-constitutional means for advancing its ends others will do likewise. (Warwick, 1982: 58).

10. *Covert methods are invisibly reactive*. Whether they intend it or not, covert participants have an effect upon the behaviour of the group. It may be judged either a help or a hindrance according to the criteria used by subjects. Attendance of religious and political groups is interpreted as support for their causes and the participant may also contribute materially through an offertory or subscription; the smaller the group, the greater such support in spirit and in kind will be valued. Fielding (1982: 87) went further in his offer of help to the National Front during an election campaign.

Overt research is reactive in the same way. An educational researcher who approaches a school with a particular interest in drama or multicultural education or information technology signifies thereby the direction of current interest and is likely to boost teachers in the school who share that special interest. The difference is that where the method is overt and the reactive behaviour of the investigator is explicit, the influential factor is identifiable and its effect notionally measurable. The covert researcher will be able to attribute effects to his or her intervention but subjects will not recognise that this participant is neither normal nor permanent.

This argument is ethical in its concerns for the false hopes or fears of subjects but pragmatic in that it concerns the inevitability of an element of reactivity.

11. *Covert methods are seldom necessary*. It is argued on pragmatic grounds that the resort to covertness is seldom warranted and that

in many cases the results sought could be achieved by a more honest and consultative approach. While Jason Ditton (1977) used covert observation and argued cogently that he could not have penetrated the real world of his subjects by being overt, Stuart Henry (1978: x) interviewed another constituency of 'fiddlers and pilferers about their dodges and deals and they allowed him to tape-record their interviews.

12. *Covert methods have the effect of confining the scope of research*. Rose Barbour (1979: 9) is among those who make the point that the assumption of a participant role disqualifies the investigator from asking questions from a position of ignorance. The style adopted by Homan (1978), whom she criticises, was to arrive at pentecostal meetings using the greetings and pass-words adopted by initiated members; while this posture event-ually afforded access to the transactions of nuclear members, it precluded any collection of data on strategies of introduction, initiation and initial socialisation.

13. *The covert researcher suffers excessive strain in maintaining the cover*. More simply, the risk of being caught is a major and distracting concern. Several covert observers have come near to having their cover blown and their research terminated. There was an occasion during Fielding's National Front research when national officers to whom he had presented himself as a researcher were attending a meeting with branch members among whom he worked covertly: in the event, his association with hierarchs enhanced his standing in the branch but it was a moment of some strain. Ken Pryce (1979: 286) lost one of his field notebooks and found one of his subjects reading through it. Rosenhan and colleagues were never suspected of being sane by doctors but they were so diagnosed by fellow patients. When working among the police, Holdaway (1982: 71–2) was always checking his back pocket to make sure his notes were still there, then

> One afternoon while working in plain clothes, I got on a bus and wrote some notes. I looked across the aisle and noticed the night duty telephonist sitting next to me.

5.4 IN DEFENCE OF COVERT METHODS

5.4.1 Deception in social context

The experimental work of the social psychologist Stanley Milgram (1974) is discussed both in this volume (7.1) and in the literature generally as an example of harm and stress being suffered by sub-jects. The playwright Dannie Abse is, however, equally enraged that Milgram 'cheats' and 'hoaxes' his subjects (Abse, 1973: 22–23) by misinforming them on the nature of the experiment and of the identity of another person who was presented to them as a volunteer participant; Milgram also misled his subjects into thinking that they were choosing the roles they should play whereas these had been orchestrated as part of the experimental design. Milgram is unrepentant in his response to this charge. Illusion, he argues, is merely a device as legitimate in a psychology experiment as it is in Abse's genre of theatre. It is also pertinent, Milgram submits, that his subjects – who were comprehensively debriefed – gave positive feedback on their experience both at the time and in response to a subsequent enquiry (Abse, 1973: 38–41).

The point raised by the dispute between Milgram and Abse is pertinent to the general disapproval of covert methods in social research. Lying, deception, camouflage and disguise are thought unworthy practices in an honourable profession. But as Bok (1978) demonstrates in her cross-cultural survey of the practice of lying and Barnes (1983) in his examination of lying in other professions, many forms of deception are widely acceptable: the implicit question is whether social research should be any different.

While lying in the House of Commons is seen as a sufficient cause for resignation, it is pardonable as a strategy of self-defence deployed by prisoners in the dock. In researching a community in the Lebanon, Michael Gilsenan (1976: 191) found that lying was 'a fundamental element not only of specific situations and individual actions, but of the cultural universe as a whole'. Again, the social anthropologist Ernestine Friedl (1962: 78–81) found that parents in rural Greece deliberately lied to their children in order to encourage scepticism in other people's actions and words.

Lying is already accepted in a number of social transactions including entertainment and story-telling. These have in common with examples of social research that they are identifiable and separable from the experience of everyday life. It is also sometimes pardoned in the protection of sensitive or confidential information; social researchers who are challenged for deceiving their subjects may nevertheless be excused for deceiving those who press them to declare their findings or sources. Deception is tolerated in varying degrees from one country to another according to the importance attached to intelligence and security. Trickery is expected in some forms of entertainment and it may be submitted that it is also part of the bargain when subjects offer themselves for psychological experiments. If so, Abse's indignation is out of place: an element of misrepresentation is already standard and tolerated in psychological research as in other professional practices. What needs to be established by the critics of covert methods is why social research should be expected to conform to standards not honoured elsewhere.

5.4.2 Covert methods in social research

While the professional consensus weighs heavily against the use of covert methods and invokes in codes and guidelines the established principle of informed consent, some adjudicators such as Martin Bulmer (1982a: 231ff) deem covertness to be allowable in a limited number of special circumstances. For example, Bulmer would allow social scientists in academic posts to reflect upon previous experience in national service or some other profession and to interpret that experience within the terms of their discipline. Such a procedure would be constrained where the Official Secrets Act applies but elsewhere has yielded valuable material and has seldom been charged with offences against ethical principles.

However, there is not a straightforward case against the more obvious transgressions such as lying, deception, disguise, role pretence and betrayal; it is the purpose of this section to comment in defence of such methods.

First, the argument about the quality of data which is made in support of explicit observation and interviewing runs both ways. Dingwall has it that 'contemporaneous notes yield better data' (Dingwall, 1980: 878) but the consequence of openness in his earlier research on health visitor training was his exclusion from key transactions and information (Dingwall, 1977: 20). The limitations and reactivity of open methods are still more dramatically illustrated in the comparison of Jason Ditton's covert research of bakery workers and the earlier work of Daniel. Daniel (1963: 108) avoided deceiving his subjects and so allowed them to deceive him: when he overtly interviewed bread salesmen they denied making dishonest gains from their rounds; with this assurance he explained the anomaly that roundsmen drove their own cars whereas inside workers rode bicycles in terms of differential expenditure preferences (see Ditton, 1977: 10). In such circumstances, data openly sought and honestly acquired afford an inadequate analysis: open methods place the investigator at the mercy of subjects and mock the profession of research. They surrender to subjects or gatekeepers the selection of what may and what may not be researched. The limitations of Daniel's insights illustrate how heavily loaded are the odds against social research conducted according to established principles and how impotent is the research enterprise likely to be rendered by too deferential a view of the rights of subjects.

Another example of the reactivity of overt methods is to be found in the now classic work of Hargreaves in the sociology of education. Hargreaves adopted the standard posture of sitting at the back of the classroom. Pupils affirmed that they soon forgot he was there, being behind them and largely out of their view, but they told Hargreaves that the behaviour of teachers changed dramatically:

When you're in he tries to act calmly as though he's a little angel and all that.

Like if Mr O's getting mad 'cos someone's ripped a book or something, but if you're in he seems to stop it. If you weren't there he'd get real mad (Hargreaves, 1967: 197).

What is at issue is the right of subjects to refuse access and it has often been the expectation of this that has inclined researchers to go underground. Even the critics of covert methods, however, would not allow the right of refusal to all communities. Robert Dingwall, a 'liberation socialist' (Dingwall, 1977: 17), would condone the infiltration of the National Front (Dingwall, 1977: 7). Many would agree that the Broderbond in South Africa should have no right of protection from research and that the Jones sect might well have been spared the fate of mass suicide had some social researchers been able to detect its tendencies. Norman K. Denzin is reluctant, therefore, to accept a position which would restrict his activities to the interviewing of volunteers (Bulmer, 1982a: 147).

The emphasis in the literature upon the right of subjects to know that research is being conducted in their midst has not been balanced with a discussion of the right to remain ignorant. Patients with terminal diseases are entitled either to know or not to know. So it is in the fields of social research. Homan (1980: 55) has suggested that the pentecostals he observed in worship were entitled to freedom from the inhibition and self-consciousness that would be an inevitable consequence of the information that they were being observed by an outsider. The argument here is not that covert methods are less reactive and therefore yield more natural data – although that might be so – but that overt procedures have the effect in certain situations of reducing for subjects the value of their own behaviour. In those situations, covert methods are arguably the more sensitive of subjects' interests and are calculated with a higher regard for their comfort.

It is furthermore possible that covert researchers are in some events such as publication more sensitive of subjects' interests. Just as the informing and acquisition of consent may be taken as a licence to pry and intrude, so may adherence to established principles of openness incline researchers to feel that data fairly obtained are freely at their disposal. The covert researcher, by contrast, may treat the private worlds of human subjects with greater caution. When observing with consent and ostentatious use of the clipboard in pentecostal meetings, Homan witnessed the death of a woman in the course of a ministration of healing which she had declined and, on another occasion an expression of ecstatic utterance which was recognisable as orgasm: had these been covertly observed he would not have felt free to report them but in the event he had no scruples about publishing a paper which offered a sociological interpretation (Homan, 1981). Rosenhan was scrupulous in eliminating all clues that might identify subjects (Bulmer, 1982a: 262), Ditton even changed irrelevant details on which identification might have been made (Ditton, 1977: 9) and Laud Humphreys kept his data securely in the bank. These measures are not the marks of unprincipled snoopers who care nothing for their subjects or the reputation of their colleagues.

Nevertheless, covert researchers are charged with getting the profession of social research a bad name. Dingwall (1979: 7) asks what kind of a reception old-time pentecostals will give the next 'legitimate researchers' after they discover that Homan was among them in disguise. The fact was, however, that overt observations in 79 assemblies had shown that sociologists were already held in very low esteem and the possibility of cooperation was remote. Some pentecostals based their low expectations of sociology upon some very scholarly and responsible work by Bryan Wilson (1961), whose interpretation of pentecostal history they did not share. Their disapproval was based not on method but on publication. Covert observation which issued in neutral interpretations of pentecostal behaviour (such as Homan, 1978) was more likely to enhance the research environment in that case than to pollute it. Denzin makes the point that the research environment is equally spoiled by overt practitioners: 'The community surveyed twice annually for the past ten years can just as easily develop an unfavourable image of sociology and refuse to be studied as can a local Alcoholics Anonymous Club studied by a disguised sociologist' (Bulmer, 1982a: 144).

It may also be argued that public data available in public places are up for grabs and that those who write, speak or behave publicly bargain for the possibility that they will be observed – even by a social researcher. The content analysis of publications such as the National Front's *Bulldog* or of curriculum materials for schools is, understandably, not regulated by codes and guidelines requiring consent. In the same way, behaviour in public places is not regarded as unobservable except by permission. It would be absurd to announce to the audience of a Billy Graham crusade or to a football crowd that there was a student of sociology among them collecting material for a dissertation in anthropology or sociology of social psychology.

Again, students of these disciplines are not always aware that they are collecting data. Goffman did not sit on beaches or trains to observe the use of towels and newspapers and to interpret this as territorial assertion: rather, this was what he had observed in the course of his daily life and he reflected upon it in or after the event. Again, the anthropologist Rosemary Firth took informal notes in her hospital bed without intending to produce the essay on routines in a tropical diseases hospital which was published ten years later:

> Boredom suggested keeping a diary and habit and training prompted some very simple analysis (Davis and Horobin, 1977: 143).

Short of posting notices that there are social researchers about after the model of warnings about pickpockets, there seems to be no defence against the unpremeditated collection of data.

Data collected by the 'sociologist as citizen going about his business' are allowed by Bulmer (1982a: 233). But concerns such as the harm done to subjects and their attitude to future researchers are not likely to vary much according to whether data were collected purposely or by accident. 'Is it moral,' asks Julius Roth, 'if one gets a job in a factory to earn tuition and then takes advantage of the opportunity to carry out a sociological study, but immoral to deliberately plant oneself in the factory for the express purpose of observing one's fellow workers?' (Roth, 1962: 284).

Another apology for covert procedures is illuminated by the distinction of private data and private space explored in Chapter 3. The methods which have caused the most disquiet both within the community of researchers and outside it have been those that have involved concealment, whether of researchers under students' beds or by technological means such as hidden cameras and telephone tapping. It must be recognised that these unashamedly intrusive measures are not necessarily used to collect personal data. If the researcher is only monitoring hesitation phenomena or the grammatical structure of sentences, it is hardly as outrageous as if the object of the enquiry is to collect information on the recruitment procedures of a trade union or political sect. Of course, professionals fear with some justification that methods sanctioned for use in one situation may then be adopted in another. We must therefore stress here the need to assess the appropriateness of all research methods in the light of the circumstances in which they are deployed.

Covertness is defended here and there by various formulations of the argument that the end justifies the means. The infiltration by social researchers of the National Front 'might be warranted by higher ethical considerations' (Dingwall, 1979: 7). The case of eight pseudo-patients who simulated certain symptoms to gain admission to mental hospitals and might well have taken the beds of other genuine cases is justified by Rosenhan and Bulmer after him on the grounds that the data collected were valuable and could not have been secured by other means. The study was said by Rosenhan to have contributed to a situation in which too few mental health professionals had much previous insight of patient experience (Bulmer, 1982a: 17) and to have demonstrated 'the stickiness of psycho-diagnostic labels' (Bulmer, 1982a: 22). Bulmer judged that the Rosenham study provided 'important evidence about the process of psychiatric diagnosis, the labelling of patients and the interpretation of their subsequent behaviour in the light of this diagnosis (Bulmer, 1982b: 820).

There are difficulties with these justifications. They are, of course, closely related to the cases of research which are used to illustrate them and neither Rosenhan, Dingwall nor Bulmer are arguing that covert methods should be used more widely. Justifications on the basis of the value of data can only be retrospective; in choosing a method one has to be guided by the data one hopes to obtain and in a hazardous design such as Rosenhan's there was no guarantee that some serious mishap would not frustrate the collection of the useful data sought. Again, the researcher or student or supervisor is more likely to be convinced either that the data sought are unique or that higher ethical considerations prevail than are the community of fellow professionals. Those who deploy covert methods must expect to stir a reaction within the profession if and when they go to press.

5.5 THE ETHICS OF OVERT METHODS

The habit of critics of covert methods is to focus upon particular cases and to suggest by example that the purposes of covert research were equally achievable by open methods. However, it is demonstrable that those virtuous exemplars have vices of their own.

For example, it is claimed that openness is possible even in the most intrepid of research fields. 'Klockars' study of the professional "fence",' it is said, 'encountered few problems despite the fact that its author was open about his research intentions' (Bulmer, 1980: 64). The reality is that if Klockars had few problems with his primary contact 'Knuckles Jones', it was because this man was in hospital with diabetes at the time and was not expected to live long. Klockars 'decided to try to take immediate advantage of what seemed like a perfect opportunity', so he contacted Knuckles in hospital and offered him 'a kind of anonymous immortality in exchange for information' (Klockars, 1975: 201). He later made contact with 'Vincent' who was to become his principal informant and whom he briefed for the research by letter. In this he styled himself as a professor 'on the assumption that Vincent would not be familiar with academic rankings', said he had read everything that had been written on the professional 'fence' when he had not read anything, and appealed to Vincent by dismissing it all as 'junk', which was not his true judgement. Klockars assured Vincent that nothing he said could be used in evidence against him: this assurance was 'totally false' (Klockars, 1975: 216).

Similarly, Bulmer (1980: 64) cites the work of Ned Polsky to demonstrate the need of a social researcher working among criminals in their natural surroundings to maintain a clear distinction between himself and those whom he is studying. Polsky, however, took pains to remove from the situation those symbols of the social researcher such as the notepad or the tape-recorder which might contaminate the environment or remind subjects of what he was doing. He trained himself to remember transactions until he got home and could write them up. His strategy was to keep eyes and ears open but mouth closed: asking questions could prompt suspicion (Polsky, 1969: 126). He was a recognised pool player of 20 years standing and had fraternised regularly with the criminals he was now studying (Polsky, 1969: 46–8). It should not be thought that there was any ostentatious advertisement of the fact that he had turned researcher.

Whether or not Polsky was genuinely open with his subjects and whether Klockars came clean but offended in some other respect are, however, incidental to the deeper problem of how pervasive of open methods are practices that are not only unethical but immoral.

It has been suggested in earlier chapters that much of the counsel available to those entering fieldwork and a good deal of the practice that is reported in the literature satisfies established ethical principles rather more in the letter than in their spirit. In particular, the principle of informed consent is the theme of lip service at the outset of observation or interviewing with human subjects but the investigator then practises skills that incline the subject to lose sight of the content of information and the conditions of consent. Investigators report that some of their most useful data were collected once subjects forgot that they were speaking on the record (Barbour, 1979: 9) and children told Hargreaves that after a short time of his sitting at the back of their classroom they forgot he was there (Hargreaves, 1967: 197). On the one hand responsible researchers give notice of their role and on the other, to be effective, they retreat into the cover of participant behaviour (see 4.6).

The other taboo which is not protected by the adoption of overt methods is the invasion of privacy (see 3.5). Here it was noticed that a principle of questionnaire design is to establish such a credibility that the respondent will then cooperate with intrusive questions that might have 'shocked' had they been asked at the outset. The skill is to soften up the respondent so that he or she will be less likely to exercise their prerogative not to respond.

Although professional principles pay some respect to the privacy of individuals, the rule in practice is that invasion is allowable if it is done with the cooperation of subjects.

In addition to these there are various ways in which ethical principles are to some degree compromised by what are widely accepted as open methods.

5.5.1 The use of informants

Interviewees are not only used as respondents who answer questions concerning their views, attitudes and behaviour but also as sources of information. Questions seeking information may concern the basic demographic variables such as date of birth, occupation and so on of which the subject is the most reliable source. They may also legitimately concern aspects of a situation over which the interviewee is a responsible custodian; for example, a director or personnel manager may be asked the number of employees in a particular enterprise, details of distribution by age and gender, methods of recruitment, training, labour relations and so on.

A problem arises, however, when investigators use informants as an alternative to addressing questions to third parties to whom access might be difficult, hazardous, expensive or even impossible. Access to the lapsed members of a community is often easier than access to the community itself. Thus Zaslavsky and Brym (1978) used emigrés from the Soviet Union to obtain insight of the role of the agitator in getting voters to polling stations. Beckford (1985: 149) interviews 26 ex-Moonies, most of them voluntary defectors, and even the former spouses of Moonies (Beckford, 1985: 170–1). For social research purposes, the perspective of former members of a constituency is an interesting one and quite as valid as that of the official representatives of that community. But there are two problems associated with such a method. First, it is likely to be ill-favoured by those of the community who consider themselves to be the real subjects of the enquiry; for the Scientologists, Gaiman made the complaint that Roy Wallis had conducted extensive interviews with 'apostates' (Gaiman, 1977: 168). The second problem is really an articulation of the first in terms of established ethical principles for social research. In using informants for data on third parties one is by-passing the requirement of obtaining consent by those who are the subjects of the research. At the time the data were collected by the informant, there may have been no notion that he or she was acting as a surrogate field-worker.

There is a further difficulty in that responses on attitudes and behaviour often imply information about third parties which may then be accumulated to the point at which the third party becomes the subject of the research. Hargreaves asked boys in a secondary school 'Do your parents expect you to do jobs around the house?' and 'How often do you go out with your parents?' (Hargreaves, 1967: 211–2). He also used a sociogram technique to build up a picture of which boys were leaders and which were particularly unfavoured by their peers:

> write down the names of the boys that the lads don't pay much attention to, the kids that are ignored, that are unpopular, who get teased, who never take the lead in things and don't follow what the rest do (Hargreaves, 1967: 209).

These enquiries apparently accord with the accepted norms of research method. If the parents were approached directly, however, it would be appropriate to explain the purpose of the research and to secure their consent; these measures and safeguard are not available when information about them is being given by intermediate informants.

5.5.2 The uses of children

There is a notion that minors are among those for whom vicarious consent by a gatekeeper or parent satisfies the professional requirement. The common procedure for access and the informing of consent is exemplified in some detail in the report of the research project on the use of drugs among schoolchildren which was conducted from the London School of Economics. A questionnaire was administered to children in their schools and official approval was sought for this procedure. Letters to local education authority, probation officers and headteachers presented the enquiry as 'a social survey of drug-taking' (Wiener, 1970: 216–18) and reminded them of the urgency of the problem and of the need to acquire accurate information to inform subsequent policy. However, headteachers were asked not to inform their pupils of the purpose of the enquiry:

> We would prefer the children not to have any previous information about the subject matter of the survey as this can influence their replies and I should be obliged if you could ask any members of your staff whose timetable might be interrupted not to mention the main purpose of our visit to the children (Wiener, 1970: 218).

The explanation of the purpose of the survey was then given much more selectively to its subjects than to their gatekeepers:

> Good morning/afternoon. My name is . We come from the London School of Economics. Part of our work there is to do surveys about the way different people live and the opinions they have . . . Today, we are going to ask you some questions about yourselves, about what you do in your spare time and also about what you think of various things (Wiener, 1970: 218).

This studiously anodyne explanation of purpose was part of a strategy 'to disguise the fact that this questionnaire was aimed primarily at drug-taking' (Wiener, 1970: 80). Another attempt at disguise was in the design of the questionnaire which had only three items on drug-taking in the first half. This 'ruse', as Wiener calls it, seemed to have been successful in that only 3 per cent of subjects guessed what the survey was really about.

This is an example of the overt methods which exposes some procedures that are arguably as unethical as those of covert researchers. Wiener and his colleagues obtained consent from responsible parties and this was fully informed. It was on the basis of the sensitivity of the subject matter that this information was withheld from respondents although their being children meant that such non-disclosure was in any case fairly standard practice. The research was overt in the sense that everybody was told who the investigator was, where he came from and, in vague terms, what was the object of the exercise. The administration of a questionnaire is an explicit method of enquiry.

But Caudill and Rosenhan, whose researches go down in the history of social research as unethical procedures, obtained consent from hospital authorities senior to the practitioners who encountered and diagnosed them and the nature of Ken Pryce's work was known to his pastor. We have to ask whether the use of a group of children, who in a classroom situation were unlikely to decline to do what was asked of them and who were deliberately excluded from the salient facts about the purpose of the research, is any more ethical for being 'open' according to the letter of the law than were some of the covert observations which have been the case material of this chapter.

5.5.3 The authority of the researcher

There are circumstances in which subjects are compelled to yield to the demands of an investigator either because there is a legal obligation or because there is a formal relationship outside the project which the investigator can bring to bear upon potential subjects.

The census which is conducted in Britain every ten years by the Registrar General is an example of an enquiry which has the force of law. There are leaflets accompanying the census form which explain its purpose and there is often a public discussion at the time about particular questions such as those about place of birth. Subjects are therefore informed to an acceptable degree but they have no option of withholding consent. Nor do teachers and the staffs of schools when they hear that they are to be visited by Her Majesty's Inspectors who subsequently write a report which, under the terms of the 1980 Education Act, has to be made public.

In the case of HMI, there is often little or no explanation about the purpose of the visit and this can only be surmised from the questions they ask and the special interests they show.

Even where there is no legal obligation on the part of the respondent, investigators may use a role or status to prevail upon subjects and secure their compliance. This commonly happens when teachers are required to do a dissertation in connection with a degree or other in-service course and elect to base the project in the school in which they are employed. Anne Sutherland (1975), for example, called upon her reputation as a respected and well-liked headteacher of a school with gypsy children to gain an entrée into the gypsy community.

Pat Sadler's work was conducted in her own low ability tutor group in a large comprehensive school: her method was to place a live tape recorder in group sessions every Monday morning from the first session of year one and then, selectively until the end of the second year. Neither children nor parents challenged the use of the recorder nor did they question other methods of collecting data: consent was not sought. Sadler's account (1980) is sensitive of the wide range of ethical issues which attend such research conduct. There is a sense in which the tutor group becomes an intimate community and in which confidences are shared: the children talk of home and leisure activities, financial affairs and health and convey to the group their perceptions of other teachers. During the tutor group session the register is called so that the names of the children are also recorded. The recordings are then stored to enable any readers of Sadler's report to challenge her interpretations (1980: 79).

There is an ambiguity between the role and authority which a person acts and enjoys in everyday life and the relationships which a principled investigator is expected to cultivate with subjects. The researcher–subject relationship is not prescribed in the codes as one of authority but one of cooperation in which the rights are accorded to the subject to whom the researcher must be obliged. One of the major criticisms that Warwick (1982: 57) makes of Laud Humphreys in particular is that he picks on a powerless group who could not fight back. The introduction of an authority relationship to the business of research renders the subjects of overt enquiries relatively powerless to refuse to take part.

5.5.4 Open methods and the credibility of research

The reputation of social research is related to a number of factors including its capacity to provide accurate and scientific data for the consumption of a public or of a client. Researchers are accountable to their profession which will go out of business if ever people stop taking notice of research findings. Critics of covert methods are inclined to the view that deception in the pursuit of data is not likely to be approved by the public or that data so obtained are of questionable worth.

We may now ask whether research findings improve or diminish in value when they have been controlled by subjects, either in manipulating the access of the researcher or in screening reports before publication. The right to do so and the sense that the researcher will only get a full picture if subjects are granted this right are represented by the Scientologist David Gaiman (1977) in response to the work of Roy Wallis.

The sociologist Eileen Barker is always punctilious in consultations with her subjects in the Unification Church, the Moonies. For those who disapprove deception and concealment, Eileen Barker's overtness with Moonies has been exemplary.

But this backfires and the reputation of sociological research has been challenged because openness and rapport are perceived as collusion with subjects and manipulation by them. In 1987 Eileen Barker was granted £120,000 by the British government to set up a research centre on the new religious movements which subsequently became known as 'INFORM'. The former Attorney-General Lord Rawlinson criticised the Home Office for making the grant to a person whose association with the Moonies was so close. The Unification Church had paid Dr Barker's expenses to eighteen of its conferences throughout the world, sparing the tax-payer this expense. Politicians wanting a more distant relationship between researcher and subjects – and perhaps disappointed that government investment in research had not issued in a more damning indictment of the new religious movements – interpreted money from the Moonies as an investment in the one thing that any cult craves, respectability (BBC radio programme, 'Face the facts', 24 May 1989).

5.5.5 Breaking down subjects' defences

Once subjects are notified that research is going on and what it is about, every effort may be made to achieve a position in which they forget the reality of the situation. They may be told at the outset that they are entitled to decline to answer a particular question if they wish, but open researchers design their schemes to put them in a more cooperative mood so that they are unlikely to exercise that prerogative.

Such a practice is not merely an abuse of professional conduct to be found here and there: it is standard in the training of social researchers. In a time-honoured classic among textbooks on research methods, Margaret Stacey advises that interviewers can use a series of innocuous questions to build confidence and then try more sensitive items at the end:

Having already answered so many questions, respondents may well be prepared to answer a final one or two rather 'personal' questions, which might have shocked them at the beginning (Stacey, 1959: 81).

The techniques of relaxing subjects and putting them into a cooperative mood are often more enterprising than questionnaire design. Belson (1975: x) fed his subjects before interviewing them about their experiences of thieving. Dingwall, who is noted above for the high moral tone he adopts in his commentary on covert methods, was involved in drinking sessions with his subjects (Dingwall, 1977: 17). Kinsey and his colleagues (1948: 58) developed special techniques for interviewing children under eight years: they used games, puzzles, stories, 'romping' and acrobatics . . 'tucked into which were questions to yield data on the child's sexual history.' Dicker and Gilbert (1988: 70) found that 'tactful responses by the interviewer' had the effect of squeezing information out of telephone survey respondents who had refused to talk on the grounds of not being able to spare the time.

The skill is to achieve the condition enjoyed by Hargreaves (1967: 197) and Sadler (1980: 79) when subjects forget that the tape recorder is present and live. It is in this state of semi-consciousness that the subjects of open research give their best value:

Some of my most valuable data have been collected when my respondents have opened up on social occasions, having forgotten about my research involvement (Barbour, 1979: 9).

This desirable lapsing of subjects' awareness is defensible on ethical as well as utilitarian grounds:

perhaps it becomes unethical to constantly remind people that their every action, word and deed is under close sociological scrutiny (Barbour, 1979: 9).

CHAPTER 6

Writing and publication

6.1 OWNERSHIP OF DATA

When access has been responsibly negotiated, the consent of subjects informed and given, the boundaries of privacy respected, the interests and welfare of respondents properly considered and all the professional codes scrupulously observed, there persist conflicts over the rights to data.

The desire of subjects to control data that relate to them is prompted by their wishes to be represented in the most acceptable light; this may not be the same as being represented faithfully. The Church of Scientology, for example, cares greatly about its public image and is not alone in being disappointed when published accounts do not accord with its perceptions of itself. Teachers, police, bakery workers and others stand to gain or lose not only in terms of the standing of their professions but at the individual level in terms of job security and career prospects. The more explicit is the identity of subjects in a report prepared for publication, the greater will be their motivation to set the record, as they view it, 'right'.

Responsible researchers value truth and will welcome correction on points of fact. On the other hand, they may for the same reason be reluctant to omit data they observed or received merely because subjects do not want them to be reported. Many research reports are informed by groups in various degrees of conflict, albeit within the same community, and the researcher may take account of a range of respondents. For example, Wallis (1976) achieved some of his insights as a student of a Scientology course but he also made contact with ex-Scientologists; predictably, the hierarchy disapproved the interviewing of 'apostates' (Gaiman, 1977: 108), although Wallis and other sociologists of religion regard such a strategy as beneficial to the research.

There is, then, both the possibility of a conflict of interest between researchers and their subjects and a procedural problem in many cases of identifying which subjects should be consulted at report stage and whether official representatives of subjects are admissible. This is the context in which questions over the ownership of data are raised and must be resolved. And nothing concentrates the researcher's mind more wonderfully than the prospect of litigation.

There are, however, other claimants to data collected in research projects. Undergraduate and research students normally operate with greater freedom and the likelihood is that in their cases negotiation over data may be a matter for investigator and respondents alone. Where research is funded, however, or where the researcher operates as an employee of an institution which directs the research, or where it is commissioned by a client, the researcher normally yields rights over data to the client or sponsor. For example, the guidelines for Development Fund projects drawn up by the Council for National Academic Awards (1986: 3) states,

> The owner of data generated by DES [Department of Education and Science] funded research projects (and the copyright thereof) is CNAA.

In the effort to make it clearer that the researcher has no rights, the potential claims of subjects are excluded.

The rights of subjects over their own data are also denied in researches conducted under statutory powers in which non-response is a criminal offence. The effect of the law is to grant the census authority absolute rights over certain data. The antithesis of this procedure is the 'democratic' approach to subjects elaborated by Barry MacDonald and deployed extensively in evaluation projects, frequently as part of the activities of the Centre for Applied Research in Education based at the University of East Anglia. The democratic principle established by MacDonald was discussed in Chapter four (4.3) and is operationalised in the form of ethical guidelines by Helen Simons (1984). Simons' guidelines are distinguished by her neutrality and distance and her willingness to represent subjects' views without interference:

> The evaluator aspired to represent all views fairly; differences of view were regarded as data to be communicated, not matters on which the evaluator arbitrated.
>
> The evaluator adopted the role of documenting events accurately and fairly . . .
>
> The evaluator does not have a vested interest in the subject under investigation (Simons, 1984: 89). Interviews, discussions, group meetings, written statements were all potential data for the evaluation; but individuals had the opportunity to check the accuracy of the reportage, to correct or improve attributable interview statements to suggest amendments (Simons, 1984: 91).

The democratic principle was also operationalised by the research project SAFARI who established that

> data is the property of interviewees and should only be made accessible with their consent (Simons, 1980: 144).

The granting to respondents of rights over data means that they may alter or withdraw data up to the point of publication. It constitutes a concession by the researcher and many find this position untenable as it implies too great a surrender of information collected and allows the concealment of information from those who are entitled to be its audience.

Social researchers working in institutions of higher education have in recent years experienced changes in the initiation and support of research with a further loss of control over data. The time was when academic staff could set their own research agenda and find the means of carrying it out. The recent pressure to finance universities and colleges from outside funding has meant that those who want to undertake social research must look for sponsors. Simultaneously, the funding bodies have reduced their support of research projects submitted to them on the basis of problems identified by the applicant and have tended to specify areas within which they are prepared to receive applications. In times of scarce resources it is no longer possible to spend three years observing the formation of bus queues except by supporting oneself. Further, the areas specified are often related to policy intentions and government departments may not want to fund and have published research reports with findings contrary to their own statements. In these cases there might well be clauses in a contract that give the sponsor rights over the data: a discussion of research contracts follows (6.3).

Now much of the debate about the ownership of data is based around a misapprehension of the nature of research, the nature of data and the role of the investigator. If research were only about collecting facts and figures and writing down faithfully and double-checking what each of several participants said, and then, after all that, of allowing them to revise or withdraw their statements, it would be a singularly uncreative activity that would not for long satisfy those who engage in it. The collection of hard and raw data involves the resolution of enough methodological problems for it to be intellectually stimulating but it is a small part of social research as we understand it. What is required of the researcher is the selection of data, the classification of responses, the insight of principles which relate key data, the sorting of worthwhile observations and the recognition of patterns and processes.

That data are only a small part – albeit a necessary part – of a research report may be illustrated by two examples, both of them concerned with the notion of the definition of the situation. Joan Emerson (1973) worked as a nurse attending gynaecological consultations and subsequently wrote a sociological paper aptly entitled 'Behaviour in private places'. The data she noted were snippets of the exchanges between gynaecologists and the patients they were examining. She noticed an avoidance of eye contact and observed that '"spread your legs" is generally metamorphosed into the innocuous "let your knees fall apart"' (Emerson, 1973: 63). Emerson's thesis is that a clinical and impersonal language and behaviour are rehearsed to define the situation as a medical encounter and not as a romantic flirtation. It is a creative and inspiring paper, not because of the (very few) data that an untrained observer might equally have collected from the consulting room on a tape-recorder but for Emerson's discovery of the significance of clinical behaviour, of which the data she reports are but a few examples.

The second illustration is Homan's (1978) study of interaction in a pentecostal prayer meeting in which he noticed that petitions addressed ostensibly to the Almighty were intended for the hearing of other participants, who in turn would retaliate, again in the medium of prayer. There was a dialogue about the leadership of Rhodesia with one side praying for Ian Smith and a black member following this with a prayer for her 'brothers and sisters'. At the end of the prayer meeting members would all greet each other in the usual way and the issue was not allowed to surface except in prayer. While members could agree that the statements quoted had been uttered, they did not share the interpretation put upon them.

The distinction must be made, then, between data and insights or interpretations. If in a given situation the ownership of data is granted to respondents and release of data negotiated with them, that need not imply that they are also entitled to approve or disapprove and thereby to control the interpretation that is put upon them. In any case, data may be vital to the communication of an insight so that subjects' control over data can itself be a serious setback to a researcher operating on the fringes of new knowledge. In the terms of the ethical principles of SAFARI, interpretations are negotiable as well as data; the critic of SAFARI ethics David Jenkins quotes from Rob Walker:

> Democratic evaluation places the case study worker in the position of having to *negotiate* his interpretations with those involved in the study, rather than being free to impose them on the data (Jenkins, 1980: 150).

The situation is in many respects different where the ownership of data is claimed by an employer or client. Market research agencies are bound by their *Code of Conduct* not to release any data without the permission of the client, except where partial or distorting information has already been released (Market Research Society, 1986: 21). Much of the work governed by this code will be represented as raw data, possibly with some statistical correlations. However, research funded by government agencies and other sponsors is often of a more qualitative kind; here the rights over the final report may constitute a claim over interpretations as well as data. To the extent that the funding body has hired its researchers, it may have both a moral and a contractual claim upon their insights. To withhold interpretative findings or to release them independently would be like working for Cadbury's and taking home chocolates. This does not mean that researchers will find congenial a situation in which they are prevented from uttering what they have discovered in the course of an investigation that may have lasted two or three years. They are therefore wise to be circumspect when considering the obligations of an otherwise tempting research contract.

6.2 THE OBLIGATION TO PUBLISH

Jennifer Platt gives details of cases in which a veto has been exercised upon the publication of research by the sociologists she interviewed: not too much significance should be attached to the detail because she states that she has altered it in the interests of anonymity (Platt, 1976: 7) but the principles are still of interest. In one case, a researcher 'Frank Brown' gave notice of his findings to senior members of the institution in which he was researching; these reflected badly on their practice and they were mindful of their dependence upon resources from outside, so they asked him to discontinue his research and paid him to take up another project. As his research was registered for a doctorate, this had serious personal implications but it was later agreed that he could continue to work within the institution as long as he confined himself to historical aspects (Platt, 1976: 47–9). Another researcher let managers of the institution in which he was working see his findings, which included the observation that numbers of clients were being dealt with by unqualified staff; the researcher was told that he had abused his position and the continuation of the research was made conditional upon the destruction of all copies of the report and the notes on which it was based (Platt, 1976: 49–50).

It is apparent in both cases that economic and perhaps other interests of the institutions being researched would be jeopardised by publication. This was so whether or not the research findings were true. However, if they were true we must consider other forms of interest than those of the subjects concerned, in particular the clients and benefactors upon whose goodwill these institutions depended. It might be thought that the researcher has a moral duty to publish so that these parties can inform their behaviour and policies. Further, both researchers concerned had invested time in pursuit of a doctorate: their careers were affected by withdrawal from their projects just as their institutions stood to be affected by continuation. The issue of the release of data thus relates closely to other issues. To grant subjects rights over these is to exclude the rights of other interested parties while the right of veto over adverse findings is to place a heavy constraint upon the freedom and integrity of social research.

Issues relating to the obligation to publish are also raised by the tendency of government departments to use research contracts as a means of controlling the dissemination of results, as illustrated by examples of such contracts quoted in an earlier chapter (2.5). In the contracts of the Department of the Environment cited by Willmott (1980: 9–10), the trend is to give the Secretary of State the right of approval, and thereby of veto, over any publication, report, paper, lecture, seminar contribution, open-day exhibition or any other means of dissemination planned by the research team. These initiatives would only be impeded by the Department if they were judged to be other than in the 'public interest' or the 'national interest'. Willmott raises a number of pertinent questions in respect of the trend toward greater government control. Since public funds are being invested in research, he suggests, it is important that the public should be given access to results, and perhaps even more important that these should be available to policy makers such as Members of Parliament. The constraint upon publication is, Willmott argues, bad for research because it may discourage researchers from accepting government contracts, bad for government in preventing public discussion and bad for public debate which is the essence of a democratic society (Willmott, 1980: 10).

What makes a number of researchers rather uneasy about the rights reserved by government departments is the ambivalence of the notion of 'the national interest', on the basis of which publication can be forbidden. A minister committed to government policies is likely to have a partisan view of the national interest and to regard not only as embarrassing but even as against the national interest research findings that contradict that government's claims. The principle governing what is termed 'public information' is that a government is free to invest in advertising to communicate its policies only after those policies have received the Royal Assent and become law. The communication of a 'message' before that moment is not 'public information' but 'propaganda' and must be paid for by the party rather than from public funds. A similar ethical principle might be thought to apply to the control of such information as research findings. The prohibition or embargo of research results is a method of selecting the basis of information on which public discussion takes place; that kind of selection might be allowable in a political party's communications but is not the prerogative of a public servant who commissions research from public funds.

By the same standard, it might be considered improper for a public servant to use public money for research of which the results are expected to legitimise the policies of a particular party. In the approach to the 1987 General Election, much was made of what were regarded to be the excesses of particular local authorities and Conservative policies relied upon the demonstration that local government was widely deviant or incompetent. The interest that was stirred settled upon a small number of local authorities, including that of the London Borough of Brent, into which the Secretary of State for Education Kenneth Baker sent a party of schools inspectors. That education in Brent should come under such close scrutiny was not remarkable in view of the public concern that by then had been stimulated; what was remarkable was the speed and timeliness with which the report was made public while other reports by Her Majesty's Inspectors waited many months and even years (*The Times*, 25 April, 1987: 2). In the following months Mr Baker was to publish the Bill which as the Education Reform Act of 1988 substantially reduced the powers of the local education authority. It is, then, the practice of a government department to promote some kinds of information and to withhold others according to the policies being formulated.

The need for information to be publicly available is expressed by John Stuart Mill in his essay *On Liberty* written in 1859; this is often taken to be the classic formulation of the right to know and Mill's thinking is based on what is good for a society. A principal purpose of Mill's essay was to fix a limit 'to the legitimate interference of collective opinion with individual independence' (Rees, 1985: 138). Mill contended that a prevailing opinion should, if false, be displaced by others that were true, and if true, had nothing to lose by the open expression of contrary opinions. The terms in which Mill expresses his argument apply directly to the circumstances of government control illustrated by Willmott:

> First, if any opinion is compelled to silence, that opinion may, for aught we can certainly know, be true. To deny this is to assume our own infallibility.
>
> Secondly, though the silenced opinion be in error, it may and very commonly does, contain a portion of truth; and since the general or prevailing opinion on any subject is rarely or never the whole truth, it is only by the collision of adverse opinions that the remainder of the truth has any chance of being supplied.
>
> Thirdly, even if the received opinion be not only true but the whole truth; unless it is suffered to be, and actually is, vigorously and earnestly contested, it will by most of those who receive it, be held in the manner

of a prejudice, with little comprehension or feeling of its rational grounds (Mill, 1975: 65).

Mill is widely regarded by his critics to lack a sense of the interdependence of individuals and human groups and of their actions (Rees, 1985: 140–4). Certainly, there is an element of political *naïveté* in the notion that dominant groups are more concerned about truth than about consequences. Nevertheless, Mill expresses clearly the case for open access to all available evidence to the end that this may be seen to be taken into account before decisions are made.

At a lower level than government, the right of access to the best available information is implied in the principle of accountability which in recent years has been applied to various professional groups. For example, access to medical records may be necessary if a judgement is to be made on the professional behaviour and competence of a general practitioner. Again, the rights of parents to choose schools for their children, which are confirmed in the 1980 Education Act, necessitate the availability of such information as examination results and the publication of inspectors' reports of particular schools. The right to know is pressed most urgently where there is public interest, either because those researched are paid from public sources or because lives, whether of children or of patients, are at stake. It is in this vein that Jenkins (1980) stresses the obligations of researchers to their audiences and takes issue with the SAFARI group for whom obligations to subjects are paramount.

Richard Pring is among those who for a number of reasons are reluctant to concede the public right to know as a justificatory concept for the conduct of research and he suggests certain obligations upon the researcher on which it should be contingent. While research may be allowable if disinterested, Pring observes that this condition is seldom satisfied. The effect of educational research has been intrusive and potentially damaging:

> Under a misguided belief in the right to know, schools have been observed, teachers and pupils interviewed, classroom conversations and interviews minutely examined, and all reported upon to the public at large, irrespective of the consequences to that school or to those teachers and pupils (Pring, 1984a: 42).

Second, Pring insists that the knowledge or information to which a right is claimed must first be submitted to the most severe and critical scrutiny; he doubts whether what passes for research often or ever satisfies this standard:

> The exposure to particular facts or to particular statements or to a selection from the data can so easily distort an understanding of what then is made public; for it removes that which is to be known from the

context in which it must be understood or from the process of enquiry to which it is logically related (Pring, 1984a: 42).

Third, the right to know conflicts with other rights that are seemingly as fundamental, such as respect for persons. It may have the further effect of inhibiting the professional judgement of such as doctors, priests and teachers which had previously not been available for public scrutiny: this, of course, may be a good thing or a bad thing but it is an effect that must be taken into account in evaluating the public right to know.

Elsewhere, Pring sets out the obligations which a researcher should honour when providing the public with research findings. At the outset of a research project, the investigator should set out clearly the kinds of knowledge sought and renegotiate these as the project evolves. Second, the researcher is obliged to declare throughout the project the data being collected and the interpretations being put upon them. Third, the researcher should be continuously open to cross-examination by subjects on points of objectives, methodology, interpretations and so on. And fourth, those researched are entitled to have their response included with the published report (Pring, 1984b: 14).

Whether or not it is in the interests of those who are affected by research to exercise their right to know will vary from case to case. Teachers and pupils who are not performing well may do worse by losing confidence if they and others are informed of this finding than if they remained oblivious and kept on trying. As with patients who are terminally ill, subjects may also have a right not to know. The researcher may be the one who must decide whether revelation or concealment are in the best interests of subjects. On this point John Barnes inclines to the view that the right to know must be satisfied if desired by adults but that a more paternalistic judgement may be applicable where the subject is a child (Barnes, 1979: 154).

6.3 A NOTE ON RESEARCH CONTRACTS

6.3.1 Cause for concern

Social researchers have recently become increasingly concerned at the imposition of various restrictions on the conduct of research which have been written into research contracts and letters of agreement. It is believed that these in some ways constrain the scope of research, reduce its validity and compromise the integrity of the research discipline. It is assumed that who pays the piper calls the tune and that researchers are relatively powerless to negotiate satisfactory conditions with sponsors. Our purpose here, however, is to take stock of the seriousness of contractual obligations for the future prospects of social research and to indicate strategies to conserve and even recover ground that is being lost.

Perhaps the major irritant for social researchers is the claim of sponsors – and of government departments and agencies in particular – to approve all forms of publication, including reports of research in progress and papers delivered to conferences and seminars. Contracts now being issued exceed the expectation that advance copies of reports will be submitted to the sponsoring body for courtesy or comment: grant-making bodies assert the right to withhold from publication findings which they do not approve. For example, a research contract issued by the Department of Education and Science (1985) requires:

> The Secretary of State shall be consulted before any written paper, statement or press notice is published, or press or other conference held, in connection with the project or the said materials. A draft of any such written statement, paper or press notice shall be sent to the Secretary of State in sufficient time to allow him a reasonable opportunity for him to comment on it before the proposed date of publication, and any such publication shall be subject to his approval.

Similarly, the rules of the Health Education Authority (1987) provide that:

> No information concerning work undertaken by the grant-holder at the Authority's expense may be published or released to the press in any form without the prior agreement of the HEA project officer.

Until 1987 the standard contract issued by the Department of Health and Social Security had required that notice of any intended submission to a journal be given by the investigator to the Department within 28 days to allow for a response but the contract allowed the researcher an element of freedom and discretion:

> Any comments which the Secretary of State makes shall be considered by the Researcher but the Researcher shall nevertheless be free to allow publication to go forward as he thinks fit (quoted by Boddy, 1988: 1).

The new DHSS contract, however, subtracts that freedom by making publication subject to the consent of the Department which may allow information to be released only upon the satisfaction of certain conditions (Boddy, 1988: 1).

The issue of the ownership of data is closely related to that of control over publication. In the strictly legal sense it may be reasoned that data – or at least the paper on which they are recorded – are the property of the sponsor (Heasman, 1982: 35). However, there are variations in the assertion of this claim between government sponsors who uniformly claim copyright and foundations such as Nuffield, Rowntree and Leverhulme which regard copyright as residing with the researcher (except that Nuffield claims copyright in respect of projects initiated by itself) (Social Research Association, 1980).

Contractual controls upon the conduct of research now go still further in relating to aspects of methodology. Elliott (1989: 14) found evidence of a tendency to impose restrictions on such aspects of the conduct of research as the questions to be addressed, the methods of data collection and analysis. The revised Standard Contract of the Department of Education and Science (1985) states:

> No person shall be asked to answer any questionnaire unless the terms of the questionnaire and its use have been approved by the Secretary of State.

6.3.2 Issues

The issues that arise from these contractual conditions affect not only the integrity of research but also the balance of political forces in the society it serves. In a democratic society, it can be argued, citizens should have a right of access to the uncensored findings of publicly sponsored research (Bridges, *et al.* 1988: 12). If there are security implications in affording public access to research concerning sensitive matters such as defence, intelligence and arms procurement, these cannot be contended in the same way in respect of social services, health and educational provision: in defence of freedom for educational research, Bridges, *et al.* (1988: 2) comment that

> It is difficult to imagine any sphere of government in which a case for governmental restriction upon what the public may know is more difficult to maintain.

Within the social research community the most persistent concern is for the maintenance of academic freedom because it is supposed that the quality and validity of research are dependent upon it. Government investment in research, it is feared, too often has the motive of legitimising intended policy and is too seldom open to findings that would contradict or embarrass policy intentions. Academic freedom is a principle that espouses the discovery of truth without fear or favour. In conditions of competition for research contracts, which are sought both because institutions need money and because individuals have career aspirations, there is a 'temptation . . . to accept sub-optimal contractual conditions which compromise the principle of academic freedom and other canons of intellectual inquiry in a free society' (Elliott, 1989: 14).

Where the freedom of the researcher is inhibited by the terms of the contract, it is submitted, the integrity of the research is impaired and its value reduced. It cannot command the most serious notice of the scientific community: Boddy observes that the effect of revising DHSS contracts to exert greater control over investigators was to devalue the research in which the Department was investing:

> the fact that research has been conducted under the terms of the new contract must inevitably mean that its publication *may* have been subject to 'conditions' – with the consequence that the integrity and validity of *all* DHSS-supported work will be regarded as suspect; more fundamentally, the issue is that of academic freedom and the assessment of the work on the basis of its scientific merit (Boddy, 1988: 2).

The procedures for the validation of research are also prevented by contractual conditions which control the circulation of research findings. It is by exposure to criticism and the appraisal of the wider scientific community that social research stands the test of validation. The filtering of findings through a sponsor, controls over what findings and interpretations will be released and the locking of data within closed systems mean that the research does not have the benefit of a more general scrutiny and the recognition that is due when the test has been passed. In short, the research process is 'incomplete' (Bridges, *et al.*, 1988: 14) and what is delivered to the sponsor is the less worthy.

6.3.3 Strategies

In the encounter of sponsors and researchers, the researchers are perceived as the relatively powerless party. Non-acceptance of contractual conditions may mean only that a research assignment goes elsewhere to an institution which is prepared to undercut the standard of more scrupulous bidders. It is therefore difficult to find initiatives which researchers may take in order to improve the terms on which contracts are settled.

A lead taken by the professional associations in establishing standards is likely to have a limited effect since – as is several times explained in this book – membership tends to be voluntary and the sanctions available are few. When Boas complained that fellow professionals who offered their expertise in connection with espionage did not deserve to be recognised as anthropologists, the remark backfired on him: but in due course the American Anthropological Association has taken his point and in the wake of Project Camelot has advised members that before entering a contractual commitment they should examine the behaviour and record of intended sponsors and should not accept conditions contrary to professional principles (Weaver, 1973: 46–8; Akeroyd, 1984: 134). In particular, the Association's code (1971: 3a) recommends the rejection of research contracts 'where results cannot be freely derived and publicly reported'. Such a position may only be sustained if it is generally honoured by the professional group so that unreasonable sponsors fail to find contractors at any price.

Another possibility is the development of relations between the group of government departments which sponsor social research and the professions which undertake it, with a view to establishing general standards. If the research academy is to lend its approval and warrant to research that is undertaken, it must make the conditions clear and be prepared to disown research that falls short of the accepted standard. The fact is that sponsors derive benefits from the research they support and that the research community has more bargaining power than it may have supposed. Bridges *et al.*, (1988: 14) note with approval a clause in a Department of Employment contract which might provide a meeting point between those who stand by sponsor control and those who assert the freedom of the researcher:

> A draft of any proposed book, article or other publication shall be submitted to the Department for comment prior to publication, and any such publication shall, unless agreed to the contrary, acknowledge the Department's assistance and/or carry such disclaimer as the Department may require, in a form to be agreed with the Department.

This formula allows both for the perspective of the researcher and for the sponsor's case to be represented. Boddy suggests a further way in which a researcher may achieve a distance from the sponsor and publish with a relatively clear conscience: in order to protect the integrity of research, authors might consider including in any report or publication a statement to the effect that the report has not been subject to conditions or to indicate what these have been. It is suggested that this would not detract from but enhance the quality of the research report (Boddy, 1988: 4) and scientific journals could require such a statement in respect of all funded research. Devices of this kind have in recent years been used by broadcasters reporting from South Africa and Northern Ireland, reminding listeners and viewers that their reports have been compiled under government restrictions.

Particular concern over implications for the quality of research has been expressed in the British Educational Research Association which set up an invitational seminar in 1988 to review and respond to trends in the contracting of research. At its 1988 conference there was a symposium on this issue in which a paper by

Nigel Norris (1988) on 'The contractual control of social inquiry' drew from several standard contracts to present a bleak picture of control and compromise.

Subsequently, John Elliott (1989) has written a draft code of practice for funded research which suggests standards, and looks to the professional association to lead, honour and implement.

6.4 CONFIDENTIALITY AND ANONYMITY

Confidentiality has a number of aspects in the conduct and publication of social research. It arises in respect of sources of data such as documents which may be sealed as confidential but in certain cases cleared for use by the researcher under certain conditions; or else researchers may come by confidential documents without such clearance. Secondly, confidentiality takes the form of a contract between researcher and subjects in which the researcher agrees so to report the enquiry that the identities of participants will not be disclosed. Thirdly, confidentiality may be a condition governing the circulation of a research report; it may be made available only to those who commissioned it, in which case those who were its subjects will not have access to findings; for example, the report of a curriculum evaluation might be confidential to its author and the Chief Education Officer in whose authority the evaluation was commissioned (Pring, 1984a: 38).

To the extent that confidentiality represents a constraint upon publication, it contradicts the right to know. A report deemed confidential is not available to a wider audience: the human subjects of research may enjoy this as a privilege and use it to deny to those who read a report the knowledge of who they are.

The concern of John Stuart Mill cited above is that the public should be entitled to hear all opinions and that opinions are enhanced by standing the test of public debate. Within social research, however, confidentiality is less related to concealing opinions than with protecting the identities of human subjects. It is possible to report what Mill calls opinions without having them attributed. As Barnes (1979: 134f) has demonstrated, the value of publication is more easily accepted by the scientific community than by those upon whose participation social research depends. The social reality of research is that one cannot compel subjects to speak openly and honestly. The assurance of confidentiality is introduced not because researchers dispute the public right to know but as a factor in negotiating with potential subjects for their participation. Confidentiality is offered as a condition in the acquisition of consent. It was found by Boruch that respondents were much more likely to yield sensitive information if confidentiality was offered, understood and believed (Reynolds, 1979: 167; see also Turner, 1982). Singer tried to measure the effect upon subjects of offering various assurances of confidentiality, promising absolute confidentiality to a third of her subjects, conditional assurances to another third ('we'll do our best') and said nothing to the remaining third. Although findings were not statistically significant, it appeared that absolute assurances eased responses to sensitive questions (Singer, 1978: 146, 151).

While confidentiality is prescribed as an ethical principle, then, it also has a pragmatic function. And there are other advantages in offering respondents confidentiality: their responses are likely to be more candid and they will be less susceptible to the 'halo effect' if there is no purpose in creating a good impression. It is in these terms – and not in terms of the rights of individuals – that the importance of confidentiality is stressed with regard to the population census:

> The public's perception of census confidentiality has important implications both for public co-operation with the census and for the quality of the data collected. The accuracy and completeness of the information collected in the census forms may be prejudiced if respondents are not fully reassured that the information is completely confidential and this will affect the validity and reliability of the statistical data collected from the census (Hakim, 1979: 133).

In the United States too the minds of social researchers have been much exercised to increase public trust in the assurance of confidentiality (Turner, 1982).

There are, however, other considerations than enhancing a response rate which lie behind the offer to respondents of confidentiality in one form or another. This pledge has the effect of defining in a specific way the situation in which researcher and subject interact: an interview is normally an encounter between strangers of a type which would not otherwise be governed by any principle of secrecy: the function of the pledge of confidentiality is therefore to define the encounter as an exchange for scientific purposes in which peculiar rules are respected (Sudman and Bradburn, 1982: 8). Again, the principle of confidentiality has been regarded in the past as a feature distinctive of responsible social research; it is symbolic of the professional style that is not shared by investigative journalists or 'muckrakers' (Lofland and Lofland, 1984: 29). Social research, it is said, has the purpose of exploring and understanding phenomena but not of accusing individuals and presenting the case for prosecution. In recent years, however, the media have made increasing use of methods of concealing the identity of informants, such as interviewing them in silhouette and disguising their voices.

While the assurance of confidentiality has some power in the negotiation of consent, it may equally be respected where consent is not sought, either because the investigator is using covert methods or because the enquiry is conducted under statutory powers. During his observational study of police behaviour, Holdaway was aware that publication could result in disciplinary action and the ruin of some careers; this did not inhibit his collection of data but he would not submit his data to the Chief Constable and in all publications he has rendered individuals and locations unidentifiable (Holdaway, 1982: 72, 77).

In practice, confidentiality is differentially granted to individual respondents and communities. It was over sixty years ago that the Lynds protected the community they studied with the pseudonym 'Middletown' but since then there have been named studies of Banbury, Sparkbrook, Bethnal Green and the St Paul's district of Bristol, to cite but a few. Studies of schools have normally used false names, that of Elizabeth Richardson (1973) being a conspicuous exception. Schools and small towns, it might be argued, have generalisable features and studies of them are valuable for their application to others of their type. The same could not be said of the Church of Scientology or of Jehovah's Witnesses, research about which would be seriously restricted and of rather less interest if its authors were not allowed to name their subjects; the tradition in the sociology of religion, therefore, has been to name national organisations but in general to refrain from identifying congregations or individuals. Despite the lead of Margaret Mead in publishing in 1932 *The Changing Culture of an Indian Tribe* without disclosing its real name (Barnes, 1979: 136), anthropologists continue to name the groups they study, give maps to show where they may be found and include photographs of individuals, sometimes participating in secret rites (Chagnon, 1983; Herdt, 1987). Of course the Yąnomamö and the Sambia are not likely to read monographs published in English and this might affect the way in which they are treated. Certainly the reverse is true: where subjects are likely to read a research report – for example, because they are professional sociologists working in universities – special care is taken to render them unidentifiable (Platt, 1976: 7).

6.4.1 Confidentiality procedures

Access to data collected in the course of social research and the selection of data that are presented in any report are controlled by a variety of methods which may or may not be specified in the offer of confidentiality to respondents.

The most common guarantee is that of anonymity, which means that the names of subjects will not be published. In the event the notion of anonymity is broadened so that the researcher undertakes to withhold all details by which respondents may be identified, such as institutions to which they belong or their places of employment. Many surveys, such as censuses, are reported in terms of statistical data relating to large constituencies. In 1971, for example, respondents to the official census were assured:

> The information you give on the form will be treated as CONFIDENTIAL and used only for compiling statistics. No information about named individuals will be passed by the Census Office to any other Government Department or any other authority or person. If anyone in the census organisation improperly discloses information you provide, he will be liable to prosecution. Similarly, you must not disclose information which anyone (for example, a visitor or boarder) gives you to enable you to complete the form (Hakim, 1979: 136).

The penalties for such disclosure are provided by an Act of 1920 and involve imprisonment for up to two years with or without hard labour (Hakim, 1979: 137).

Trust in the assurance of confidentiality is most effectively secured where the names and identities of subjects are not sought in the first place. This is the common practice of opinion pollsters and market researchers whose interviewers stand in the street and outside shops with clipboard at the ready. In other cases it is helpful to identify responses, whether to avoid interviewing the same person twice or to chase non-respondents to postal surveys. This does not mean that the name of a respondent must stay attached to the response form beyond the minimum period necessary for the purpose. Questionnaire forms sent through the post or collected at a central point may bear index numbers which correspond to names; by tearing off the number and deleting the name simultaneously, the investigator can know who has not responded without identifying those who have. Another method of achieving anonymity is to assign false names to respondents (Belson, 1975: x) or to allow them to invent their own (Reynolds, 1979: 169).

Pseudonyms may or may not appear in the published report. Where a community is pseudonymously represented, the intention is to spare it the effects of publicity and embarrassment. That does not prevent the possibility of subjects exposing themselves: Vidich and Bensman called the town they studied 'Springdale' but its citizens 'came out' and retaliated in a Fourth of July parade (Vidich and Bensman, 1968: 315–475). In a useful historical account and discussion of the use of pseudonyms in social research, John Barnes makes the point that they diminish a report by depriving it of some data that might have been instructive but they do not distort it (Barnes, 1979: 139).

A third option is to refrain from publication. This may be a realistic option for a student conducting research as part of a first or master's degree and some university libraries, which normally ask for bound copies of theses to be placed on their shelves, are prepared to waive this requirement if they include sensitive or confidential material. In cases where a project has been funded or has been conducted in response to an identified need, the dissemination of findings may be seen as a professional obligation. To offer these in confidence to a closed group is undesirable not least – as we discuss below – because it may deprive decision makers of the benefit of a more public response to findings.

The assurance of confidentiality is regarded by some to have implications for the secure conditions in which data are stored. Precautions taken include the responsible use of lock and key and the omission of identifying labels on files and tapes. Records should be purged of the names of subjects before outsiders or new users are given access to them and at this stage consent for release may be re-negotiated with subjects – a requirement that implies that names and addresses be stored somewhere, if not with the data. All staff engaged on a project should be fully briefed on the principle of confidentiality as it has been formulated and offered to subjects. As a general rule, investigators are urged to detach names, addresses and – in the United States – social security numbers from records at the earliest opportunity (Sieber, 1982a: 112–15).

Although he will not go down in the annals of social research for the rigour or his ethical principles, Laud Humphreys operates a useful acid test on the issue of confidentiality:

> The question I have always asked myself in this connection is: Could the respondent still recognise himself without having any other recognise him? I may have failed in a few cases to meet the first part of this standard, but I am confident that I have not failed to meet the second (Humphreys, 1975: 172).

In some research reports there is a pretence of confidentiality but there are enough clues to inspire guesses. For example, Cecile Wright introduces an ethnographic study of two Midlands schools which are three miles apart: School A was originally a boys' grammar-school which merged with a boys' secondary-modern school in September 1972 and School B was a girls' grammar-school which at the same time merged with two girls secondary modern schools (Eggleston, *et al.*, 1986: 128–9). If these details are correct, the schools would no doubt be easily identified. The disguise used by Verma is equally transparent if the details are true:

> School B
> One of the two original purpose-built comprehensives in Bradford, which has been under the same headmaster since 1962.

School C
Located in a village six miles from the centre of Bradford, this school was an ex-grammar school turned comprehensive in 1967 (Verma, 1986: 59–60).

Again, Clift (1988) offers a study of the attitudes of first-year undergraduate students in a college of higher education in south-east England: his subjects were students of a course in Radio, Film and Television Studies (Clift, 1988: 36). There is only a small number of such colleges in this region and still fewer that offer such a course so that readers may infer which one it is, not least because the author's institutional affiliation is given as one of them. The contradiction of the effort of concealment by the supply of clues is nowhere more exaggerated than in the study of Plainville in which the researcher changed his own name as well as that of the town he reported and yet, as one plaintiff resident remarked to Gallaher (1964: 288):

> Why, he had a map drew in the front of his book so's anyone who read it would know it was [Plainville].

Of course, it may well be argued that none of these studies warranted a more rigorous protection of confidentiality and even the best attempts to conceal identities may be frustrated. Robert Dingwall (1980: 877) tells the story of a sociological study of an independent school conducted with all the assurances of anonymity and confidentiality. But a daily newspaper rang round the members of the Headmasters' Conference for comment, until 'one of them exclaimed, "Good God. How did you find out?"'

One of the measures taken by some researchers – and for all we know Wright and Clift may be among them – is the alteration of details that are not significant in the analysis but may tempt or facilitate detection. The Lynds took the precaution of rounding down statistical data relating to 'Middletown' (Barnes, 1979: 138). Ditton purposely sought to protect the identity of the bakery in which he conducted his research by changing irrelevant facts and omitting names (Ditton, 1977: 9). A developed form of this practice was adopted by Jennifer Platt who was mindful that the professional sociologists she was studying were likely to read her report:

> I have . . . gone to some lengths to make it difficult to identify individuals or projects in the text, though I have always been conscious of the danger of concealing relevant information by doing this. All names have been changed, and sometimes sexes; institutions, affiliations and research topics have been changed or described in general terms . . . If the same name appears in more than one place it does not refer to the same individual (Platt, 1976: 7).

The reader may at this point be left wondering whether there is anything that has not been falsified and what remains to be believed. 'With such circumspection,' John Barnes observes, 'we might well think we were about to hear something really iniquitous; alas, all that is offered is an account of the *Realities of Social Research*' (Barnes, 1979: 140).

6.4.2 Problems with confidentiality

However desirable as a basis for the researcher-subject relationship and effective in negotiating the agreement of subjects to take part, the assurance of confidentiality is not universally offered and there are situations in which it is regarded as inappropriate and effects that may be thought adverse.

One of the objections to the principle of confidentiality is that in certain circumstances subjects may take cover behind it. This argument is made with regard both to decisions to conceal research findings and to allow anonymity to respondents. Barry MacDonald suggests that it is wrong to allow the conditions of a contract to prevent researchers from conveying findings to those who may be most affected by them; he cites the case of a piece of American research which endorsed on educational grounds the practice of bussing children to schools outside the immediate neighbourhood, but the policy makers were able to discontinue the practice because these findings were not made known (MacDonald, 1976: 126–7). The ability to withhold or disclose research findings is a facility that enhances the power of those who already have it. In a similar way, anonymity is a 'cloak' behind which power elites operate (Horowitz and Katz, 1975: 120). The concealment of data and identities does not serve the quest for greater accountability in situations in which policies are formed; in these circumstances the respect of anonymity and confidentiality is an obstacle to the free flow of information (Pring, 1984b: 8–9).

Discussions concerning the issue of confidentiality as a right claimed by the subjects of social research have dwelt upon subjects who are either powerful or accountable or in the public eye. Spector (1980) has seriously questioned whether anonymity should be offered by researchers to public figures. Rainwater and Pittman (1967: 364–5) have suggestd that the facility of confidentiality may be both unnecessary and a bad strategy on technical grounds since it functions as a gag upon the researcher at the reporting stage. And it was found by Spector (1980: 106) that informants who had been in the public eye were accustomed to speaking on the record, did not expect the offer of anonymity and were even motivated by public attention. What this may mean is that public figures reckoned that they could manipulate all interviewers to their own ends and the ethical question is then one of whether social research should afford them the publicity and credibility they hope to derive from it. It is, however, worth noting the practice of the British press which makes considerable use of information derived from unnamed persons such as 'sources close to the Prime Minister'.

Of course, respondents – and especially respondents in positions of power – participate in most research enquiries only when assurances are made and trusted. Except when research is being conducted under statutory powers, their cooperation is voluntary. If such assurances were not given the likelihood is that they would not take part. If so, the investigator has the choice of collecting data that are bound by confidentiality or not collecting the data at all. The third option that is sometimes entertained (Galliher, 1973, 1974; Warwick, 1974; Reynolds, 1979: 351–2) is that pledges need not be honoured if disclosure were thought to discourage some kind of malpractice. Of course, the exercise of such an option would jeopardise trust in promises made by other social researchers. It would also entitle the investigator to be the judge of what is and what is not in the public interest.

In considering the conditions in which promises of confidentiality might be dishonoured, Reynolds has in mind social researchers of what he calls a 'social activist orientation' (Reynolds, 1979: 352). Perhaps those with political motivations would be particularly tempted to break promises. However, the researcher is likely to be burdened with a wide variety of confidential data which may be burdensome. What if the researcher in the course of enquiries is told of child abuse, or a terrorist plot or the source of a campaign to contaminate foodstuffs or they observe the force-feeding of geriatric patients? It may be hoped with some confidence that there are few social researchers who can maintain indifference and scholarly interest in these circumstances and investigators may feel shackled by assurances they have given.

Of course, other professionals than social researchers agonise over dilemmas such as these. Priests hear such things in the confessional; journalists are allowed to glimpse terrorist capabilities of aggression; doctors and counsellors have professional and ethical protocols of confidentiality and faith in their ministrations is dependent on the scrupulous exercise of these. Perhaps social researchers do not yet have the public standing that would afford them much sympathy if they declined to disclose information as sensitive as these examples. They have to ask themselves before giving assurances of confidentiality in what circumstances they would divulge data, whether they would refuse to give evidence to a court of law and what other ethical principles would prevail when in conflict with that of confidentiality.

Confidentiality and anonymity offer cover not only for the subjects of research but for the investigators themselves. It is for the protection of researchers that Lofland and Lofland (1984: 29) advise 'disguise and obscure'. And it was because Elizabeth

Richardson regarded the assurance of anonymity as a cop-out by the researcher that she resisted from the start the pressure to grant it and determined to name Nailsea School in which she worked:

> I made it clear right from the beginning that if, as I hoped, the work culminated in a published report or book, I should want the school to be named, since 'anonymity' in research projects of this kind could never in any event be total. Moreover, my view of 'anonymity' . . . is that it can too easily be used as a protective device . . . that endangers the school while it protects the research worker (Richardson, 1973: 45).

Richardson takes the view that anonymity allows the researcher to betray a community of subjects by avoiding the 'painful process' of working through findings with subjects before publication.

It is to protect the researcher that the principle of anonymity may be advised on legal grounds. The author who publishes names and identities incurs a risk of prosecution under British libel laws. Ruth Cavendish (1982) used the convention of pseudonyms to protect from victimisation the women workers whom she observed on the production line of a vehicle components factory. But her intention was to publish the name of the company. Upon taking legal advice she recognised that in the event of litigation the burden of proof weighed so heavily upon the author as to render impossible the defence of her report. Reluctantly, therefore, she rewrote the book so that the company was unidentifiable:

> The factory is now located in West London, which is not true, and I have invented a name for the near-by trading estate . . . To name the particular motor component we manufactured would be tantamount to naming the firm so I have taken rather extreme steps to disguise that too (Cavendish, 1982: viii).

Cavendish regards the British libel laws as protective of those in power. She exercises her own discretion in anonymising and protecting women subjects but takes the view that the virtual enforcement of anonymity on legal grounds is a restriction upon freedom of speech.

Cavendish's account raises another aspect of confidentiality which relates to the accountability of the researcher. If subjects are rendered unidentifiable, research findings become less accessible to be checked or disputed. It may also prevent other researchers from continuing longitudinal studies, making linkages across files, revisiting subjects and so on (Øyen, 1976: 253).

Confidentiality and anonymity are not always perceived by subjects as being in their best interests. Of course, research is not conducted purely to serve the interests of its human subjects and it may not be possible to deliver the exact conditions they prefer. However, it must be borne in mind that anonymity may for some respondents be a disappointing arrangement. In the submission of Malcolm Spector, the guarantee of confidentiality inhibits interviews with public figures who are accustomed to and prefer speaking on the record (Spector, 1980: 103–5); they regard their contribution to the research as valuable time and expect in return to have their views reported and attributed. What is true for people in power is equally true for the dispossessed; if a survey or census reveals inequalities in the allocation of resources, poverty, inadequate housing and the absence of supportive social welfare, the best hope for those who suffer is that readers of the report will know where and among whom those needs exist. To grant anonymity in these circumstances is a disfavour to respondents. Pring (1984b: 13) makes the point that social research must maximise access to data if it is to be a useful resource for policy makers.

The maintenance of confidentiality has proven particularly stressful where an investigator continues to have daily contact with those who were for a limited period respondents in the research. This is often the case when schoolteachers conduct research in their own schools as a requirement of a degree course. What is discovered in the confidence of the interview is likely to become a factor in the continuing relationship of two colleagues. While the researcher may be determined not to refer outside the interview situation to what transpired within it, the respondent may put this principled behaviour under threat by broaching themes that were treated in the interview. Jennifer Platt experienced such strain when interviewing colleagues in her own university on such matters as career aspirations. She could not easily forget what had transpired and her colleagues did not necessarily want her to do so (Platt, 1981: 78). Once again, observance of the principle of confidentiality demands a skill that is trained in other professionals such as priests, doctors and counsellors who must not allow what they learn in confidence to affect professional relationships with clients. Notwithstanding, there are patients who choose not to see their general practitioner socially and penitents who go outside the parish for a confessor.

In societies where the information collected by sociologists and anthropologists is not regarded as privileged, the social researcher must be careful about the terms in which offers of confidentiality are expressed. A researcher who has given an absolute assurance may subsequently be in a position of having to break the promise or go to prison. Knerr (1982: 191–5) lists a number of cases of sociologists, social psychologists, economists and others who have been directed by American courts to disclose data on crime victims, police activity, business procedures, pornography and other behaviour observed in the course of research. Some acceded while others claimed a scholarly right not to disclose and were, in a few cases, sent to prison. Of course, there are precautions that can be taken so that records identifying subjects are lost before they can be demanded by a court: Jorgensen accordingly suggests a system of numbering respondents on interview sheets and then destroying the record of names (Jorgensen, 1971: 330). This procedure reduces identification but particular subjects may be recognisable from elements of their response: and it does not solve the problem of the indelible memory of observed behaviour.

6.4.3 Summary

Confidentiality is widely commended among social researchers as an ethical principle but it is also operated as a device to secure cooperation. It is normally introduced as a favour to or right of respondents. However, there are certain situations in which confidentiality can operate against the human subjects of research, reduce the obligations of the investigator and prejudice the making of desirable policy. The assurance may also prove a serious burden to the researcher who receives data, the closure of which may pre-empt appropriate action. The principle which is most widely endorsed is that assurances should not be given which the investigator may not be able to honour. The implications of the cases cited above are for the terms in which confidentiality should be offered.

6.5 COMMERCIAL EXPLOITATION

The publication in 1976 of Neville Bennett's *Teaching Styles and Pupil Progress* is an instructive case of the reception that may be accorded to a piece of research that coincides with popular feeling. Indeed, to understand and judge the Bennett report in terms of ethical issues relating to research, we must first take notice of current issues in the world of education to which the report was addressed.

By the late 1970s traditional and formal pedagogical methods were widely giving way to less formal 'progressive' methods, especially in primary schools. These new methods were marked by a higher level of individual work or group work by pupils, less teaching of the whole class, a less structured organisation of the school day, more integration of subject areas and a higher level of interaction between pupils, for example. This fashion was of some ten years standing and there was a rising backlash to it expressed most vehemently in a series of 'Black Papers'; the Conservative MP and former headmaster Rhodes Boyson and Professor Brian Cox of the University of Manchester were prominent contributors to the Black Papers. They stood for firm discipline from parents and teachers, restraint in the degree of freedom allowed to children, the place of healthy competition in school as preparation for a competitive world, external examinations, selection on the basis of ability and the preservation of freedom of speech. The ideas of the Black Papers group gathered some momentum in the course of publicity given to the case of the William Tyndale school in Islington which was distinguished for its informal ethos, from which parents had started to take away their children; eventually the headmaster was suspended and the school closed.

The educational climate of 1976 was, therefore, marked by passionate views on both sides and the debate was compelling the interest of parents who were seriously concerned for their children's education. That progressive methods were better for learning was asserted by teachers and others but there was no evidence to prove it. The research of Neville Bennett was the first thing that looked like evidence on the subject; such was the manner of its dissemination that it communicated quickly with parents and public and the verdict that it appeared to pass was unfavourable to progressive methods. Bennett had classified teaching styles along a continuum of twelve types from informal to formal; he studied groups of children taught by the extreme styles on this continuum and some of those in the middle which he called 'mixed'. On tests of reading, he found, 'the results provide clear evidence for the better performance of formal and mixed pupils' (Bennett, 1976: 88); in mathematics he found most progress among formally taught groups except among lowest ability boys (Bennett, 1976: 93); and in English, 'Overall, pupils in formal classrooms show significantly more progress . . . than those in mixed and informal classrooms' (Bennett, 1976: 96).

The newsworthiness of these findings at that time is immediately apparent. Bennett had a publisher awaiting his typescript eagerly. This was Helen Fraser who could see that after ten years of progressive education the time was right for a book of this kind (Open University, 1987). Bennett was persuaded to cut 50 pages in order to keep the price under three pounds and in the course of this excision some statistics got muddled. Press releases were written and a press conference arranged. The book immediately captured headlines like 'How progressive schooling has failed' in the *Observer*, 'The cheated pupils' in the *Daily Express* and 'Old fashioned teaching works best, say dons' in the *Daily Telegraph*.

The Black Papers enthusiasts were fortified by the findings of Bennett and Rhodes Boyson called upon parents to visit their children's schools in order to ascertain whether the teaching style was progressive and if so to keep the children at home (Open University, 1987). In October of 1976 the Prime Minister James Callaghan, making an unprecedented speech on the subject of education, picked up the issue of standards and called for a professional review to relate the standards of school leavers to the needs of industry. This was the famous Ruskin College speech which was to inaugurate 'the great debate' in education which led to legislation in 1980 and 1988, when the national curriculum was introduced.

It might be suggested that, whether by design or accident, the Bennett report was timed to appear just when the public wanted to hear it and that it was influential in the future course of educational policy. The use that was made of Bennett's research, however, was not in accordance with his own interpretation. In his conclusion Bennett avoided giving the advice to parents to take their children where the formal teaching was to be found. A few newsworthy findings from the book took on a power of their own and Bennett was left to observe that 'you lose control once your research goes out into the market-place' (Open University, 1987).

As the Bennett report went into orbit and the dust settled, there developed a more reflective and measured debate among scholars in the field. For example, it was found that the progress in English shown in the statistical tables (Bennett, 1976: 177) did not tally with the graphic representation of results (Bennett, 1976: 94). In due course Bennett and others published a re-analysis (Aitkin, Bennett and Hesketh, 1981) but this did not in the same way capture the imagination of the press.

Several ethical issues are raised by this saga. First, are we to count Neville Bennett responsible for the uses that were made of his findings, not only in energising the Black Papers contributors in 1976 but also for feeding public opinion in a way that was to lead to the enfranchisement of parents in education, the application of market forces to give the laity greater control over education professionals, the advent of the National Curriculum in 1988 and so on? The ethical codes vary on the accountability of researchers for policy outcomes. Bennett believes that social researchers cannot afford to have ideologies (Open University, 1987) and that their function is to provide accurate information. Second, then, should a researcher be regarded as accountable for policies which are inspired by faulty results or misinterpretations? Donald MacIntyre comments that he does not blame Bennett for getting wrong answers but for publishing them before other scholars had taken an opportunity to reflect and re-interpret (Open University, 1987). So third, should we establish as an ethical principle that researchers first present their work to their peers, in learned journals and at seminars, before addressing a wider audience? We know from the case of the British Association scandal (Morgan, 1972) that papers delivered in the most exclusive of circles can still hit headlines (see 6.6). Fourth, is it realistic to require a researcher to make interpretations so clear that they will not be mistaken or contradicted? It is in the nature of debate that a researcher enjoys no more authority over the implications of findings than others who are free to read and re-interpret. Nor can a researcher new to the world of publication expect to prevail against political heavyweights who are practised in the manipulation of the media. Bennett did his best by accepting a heavy schedule of speaking engagements in an endeavour to correct the record.

The problem of commercial exploitation arises in Bennett's case, as in many others, between the researcher's report and the press report. For some purists, the most professional strategy is to avoid releasing research findings that might capture the public imagination and at the very least to try findings in research seminars before disseminating them more widely. Educational research findings, however, are of practical rather than theoretical consequence; the public has a right to know and to know urgently, it is argued. In Bennett's words,

> What is the point of doing educational research if teachers cannot read it, because the only rationale for doing educational research is for the improvement of practice, and for the improvement of practice you've got to get to teachers and you've got to get to student teachers (Open University, 1987).

A not inconsiderable ethical problem glimpsed in this account of the Bennett case but also common elsewhere is raised by the involvement of the publisher. The publisher operates with a view to the market. What is likely to sell well will be encouraged. The timeliness of Bennett's work was such that he was apparently urged to rush into print. Publishers commonly ask authors and referees to help estimate the appeal of a proposed book and they take account of such demands as courses in universities and colleges. It follows that the same encouragement is not afforded to research on subjects of less interest. Publishers may trade upon the very habits which are disapproved by those who respect the familiar ethical principles: for example, the blurb on the back cover of Patrick's (1973) observation of the Glasgow gang makes capital of 'the author's hazardous double game'.

Even more seriously, perhaps, the need to find a popular theme can shape what is publishable in book form. In recent years the sociology and social theory sections of publishers' catalogues have been much occupied with themes of sex and violence and we have had titles on male fantasies, Marilyn Monroe, pornography, the sexual exploitation of children, the nudist beach and the psychology of the female body. All these have their place and there are such worthy classics as Malinowski's *The Sexual Life of Savages*. What remains a problem is whether social research that lacks this kind of commercial potential will also see the light of day and whether in the end market forces exercise as effective a control over the agenda of social research as the sponsors whose role was challenged earlier (2.5).

6.6 CONSEQUENCES OF PUBLICATION

6.6.1 Personal consequences

The publication or circulation of a research report may be the occasion of a number of sensations and experiences, not all of which will be found congenial. At this stage it is common for researchers to be troubled with feelings of guilt that they have betrayed their subjects, a condition referred to by Lofland and Lofland (1984: 154) as 'ethical hangover'. Where the release of a research report catches the tide of popular interest, the publicity can be traumatic for its authors: after months of solitude devoted to the sifting of data and the organisation of material into a coherent account, they may find themselves at the centre of a lively public debate and at the receiving end of reviews that are not all kind. Attention may be drawn by publication to the institution in which the research has been conducted so that colleagues share publicity which they have not invited. Exposure of this kind is a way of life for seasoned researchers but others must be properly prepared for it. While directors of projects need not take the full brunt of any attacks that might be forthcoming, it would be irresponsible for a supervisor to take a year's sabbatical leave in Australia on the eve of publishing a sensitive report.

One of the by-products of publishing a report is that its authors are approached as experts on its subject matter and frequently on a subject more general than that of the report. They may also be invited to answer questions pertinent to the subject of their research but framed within the language of another discipline. Tempting though radio and television interviews may be, researchers are urged to decline invitations to operate outside the sphere of their competence:

> Sociologists are wise to exercise caution in communications with the press, and particularly with radio and television, bearing in mind that their ethical standards and their interests in the subjects of study are not necessarily coincidental with those of sociologists . . . Sociologists should beware of allowing themselves to appear on T.V. or radio as experts in fields outside those that would be recognised academically as their fields of expertise . . . (British Sociological Association, 1982: 2).

Publicity can bring about dramatic changes in the life of the researcher and these are well illustrated in the account of Robert Moore (1977), whose story – like other cases cited below – also reveals some of the effects of publication upon the social and political climate.

6.6.2 Case studies

Social researchers must be mindful that at any given time their findings have the potential of affecting political decisions. During the parliamentary passage of the Video Recordings Bill in 1984, survey findings were released which were much used by supporters of the Bill and were featured prominently in the press. In particular, it was found that 40 per cent of all children and 38 per cent of those in the age group five to six years had seen one or more 'video nasty'. The research procedure used in this survey was to give child respondents a list of video titles and to ask them to signify which they had seen. Subsequently, Guy Cumberbatch used the same method with fictitious titles and found that 68 per cent claimed to have viewed video films which did not exist such as 'I vomit on your cannibal apocalypse'. Teachers who saw the questionnaire recognised at once that results obtained from it would be unreliable; indeed, one headmaster put the technique to the test by asking children whether they had ever seen a Martian and found that 20 per cent of 11-year-olds had done so within the previous fortnight. The effect was to discredit the original research, but meanwhile the Video Recordings Bill was enjoying a smooth passage on the strength of it (Harris, 1984: 140–2).

Robert Moore (1977) gives a vivid and salutary account of the events which attended the publication of the study of Sparkbrook in which he worked with John Rex (Rex and Moore, 1967). The book was completed and published under pressure from sponsor and publisher. It was launched with a luncheon for 'top people' at the Café Royal (Moore, 1977: 101). Parts of the book were serialised in the local press and there were invitations to appear on television. The authors anticipated something of the public interest stirred by the book but were disappointed that it was not being received as a serious sociological work. A leader in *The Times* argued that the book showed the urgency of rigorous immigration control which was not at all the conclusion of its authors. In Birmingham the city fathers and local government union reacted to the submission that there was racial discrimination in its housing policy by trying to seek out the informant who provided the evidence (Moore, 1977: 103–4). Even within the academic world, Rex and Moore have attributed to them the thesis that housing classes replace other types of social class, which they did not intend to convey (Moore, 1977: 105). Moore's story is a cautionary tale which deserves to be read by any social science student being tempted by the prospect of publication. It demonstrates not least that publication will afford a platform to those whose views are contrary to any which appear as conclusions or recommendations in a research report.

6.6.3 Social and political consequences

These cases serve to highlight a number of ethical problems relating to publication and to the responsibilities which social researchers may have for the use that is made of their findings. Moore was to see his findings deployed in support of a policy with which he did not agree. In contrast, those who first surveyed children's video viewing habits supplied their data to a sympathetic parliamentary lobby; according to Harris (1984: 141), there was a religious motivation behind the research and its purpose was supportive of the sentiments of the Bill. In the cases of Moore and Bennett, it might be suggested that misinterpretation of findings could have been averted if implications for policy were made more explicit in their reports. On the other hand, social researchers do not pretend to be policy makers and their expertise may be confined to the collection and analysis of data. Nor, perhaps, would it be desirable if social researchers were always to have the influence upon policy that was a feature of the timely report on children's video viewing.

Again, the more notice that is taken of research findings the greater is the moral obligation to get them right. While the sponsors of the video survey might have achieved their political ends, it is undesirable for policy to be decided on the basis of data that are false or faulty and this episode can have done no good for public confidence in research.

A further lesson to be drawn from the case of the Video Recordings Bill – which could equally have been drawn from many other cases – is that in the immediate reaction of press and public more attention is given to results than to methods. While the scientific community will examine critically the means by which results were obtained, its observations are invariably less newsworthy and they may become available some time after initial interest has waned.

What is at issue is whether or not social researchers should set out to influence opinion and policy in what they judge to be the desirable direction. The motive to explore and expose certain conditions so that they will in due course be improved lies behind much social research in areas such as race, poverty, housing and educational opportunity. This is the rationale of the enquiries conducted by Her Majesty's Inspectors of schools and of certain questions in the Registrar General's census every ten years. Social research is no less valid for being tendentious and it does not matter if the investigator has some prior notions about what will be discovered. To that extent, research is regarded by those who conduct it as a potential agent in social change. The data on children's viewing behaviour might have been exceptional for their unreliability but the way in which they were supplied to policy makers was not irregular.

Some data collected by social researchers may be very hot to handle. Whether or not investigators set out to influence opinion and policy, the release of such data is likely to invite a public response to which the investigators themselves may be unaccustomed. Information on sensitive subjects such as the competence of teachers or the honesty of public servants such as police and local government officers is of perennial interest to the media which may seize upon aspects of a research report that were regarded as incidental or subordinate by its authors.

Such attention is seldom given to dissertations by undergraduate and research students which are destined only to sit on a library shelf. However, if publication in the form of a book or journal article follows, there is a likelihood that findings will in some way become headlines. In this situation, the researcher is wise to guide the interpretations put upon the report. It is sometimes advisable to write a two-page press release which sets out major findings in the proportion that the author perceives them: this reduces the possibility of journalists picking upon something in the article or book that was obscure rather than central. With major projects, it is also a good plan to arrange a press conference at which the report can be launched; this gives those who have conducted the research the opportunity to stress the aspects which they consider to be most important. These arrangements afford considerable control over the kind of press coverage that a project receives. The principle that researchers are held responsible for the consequences of publication assumes that they have some control over such effects. Publishing research findings is not a matter of lighting a blue touch-paper and standing clear but of controlling as far as possible the dissemination and representation of findings and of contributing as appropriate to the ensuing debate.

Accountability for the uses and misuses of one's data is made most explicit in the ethical principles of the British Sociological Association (1982):

> Sociologists should be aware that they have some responsibility with regard to any use to which the results of their research may be put . . . They have the responsibility to consider the effects of their research upon further research. Sociologists have a particular responsibility for considering the possible application of research findings since this in itself is a sociological problem, being concerned with the prevention of the *misuse* of research results.

We have recorded in the previous section, and above in this one, concerns that the interpretations and uses made of research by Neville Bennett and Robert Moore respectively were not as their authors intended. This we have presented as a hazard of publication. However, the very expectation that policy makers and others should respect and follow the interpretations expressed by researchers raises another problem regarding the role of the researcher. Few would argue that those who collect data should also dictate related policies. In a free and democratic society the role of the researcher is to inform and perhaps to interpret but it is not so to present findings as to confine the interpretations that others can put upon them.

Some commentators put their trust in the select seminar as a means of dissemination among discerning academics or else in journal publication, the inevitable delays in which take the heat out of the more sensational aspects of research findings (Sherif, 1980: 411–12; Malamuth, Heim and Feshbach, 1980: 415). Even these forms of publication, however, are visited with hazards. A research team from the University of Manchester spent a period of participant observation in an electric components factory where the employees were mainly women. After the end of this period but before the publication of the final report, one of them delivered a paper to the British Association for the Advancement of Science entitled 'Women in industry – the factory and the home'. The thesis of the paper was that whereas men are alienated at work and seek consolation outside the workplace, women may suffer such alienation at home and find in social relationships at work some measure of satisfaction and reward. In illustration of this tendency, the author quoted a conversation between two women at the factory concerning the Royal Wedding of Princess Alexandra and Mr Angus Ogilvie. This paper was picked up by a number of national newspapers the following morning. While the *Guardian* and the *Telegraph* gave it fair summaries the *Daily Mirror* represented it under the headline 'A factory girl's dream of romance', the *Daily Express* used the heading 'What a giggle: When a man tells the secrets of life among the girls' and the *Daily Mail* referred in its headlines to the author as 'The eavesdropper'. Worse still, two newspapers identified and printed the name of the factory which had been represented pseudonymously by the author (Morgan, 1972: 189–90).

The following day Morgan went with a senior colleague to make their peace at the factory where the women felt betrayed and misrepresented. The relatively fair reports of the *Guardian* and *Telegraph* had not found their way on to the factory floor and one of the women felt that Morgan had represented the workers as 'a lot of layabouts' (Morgan, 1972: 190). For his subjects, Morgan and his team had exposed them to adverse publicity; for his fellow professionals, it was clear that Morgan's paper had been used for its data rather than for its thesis and it might have been unrealistic to include in a scholarly paper delivered in an academic environment only those data which were incapable of misinterpretation; indeed, it is regarded as a scholarly practice to give as full a representation of data as possible in order to afford secondary analysis.

Morgan's own reflection on this episode is a philosophical one. He regards the event as a 'social drama' which allowed researcher and subjects to exchange interpretations to the benefit of the ultimate report (Morgan, 1972: 20).

CHAPTER 7

Effects

The conduct of social research has effects upon all participants, be they subjects or professionals, and its outcomes have implications at social and political levels. For subjects and investigators there are risks of strain or harm both during the research process and in the aftermath of publication. The ethical problems in this regard are complex. Those who conduct research will want to take account of the risks that affect subjects and they are urged to inform them accordingly in advance of the research. They will want to assess the risks to which they expose themselves and their immediate colleagues; in particular, there is a problem attending the implication of students or employees such as research assistants in projects that are hazardous or likely to involve inordinate strain. The reputation of the profession of social research in its various forms relates as well to the methods of research as to its reports. Finally, publication has the effect of exposing both subjects and investigator to attention which they may not welcome and may have consequences in terms of policy or of the image of the researched community for which, in the view of many, the researchers and authors should themselves take responsibility.

7.1 EFFECTS ON SUBJECTS

7.1.1 Professional guidelines

The professional associations all counsel their members to have due care for the interests of subjects, whom they should apprise of the nature and purpose of their research and the procedures by which they sampled their respondents. Voluntariness in participation, the entitlement to be informed and to have privacy respected are principles stressed in all guidelines.

Beyond that, some go further than others and the British Sociological Association (1982) does not go very far at all. The BSA reminds practitioners of the dangers of raising false hopes and causing undue anxieties.

It is in psychology, where the work of Stanley Milgram (1974) has exercised professionals to consider ethical problems, that the code gives a better sense of some of the possibilities. The principles of the British Psychological Society (1978) stress the responsibility that psychologists have when working with human subjects to anticipate harmful effects including strain, consult with experienced and disinterested professionals at the design stage, and break off an experiment for such consultation if evident effects exceed those anticipated. Experimenters are obliged to stress the voluntariness of participation in proportion to the magnitude of physiological or psychological stress likely to be suffered. They must also observe the highest standard of safety in procedure, equipment and premises. Milgram justified his procedures by distinguishing between intended and unintended effects: what is therefore significant about the BPS principles is that they hold psychologists responsible for both.

The Market Research Society (1986) subscribes with others to absolute principles of confidentiality and informed consent as protection for subjects. In respect of the kinds of survey its members undertake, it adds principles not found elsewhere. If a survey is conducted under statutory powers, informants must be apprised of the consequences of refusal; and recognising that telephone surveys can be intrusive, members are directed not to telephone domestic households before 9 o'clock weekdays, 10 o'clock Sundays or after 9 o'clock evenings.

A similar sensitivity about the intrusiveness of much social research and the inconvenience it might cause is expressed in the discursive guidelines of the Social Research Association (n.d: 12). Researchers should question themselves on the necessity of the enquiries they plan and ask whether the inconvenience to potential subjects could be avoided by using data already available. The SRA raises further questions about the possibility of asking questions which cause offence or distress; while it is sometimes suggested that open interviewing can have a beneficial or therapeutic function for the respondent, the SRA points out that not all respondents will welcome the self-knowledge that an interview might yield.

7.1.2 The legend of Stanley Milgram

In 1954 a correspondent to the *American Psychologist* raised a number of questions concerning the protection of experimental subjects in an attempt to alert fellow psychologists to neglected ethical issues. He referred to what he called 'the miniature social situation' in which an experimenter may use dissimulation or deceit in the control of behaviour variables. He wanted to establish what were the proper bounds of deceit. He noted reports of 'standard' reassurances given to subjects after experiments implying that they went away happy but he pointed to practices which compelled the attention of conscientious professionals although, as he observed at the time, 'So far as I can tell no one is particularly concerned about this' (Vinacke, 1954: 155).

The professional concern which was dormant as Vinacke wrote came to life as reports appeared of the experiments on obedience conducted by Stanley Milgram. These were always explicit as acts of research although they involved the deception of subjects at a number of stages. Subjects were recruited by means of a newspaper advertisement which described the project as 'a Study of Memory' (Milgram, 1974: 15) and their briefing for the laboratory sessions was in terms of theories of learning (Milgram, 1974: 18). At the superficial level this was honest in that the role which the subject then acted was that of teacher operating under supervision.

However, the real purpose of Milgram's experiments was to study the degree to which subjects were prepared to administer to a 'learner' punishments in the form of electric shocks. Subjects were put in charge of a control panel from which they understood that they could administer to a learner shocks ranging from 15 volts to 450 volts. Subjects were themselves given a token shock of 45 volts before the outset. In fact, the person in the role of learner had been trained to show various reactions and was not suffering the shocks that subjects believed they were administering. That subjects chose the role of teacher was manipulated by allowing them to draw a scrap of paper from two, both of which carried the word 'teacher'. As the learner continued to give wrong answers, so the subject, following instructions, increased the degree of shock. If subjects had scruples about inflicting pain and possibly damage, they were told 'Although the shocks may be painful, there is no permanent tissue damage, so please go on' (Milgram, 1974: 21). The learner or 'victim', as he is called in the study, showed no discomfort but only mild grunts as the level of shock rose to 105 volts. Then,

> at 120 volts the victim shouted to the experimenter that the shocks were becoming painful. Painful groans were heard on administration of the 135-volt shock and at 150 volts the victim called out, 'Experimenter, get me out of here! I won't be in the experiment any more! I refuse to go on!' Cries of this type continued with generally rising intensity, so that at 180 volts the victim cried out, 'I can't stand the pain,' and by 270 volts his response to the shock was definitely an agonized scream . . . At 300 volts, the victim shouted in desperation that he would no longer provide answers to the memory test (Milgram, 1974: 23).

In this circumstance the experimenter instructed what the study calls 'the naïve subject' to treat non-response as incorrect response and continue the punishment. Those who have faith in human nature will be reassured to know that only a small number of subjects were prepared to go as far as to administer the maximum shock.

Milgram made a point of giving his subjects a debriefing or 'dehoax' at the end of the experiment when they were reconciled with the 'victim' and it was explained that their behaviour was perfectly normal (Milgram, 1974: 194). Some time later he surveyed those who had taken part and it was found that 83.7 per cent were glad or very glad they had done so, while only 1.3 per cent were sorry or very sorry (Milgram, 1974: 195).

On the issue of whether or not there was a likelihood of enduring harm to the subjects of the Milgram experiments, the discussion wants the view of an experienced psychologist. It was not long after the appearance of Milgram's first report (Milgram, 1963) that Diana Baumrind delivered her judgement that Milgram's standards of concern and care for the well-being of his subjects fell short of professional requirements. She declared herself to be alarmed by the detached and unfeeling manner in which Milgram reported the extraordinarily disturbing experiences of his subjects and she was unconvinced by his casual assurance that he was able to calm subjects before they left his laboratory. In Baumrind's professional opinion there was a distinct possibility that the emotional disturbance suffered by subjects could be permanently harmful, perhaps effecting alterations of the self-image of subjects and their ability to trust other adult authorities (Baumrind, 1964: 433). Milgram insists that there was no evidence of injurious effect and that even those subjects who were obedient to the end suffered no more than 'momentary excitement' (Milgram, 1964: 849). What is of more enduring professional interest than the indictment or acquittal of Stanley Milgram, however, is the establishment of principles which would minimise harmful effect: to this end Baumrind suggests that such experiments should be allowed to continue only if subjects are fully apprised of the possibility of harmful after-effects and if the corrective measures used were proven to be effective in restoring subjects' well-being (Baumrind, 1964: 423).

Hans Schuler (1982: 60–4) analyses the Milgram experiments not in terms of the possibility of harm to subjects but in relation to what he terms the 'social contract' between experimenter and subject, of which he judges there to have been a breach. An element of deception is widely to be found in studies deploying the method of participant observation (see Chapter 5) and to that extent it is not the distinguishing feature of Milgram's work. What also concerns Schuler, however, is the degree of power that the experimenter exercises over the subject. Sociological research and anthropological studies are normally conducted in natural settings and researchers disguise their identities or misrepresent their purpose often in order to minimise the effects of their presence upon the ambient conditions of the social situation. Experimental methods differ from other observational methods in that they imply a construction of a situation by the researcher to whom reference may be made for clarification of the rules. Milgram's subjects turned to the experimenter for guidance and the powerful position of the experimenter was still further enhanced by the appeals of the victim for mercy. Schuler (1982: 44–5) observes that in psychological experiments the power of the investigator over the situation and the subjects within it is critical to the internal validity of the research act.

One of the major objections on ethical grounds to the Milgram experiments has come from the playwright Dannie Abse who is by training a medical practitioner (Abse, 1973: 33). In his play *The Dogs of Pavlov* Abse translates Milgram's procedures to a medical setting in order to highlight the ethical issues. As Abse recognises and Milgram stresses (Abse, 1973: 126–7), the experiments in the play are not those which Milgram conducted, nor is it appropriate to judge Milgram on the basis of Abse's dramatised version. However, Abse uses his introduction to dwell upon the details of Milgram's work and he sets out three ethical criteria on which such work should be assessed. First, he questions the motives of the experimenter: while those of Milgram might well have been worthy and confined, as Milgram says, to a curiosity about how far participants were prepared to go in obedience to the instructor, a different complexion might be put upon a piece of research were the person conducting it motivated by career aspirations or the prospect of personal advancement. Second, Abse requires the free consent of research subjects which implies that they be truthfully apprised of the conditions of the experiment; in Abse's judgement, Milgram was guilty of cheating and hoaxing his participants. And third, Abse takes into account the degree of harm suffered by subjects and is prepared to hold experimenters responsible for all effects of their exercise, whether or not foreseen (Abse, 1973: 27–8).

An observation of Milgram's experiments offers an account of the distress suffered by participants which Abse cites:

> I observed a mature and critically poised businessman enter the laboratory smiling and confident. Within 20 minutes he was reduced to a twitching stuttering wreck who was rapidly approaching a point of nervous collapse. He constantly pulled on his ear lobe, and twisted his hands. At one point he pushed his fist into his forehead and muttered, 'Oh God, let's stop it.' And yet he continued to respond to every word of the experimenter, and obeyed to the end (Abse, 1973: 30).

In the response which Abse allows him, Milgram invokes the principle of subject evaluation and takes comfort in the feedback of participants both on the occasion of the experiment and in reply to a follow-up survey. The reflective assessment of participants on the distress they may have suffered is of more consequence to Milgram than the indignation of playwrights and any others who were not involved:

> The critical moral justification for allowing a procedure of the sort used in my experiment is that it is judged acceptable by those who have taken part in it. Moreover, it was the salience of this fact throughout that constituted the chief moral warrant for the continuation of the experiments (Abse, 1973: 40–1).

7.1.3 Persistent effects

The long and continuing debate over the ethical aspects of Milgram's work has drawn attention to the effects of participation in research, especially in contrived or non-naturalistic settings. The hazards have been widely heeded by psychology professionals who have endeavoured to put their house in order but the problem is by no means confined to the use of experimental methods.

We have already observed a study in which children aged 11 years and above were asked how often they experienced sexual intercourse (Udry and Billy, 1987: 852) and commented that the question itself may be interpreted as a message about what is expected or accepted as normal. The introduction of human subjects to attitudes and habits which they may not already have formed is a serious by-product of some research procedures and the problem is especially acute when the subjects are particularly vulnerable. West, Gunn and Chernicky (1975) offered their subjects $2000 to take part in burglary though they took no part themselves. Sherif (1980: 409–11) expresses a similar concern in the comparable case of Malamuth *et al*. who exposed student respondents to false depictions of rape: though available in popular pornography it was not to be known whether respondents had previously encountered such images and she wonders about the effect upon a young man who is aroused by a cruelly violent depiction and then told in debriefing that it is totally false. These are instances of the formation of undesirable habits or attitudes and of psychological damage to subjects but we must observe also that physical danger may be persistent, particularly where researchers use as informants members of a potentially hostile community who would not corporately cooperate in an enquiry: this may be the case in research on deviant groups and Warwick (1983: 327) suggests that in places like Argentina and Chile a social researcher may be endangering the lives of those who participate in politically sensitive research.

In many cases, however, the most injurious and persistent effects of social research arise not from participation but from publication. The issue of a research report can have serious implications for the lives of subjects, be they factory workers such as Ditton's subjects at 'Wellbreads' or the residents of a small town like West's 'Plainville'. Those communities of subject both felt that life could never be the same again. 'Plainville' was soon identified and became a curiosity and visiting place for sightseers. Ditton (1977) anticipated the effect of this report of fiddling and pilferage in the Preface to his book:

> I don't expect that many of the men at Wellbread's will look too kindly on the cut in real wages that this work will mean to them, and my bakery self would agree with them.

Of course, effects upon subjects may also be benign. The secretive Rom community which Sutherland penetrated had suffered persecution and other discomforts as a result of prevailing misconceptions so that there was some positive purpose in publishing a full and fair account (Sutherland, 1975: 29–30).

It is often the case that the details which make a research report most readable are also those which might most harm its subjects. In these cases a researcher might put the interests of subjects before his or her own, as did Ball in omitting information about a theft by one boy and sexual experiences of two girls (Ball, 1985: 45).

7.2 EFFECTS ON RESEARCHERS

Participation in social research often incurs strain as well for those who conduct it as for those who are their subjects. Under students' beds and inside wardrobes are not the most congenial settings for scientific observation. The invasion of political sects and criminal communities implies risks, not least as a consequence of the cover being blown. The hazard of changing one's skin colour is brought home when the condition proves to be irreversible. Humphreys' observation was so participant that it led to his arrest and imprisonment. For professing patients there are risks in medication and treatment for the conditions they profess. Some groups of subject, such as members of new religious movements, can exert severe pressure upon those who show a research interest in them in order to discredit any who may be expected to give them an adverse press.

7.2.1 The strains of doing research

Research in social fields can be lonely, arduous, inescapable and dangerous. Those who become involved may regret having done so but have no means of turning back. They may not have been realistically apprised of what to expect, which perhaps not even their directors could have envisaged.

The case which instances a number of these possibilities is the work of Rosenhan who engaged eight colleagues to experience mental health care by professing symptoms of insanity and becoming admitted to institutions. It seemed a good idea at the time but the eight had more difficulty getting out than getting in. The arrangement was that they would have to secure discharge by their own means by persuading the authorities they were sane. The psychological stress was severe and all but one of the pseudo-patients desired to be discharged almost immediately after admission. However, the average period of hospitalisation was 19 days and one of the colleagues whom Rosenhan engaged took 25 days to get released (Rosenhan, 1973: 19).

Not the least considerable source of strain, however, are the subjects themselves who may be very resentful of researchers in their midst. They may be intent either upon driving the researcher away or upon controlling or discrediting any reports that might issue from the investigation.

Pressures of this kind are vividly detailed by Roy Wallis in his autobiographical paper 'The moral career of a research project' (Wallis, 1977). Wallis had been conducting his doctoral research initially on aspects of the new religious movements and later more specifically on Scientology. He responded to an invitation by post to take a short course at the Church of Scientology's British headquarters at Saint Hill Manor, East Grinstead. To the extent that he did not declare himself a sociologist who was researching the situation, he used the method of covert participant observation, although after two days he abandoned the course and slipped away during a dinner break. He also made contact with and interviewed a number of former members. Wallis was mindful that Scientology was particularly active in the field of public relations and would have defined his interest within this field had a formal approach been made. He also wanted to know how the visitor off the street was treated, not how a sociologist from a university was received (Wallis, 1977: 153–5).

Evidently prompted by the publication of an article on the basis of his early research, the Church of Scientology then took an active interest in Wallis. According to his account, a man turned up at the University of Stirling where he was lecturing, said that he was researching religion in Scotland, asked to join Wallis's classes and even to stay at his home. Wallis recognised him from Saint Hill Manor. The man asked students whether Wallis was involved in the drug scene. Wallis confronted him and he claimed to be a defector and afterwards disappeared (Wallis, 1977: 157).

After this some forged letters supposedly by Wallis were put into the hands of his university employers suggesting in one case that he was involved in a homosexual love affair and in another that he was a spy for the drugs squad (Wallis, 1977: 158).

When Wallis published an article in *New Society* in 1973 scientologists wrote to the Social Science Research Council which had partly funded his research complaining on a number of grounds including the fact that Wallis had not secured informed consent before embarking on his research.

When the time came for Wallis to present his thesis he simultaneously found an interested publisher. Sensing that the Church of Scientology might react to its publication he copied the thesis to its officers. Negotiations followed as a result of which first 27 and then 46 and later 80 and finally over 100 changes were made to the text. In a further attempt to pre-empt litigation which Wallis would not be able to afford, the Church of Scientology was invited to write a 5000-word reply which was incorporated in the eventual book *The Road to Total Freedom* (Wallis, 1976). Wallis had no desire to cause 'undeserved harm' but recognised a dilemma between obligations to subjects and the possibility of censorship (Wallis, 1977: 160). In his experience he was dealing with 'officials whose wish it is that only their own view of certain affairs will become public knowledge' (Wallis, 1977: 165).

7.2.2 The risks of doing research

There is a sense in which researchers enter the field with their eyes open, cognisant of the risks. The hazards to which they expose themselves and their personalities are of their own choosing. For example, the police through whom Klockars made contacts with his criminal subjects gave him the name of 'Knuckles Jones' together with an undertaking:

> The promise the detective made me was that if I were killed during the course of my research, he would see to it that my killer was brought to justice (Klockars, 1975: 200).

So comforted, Klockars entered the field at his own peril. There may or may not be an ethical problem if the risk is known to the researcher but it is not of the same order as that which applies when the risk is concealed. On the other hand, the professional context in which fieldwork is undertaken may mean that the refusal to bear a particular risk will incur the disfavour of senior colleagues or prejudice opportunities of qualification and career development. For example, the famous studies of Festinger *et al*. (1964) and of Rosenham (1973) were conducted by students and others engaged for the purpose and directed by established academics. It is one thing to risk one's own life or sanity and quite another to make studentships and research posts conditional upon the willingness to take such risks vicariously.

While the standard procedure of Klockars was to conduct interviews with criminal subjects, that of Hobbs was to enter

their behaviour in a more participant way. He felt that he would lose rapport with subjects were he to start questioning the legality of any activity in which they invited him to share. Hobbs insists that this was not unethical for the ethics he adopted were those of the East End community he observed, albeit not necessarily those of the social research community. For the sake of flexibility Hobbs reckoned that he needed 'a willingness to abide by the ethics of the researched culture and not the normative ethical constraints of sociological research' (Hobbs, 1988: 7).

One night Hobbs was taken for an Indian meal by a man who had the previous evening burgled an office, only to find the safe full of luncheon vouchers. It was in a small denomination luncheon voucher that the man paid the bill of fifteen pounds (Hobbs, 1988: 9).

The suspension of personal morality in the cause of research is one crisis; the risk of being arrested is another. These considerations are particularly commended to those who design research projects for others to conduct.

7.2.3 The persistence of research habits

All learning has the effect of taking over more parts of one's life than the hours that are formally assigned to it. If the conceptual apparatus of a social science is valid at all, it will find expression throughout the daily life of those who come to terms with it. Concepts of social class are applied continuously to observed social relations, instances of anomie are discovered in every situation once the concept has been acquired.

The role of investigator is quite as pervasive of one's whole life as book learning. The method of observation becomes a way of life. A few months after completing a period of four years observing pentecostal assemblies Homan wrote:

> I have already found (in shops and lifts, on trains and at coffee with colleagues) that I am continually sifting and noting potentially significant social data: my fear is that the 'phatic communion' type of interaction that has always featured in my behaviour repertoire now has the further function of 'covert interview' (Homan, 1980: 55).

A decade of reflection has only proven that fear to have been well substantiated. In the field, one's subjects became one's friends; outside it, one's friends became one's subjects. One would always have a scrap of paper and a pen available, which got used more than once at a football match, and the first few minutes after coffee in the senior common room were spent back at one's desk writing notes.

The concern here is with the potential damage to those who are involved in field research, particularly observation, which may prejudice their chances of developing full and open relationships in their personal lives. In particular, habits such as deception which are practised for research purposes in specific contexts become a way of personal and professional life. Margaret Mead has been among those to express the concern that social researchers may too easily become accustomed to tricking, deceiving and manipulating other human beings; her concern is that the use of methods involving lying might have the effect of establishing a 'corps of professionally calloused individuals' (Mead, 1969: 376).

7.2.4 Discussion

O'Connor and Barnes have questioned whether the problems raised in this section constitute an ethical issue. The experiences of inappropriate medication or compulsory detainment which were suffered by Rosenhan's colleagues were, they argue, a normal professional hazard and part of the bargain on the basis of which they developed their reputation. Only when researchers do not consent in principle or are subject to undue pressure from supervisors is the issue an ethical one (O'Connor and Barnes, 1983: 755). After all, biting off more than one can chew, reaching points of no return, emotional and physical strain and moral dilemmas about participation in professional assignments must be confronted in some measure in many if not all occupations; in all kinds of work, loyalty and honesty are in conflict.

The sensitive issue which O'Connor and Barnes recognise is that in which the free and voluntary decision about whether and how to conduct a particular piece of research is affected by factors such as the authority of the research director and the prospect of a research post and degree, possibly in the absence of alternatives. There is here not one question but several. Is it ethical to make a research degree or post contingent upon the willingness to take personal risks or compromise principles? Is it a responsibility of a supervisor to apprise those engaged in a project of the risks involved, and in any case is this possible? Is it unethical to expose colleagues to risks to which one is not exposed personally? Ought risky procedures to be adopted only by those who conceive them? And is it possible to be responsibly protective without being paternalistic?

As with all interesting questions there are no easy answers but there are two kinds of safeguard which might be operated. First, what amounts to the exploitation of social scientists by senior colleagues is a problem that must be registered on the agenda of ethical issues in social research. Existing codes and guidelines are concerned with the exposure of subjects to particular kinds of harm and with consequences for the profession but tend to neglect the ethical implications relating to professional hazards.

The ethical guidelines issued by the University of Manchester's Committee on the Ethics of Research on Human Subjects include a statement intended for the protection of subjects: this could equally be applied to those who conduct research:

> The greatest care should be exercised when trying to recruit for experiments members of the student body or junior staff, since there is always a danger that their consent may be influenced by the nature of their relationship with the investigator . . . It should always be made absolutely clear that refusal to take part or a decision to withdraw without giving a reason will in no way prejudice the potential volunteer.

Second, extensive use may be made of documented cases to increase a predictive sense of the possible effects of different kinds of research upon those who conduct it. It is to this end that some pertinent examples are detailed in this book. Those whose activities risk exposure by the publication of social research may be prompted to discredit publicly the scholars who investigate them. While Laud Humphreys' work illustrates the hazards of being drawn into the community of one's subjects, that of Samuel Heilman (see 3.6.1) shows the way in which involvement in research can estrange an individual from a social community. In recent years there has been an increasing interest in aspects of methodology and procedure with the result that most books and articles reporting social research include some account of this kind: these offer salutary reading and enable intending researchers to reckon the hazards of research in a realistic way.

7.3 EFFECTS ON THE PROFESSION

The adverse effects which social researchers may experience as a profession are quite different from those they may suffer individually. There is concern that research may be conducted and reported in such a way as to damage the reputation of social research to diminish public interest and reliance in research findings, to discourage the investment of sponsors, to embarrass the institution to which a researcher belongs and to incur non-cooperative attitudes by potential subjects. The dominant theme of these concerns is professional self-interest: it is stressed that researchers have an ethical commitment as well to their enterprise as to their subjects.

The possibility of harm to the profession or of restrictions upon the freedom of enquiry is a consideration in the formulation of a wide range of ethical guidelines. Confidentiality is assured partly because it has the practical value of encouraging participation. If sociologists choose to avoid deceitful methods, it may be because they do not want to get their discipline a bad name.

And if psychologists are scrupulous in reducing and explaining the hazards of participation in experiments, they will be aware that recruitment of subjects in the future will be eased because there will be less fear of being duped or trapped. If they do not in some sufficient measure satisfy the conditions of their participants, social researchers may find that they are not able to practise at all. By no means is self-interest the only motive in professional behaviour, but it is a considerable one.

Wherever there is an element of voluntariness in the market, professional groups will take account of their reputation and image when seeking business. Even in some organised sports, it is regarded as an offence to behave in such a way as will bring the game into disrepute. Because the reputation of social research is shared by all who undertake it, complaints are frequently made by those active in research about the behaviour of others. It is suggested that sociology and sociological research have such a problem with so many opponents that special care should be taken in respecting the principles of professional discipline (Dingwall, 1980: 884). And researchers can do their collective cause as much harm by getting too close to subjects and being manipulated by them as they can by treating the interests of participants with too little respect: reports in which the aspirations and interpretations of particular subjects are represented uncritically may be regarded as an abuse of the scientific warrant and are more likely to damage the reputation of social research than to enhance it.

Before protesting about the behaviour of our peers, however, we should do well to heed the fate of Franz Boas, an anthropologist who had dominated his discipline in America for the first two decades of this century. Boas was filled with moral indignation when he received evidence that four anthropologists had presented themselves to foreign governments as being engaged in scientific research, which in fact they used as a cover for intelligence gathering. Boas was concerned that as a consequence those professing to be engaged in scientific research would be widely discredited and he published a letter raising this issue (Boas, 1919). The implications of uttering so public a protest are complex. Of course, the plaintiff must be certain about the evidence. The consequences of alerting the public to the fact that the profession of anthropology may have been so used must be weighed against the implicit assurance of knowing that such an event is unusual to the point of being raised and publicised. If the accused are named or identifiable, it must be decided whether the consequences for those individuals – which may be terminal as far as a scientific career is concerned – are proportionate to the offence, especially if they were young and naïve and relatively unaware of the behaviour which anthropologists expect of those who join their profession. In the instance of Franz Boas it was he whose career was terminated; his eminence notwithstanding, there was a violent reaction to his letter and he was censured by the American Anthropological Association and stripped of membership (Weaver, 1973: 71).

A second type of adverse effect which is more specific and directed is the embarrassment of a researcher's institution and immediate colleagues or of other systems of support such as sponsors. Institutions of higher education facilitate research by offering to those who work within them a network of contacts which have been cultivated over a period of time. These research fields may include schools, social service agencies, hospitals, industry and so on. It is particularly important for those who are in these institutions for only a short time, whether as students or as research staff on a fixed contract, to remember that one outrage may incline the gatekeepers of a particular field to withhold that opportunity in future years. Institutional guidelines, therefore, often pay particular attention to the fostering of good relations between the university or college and the local community. One of the more publicised cases of the projection of hostility toward a researcher's professional base involved the American town 'Plainville' which was studied by 'James West': Gallaher found that Plainvillers were highly critical of Columbia University which was believed to have been responsible for sending 'West' to their town (Gallaher, 1964: 282).

Unfortunately, in the economic conditions which currently constrain the support of social research, sponsors are frequently inclined to compromise the professional integrity of social researchers by controls upon, for example, the publication of findings: a fuller discussion of this tendency appears in Chapters 2 (2.5) and 6 (6.3).

A third kind of adverse effect is the engendering of various forms of non-cooperativeness by potential subjects. As at 'Plainville' subjects are unwilling or reluctant to participate in further enquiry or they learn from the experience of others to be distrustful. Such a consequence is sometimes referred to in the literature as 'environmental contamination' or 'pollution' of the field. Following in the footsteps of 'West' fifteen years later, Gallaher found himself treated with suspicion: Plainvillers assigned false roles to him and some of them supposed him to have been a government spy: he is prepared to learn from this that small-town populations have an antipathy to central government interventions of any kind (Gallaher, 1961: 4–5) but it is also clear that memories die hard and that the town still felt badly at what it perceived to be a betrayal by 'West' who had, in their view, portrayed the town in a negative way and found apparent amusement in their supposed backwardness. The very sight of notes being taken evoked painful memories and Gallaher and his wife had to resort to conducting shorter interviews which they could remember and write up afterwards (Gallaher, 1961: 8).

Inevitably, the deteriorating relationship affects a wider field and research community than those immediately involved in the case that is first at issue. The word gets round and a community that is aggrieved warns others. When Cohen and Taylor researched prison life without clearance from the Home Office, their book was reviewed in the *Prison Service Journal* with the comment that if future researchers or teachers in prisons encountered problems of access 'it would be clear where the responsibility lies' (Cohen and Taylor, 1977: 81).

The instances given here are indicative of the reactions that might follow incautious steps in the field. The picture that we have of the fall-out of social research is, however, fragmentary and Vinacke has proposed that it be more systematically investigated. He suggests that research be undertaken in the vicinity of social psychology laboratories to discover the feelings of investigators, their colleagues, subjects, parents and others: he wants to know what kind of 'atmosphere' results from research at these centres (Vinacke, 1954: 155).

7.4 SOCIAL AND POLITICAL CONTEXT

We treated in the previous chapter (6.6) of the consequences of the publication of research findings in terms of social and policy outcomes. Here we are concerned with the social and political context in which research is conducted. Investigators may be utterly open, inform their subjects scrupulously on the nature of the research, guarantee and honour confidentiality, take due care to protect subjects from strain or harm, be sensitive of subjects' feelings and non-obtrusive of their private lives and yet be engaged in the collection of data for a purpose which they may not regard as moral.

Market research, for example, is concerned with the systematic collection of information on the motives and habits of potential customers which is beneficial to a producer in the design of products and in suggesting policies for advertising. The expense of such research is borne by the producer from the price charged to the consumer. Consumers thus pay so much more for the product in order to enable the producer to find out how to appeal to them most effectively. This is arguably a kind of manipulation and not all persons would be happy to be involved in it, least of all those whose political views do not dispose them favourably toward big business in a capitalist society.

That research of the market or the polling of opinions can be so costly in financial terms weighs the odds heavily against the individual, the small business and the small party. This is most true when research is commissioned by an interested group which then holds findings in confidence and less true when a poll is commissioned by a newspaper or television company for the purposes of publication. Just as governments, big firms and big unions can afford the best lawyers, so they can hire researchers to secure their own interests. Catherine Marsh, in a chapter on 'the political applications of survey research' that rewards a close reading (Marsh, 1982: 125–46), cites the case of Eli Lilley, a drug company in the USA which was sued by aggrieved parties when a majority of the daughters of women who had taken a particular drug developed cervical cancer. The drug company then commissioned a firm of research associates to investigate the likely response of a jury to this case. With the information it acquired, it could calculate the risks and decide whether it would be cheaper to settle out of court. If, however, the case went to court, it would know both which jurors to reject and which arguments would sway those who were retained for the case (Marsh, 1982: 130).

Shapley (1974: 1033) details an extensive list of cases in which social scientists have been used in the procedure known in the United States as *voir dire*, which is the opportunity to question and if need be eliminate prospective jury members. Methods deployed include telephone surveys and in-depth interviews of those on jury lists. Observation by psychologists during *voir dire* of candidates for jury service and, on the basis of data yielded by these means, predictions of the dispositions of jurors to convict or acquit or in civil cases to agree levels of financial settlement. The more reliable these techniques become, the more serious are their ethical implications.

An obvious objection to jury selection in this way is that it is a manipulation of the process of justice which here and in many cases is loaded against the plaintiffs. The more dependable forms of such a service will inevitably be available only to those who can afford them and social scientists may well feel that they do not want to be a part of such activities. Alternatively, they may take with Shapley the view that since it is going on anyway, they should extend the benefits of researched jury selection to the subordinate parties.

In many ways, opinion polling serves the same purposes in politics that interviewing and observing potential jurors serves in the field of justice. A political party may invest in a poll to ascertain which policies will appeal to which groups of voter and may fashion its campaign accordingly. A government that is riding high in opinion polls may take the opportunity to seek approval for a further term of office: it was a temptation which prime minister James Callaghan resisted in the autumn of 1978 when he could have won, but he held on through the winter of discontent and then lost. In these circumstances, the rights and wrongs of opinion polling are much more debatable in Britain where the timing of a general election is in the gift of the Prime Minister than in the United States where a President serves a fixed term.

However, if it is partly true that information about public opinion enables politicians to woo the electorate in a manipulative way, it is also true that such published information healthily embarrasses politicians by demonstrating the unpopularity of the policies that come and go between one general election and another. Investment in opinion polls is made by newspapers and other agencies as well as political parties and it is seen as a means of giving the people a persistent voice.

What is at the heart of the matter in 'our new research society' (Deloria, 1980) is the relationship between individuals and powerful groups. Information is expensive and therefore not universally available, but it is often the basis of the retention of power, especially if its publication can be controlled. For their own part, powerful groups have largely been able to escape the serious study of social scientists, partly because they have been able to make access difficult and partly because social researchers have been more interested in the deviant than the everyday (Warren, 1977: 94). There emerges a pattern of unbalanced interests in the conduct of social research. Subjects yield more than data when they cooperate because they strengthen the position of those groups who control the flow of the information they collect. Social researchers must decide their own role in this process and may have misgivings about collecting data from individuals and delivering them to be held and used by powerful institutions.

7.5 ANTICIPATING EFFECTS

Times have changed since the earliest days of social research. The public is more litigious than before and the profession is more accountable. Only at their own peril can social researchers proceed without reckoning the likely consequences and implications of their work. They must know that they can be held responsible for the various forms of harm that can be sustained by participants in research, for the risks to which human subjects are later exposed and for any social changes or policies that follow the publication of their findings. So celebrated in case history are the likely hazards of conducting and publishing social research that researchers cannot plausibly claim to be unaware of possible outcomes.

Johnson (1982: 87–8) has proposed a number of ethical guidelines for proof-reading which are commended as a precaution in publication: to these we may add principles for the design of field research. Most if not all such principles will urge researchers to entertain the least desirable outcomes as possibilities and, like ethical principles in general, are prompted by a good deal of self-interest:

First, let all who enter the field first read carefully the professional debates that have surrounded the classic 'offences' of people like Milgram, Humphreys, Ditton, Morgan, Mullan and others. In a number of cases the procedures they adopted were standard and the attention they received was not predictable. The anticipation of effects is a speculation not upon what is likely but upon what is possible and case histories are most instructive in the cultivation of this skill.

Second, let it be incumbent upon intending researchers that they take counsel from experienced peers in the profession. Two minds are always better than one. This is a procedure commended among psychologists in the light of the Milgram experiments and it is often the case that more seasoned researchers have a better sense of hazards than those who are at the centre of a research design or entering the field for the first time.

Third, authors of a research report are urged to omit all that may cause gratuitous harm or embarrassment either to the subjects of the enquiry or to others who may be indirectly represented – for example, a study of one small town will provide a stereotypic image that will be generalised by its readers. It is not suggested that researchers should never embarrass their subjects but that they should expect to be engaged in a public campaign against the report.

Fourth, whatever measures are taken to conceal the identities of subjects, it should be anticipated that these will be disclosed, even by the subjects themselves. The preparation of a report with this possibility in mind will compel a standard of truth which might be more casual were the author to assume that no subject will be identified.

Fifth, an author should consider the possibility of being compelled to declare sources and identities, upon pain of imprisonment. That prospect may concentrate the mind wonderfully and the investigator may be inclined to take the precaution of destroying certain details before publication.

CHAPTER 8

Conclusion

8.1 PROBLEMS WITH RESEARCH ETHICS

Throughout this book we have referred to and explored a number of problems in the application of ethical standards to the conduct of social research. First, there have been practical issues in formulating general principles and in implementing these within the professional community. Second, we have at several points observed ways in which the prescription of normative standards encourages an observance of the letter rather than the spirit and in the end affords practices which contradict the values they are intended to enshrine. We may now gather these observations, referring the reader to the passages in the book in which they are developed.

8.1.1 Practical problems

1. The regulatory powers of professional associations are limited where there is no obligation to take up membership and the sanctions of exclusion and censure are weak (2.7).
2. Ethics committees within institutions are in a good position to apply ethical standards but there is a temptation to waive or compromise these if external funding is implied (2.3).
3. Ethical guidelines issued to students have been found to relate to single issues or narrow ranges rather than to be broadly conceived (2.4).
4. Concern about ethical issues in research is often stimulated by dramatic cases: in the absence of major offence, there is a tendency to be complacent (2.6.1).
5. Codes in social research have no teeth (2.7).
6. The evidence is that educated subjects know their rights and are competent to refuse to participate, whereas less articulate types defer; the practice of securing consent looks very like the exploitation of vulnerable groups (4.6).
7. The taboo on covertness has the effect of confining researchers to volunteer subjects (5.4.2).
8. Investigations such as surveys and questionnaires satisfy the formal standards of openness but in practice may be no more open with subjects than those which have gone down in case history as classic offences (5.5.2).

9. It is noticed that in many cases powerful groups are not subject to ethical standards: in particular, some government research proceeds without the requirement of consent and government bodies do not regard publication as an obligation (6.2).
10. Human subjects may not be aware of the means by which their privacy is invaded and are therefore incompetent to protect it (3.7).

8.1.2 The contradictions of ethical procedures

11. There is a tendency among some sponsors, especially government agencies, to invest in particular results and want to retain rights over publication; although this may be an appropriate expectation in market research, it may elsewhere seriously compromise the principle of academic freedom (2.3).
12. Regulatory and prescriptive codes are especially inclined to direct practitioners to the letter of the law rather than to its spirit, whereas educative codes and guidelines keep fundamental values in clear view (2.3.2).
13. Codes may have the effect of closing the discussion of ethical principles rather than of stimulating it (2.7).
14. In negotiations between subjects and researchers, the professionals are likely to have the more practised skills and therefore to be the more powerful party (3.1).
15. The taking of control by subjects, as over privacy or in the giving of consent, may incline researchers to suppose that their moral responsibility has been discharged (3.1).
16. Informant interviewing again transfers moral responsibility from investigator to informant (3.6).
17. Though approved for its openness, the method of interviewing is widely practised as a strategy of invasion (3.4).
18. A variety of methods approved as ethical involves the off-loading of moral responsibility from researcher to subject (3.4).
19. The voluntariness of participation is belied when researchers practise techniques to erode the human subject's ability to resist or decline (3.5).
20. What passes for the informing of consent is often designed more to allay the suspicions and fears of intended subjects and to encourage their participation than to appraise them of hazards and rights (4.2.2).
21. The principle of consent is widely operated as a moment at the outset of research rather than as a continuing option once it is in progress: researchers often encourage their subjects to forget that research is taking place (4.2.2, 4.6).
22. The refusal of subjects to participate may be seen as an obstacle to be overcome rather than as a legitimate position to be honoured: the desirability of a high response rate disposes researchers against refusal (4.2, 4.6).
23. Informants, surrogates and gatekeepers (3.6, 4.4) are used to by-pass the rights of subjects.
24. In its operation the principle of informed consent affords more protection to researchers than to subjects (4.6).

25. Informed consent is seen as a means of indemnifying the researcher (4.6).
26. The taboo on covertness allows subjects, informants and gatekeepers a control over the release of data not conducive with the public right to know (5.4.2).
27. Codes have stressed the subjects' right to know that research is taking place: they have neglected their right not to know, respect for which may in some cases be more sensitive of their needs and interests (5.4.2).
28. Researchers who abide by established ethical formulae may feel exonerated from further responsibility, whereas those acting covertly may respect subjects' interests at a deeper level than the codes prescribe (5.4.2).
29. Too overt a relationship with subjects invites the criticism that one is being controlled by them (5.5.4).
30. Notions of subjects' ownership of data may compromise the integrity of published research as may excessive control by sponsors (6.1).
31. Confidentiality is widely offered to respondents not because it is their right but as the means of securing their cooperation (6.4).
32. Confidentiality affords subjects the chance to conceal data on which they might arguably be accountable (6.4).
33. Confidentiality may operate less as a protection of subjects than as a licence for researchers by reducing their obligations to verify findings with subjects (6.4).
34. The principle that researchers are in some way responsible for the uses that are made of their findings is problematic in that it accords to social researchers an inordinately powerful and responsible role in policy formulation (6.6).

8.2 TOWARD A MORALITY OF SOCIAL RESEARCH

Codes of practice share with ethics education and other measures the positive function of establishing an ethical milieu for professional practice. It may well be that guidelines are not applicable in points of detail and that exceptions can always be found to rules that are expressed in absolute terms but the combined effect of codes and other attempts at control will be to heighten the awareness of researchers in respect of ethical considerations. This is best illustrated by an example of the practice that is possible where such a moral milieu does not exist. In 1971 a number of Mexican-American women applied at a family planning clinic for contraceptives. The physician took the opportunity to monitor the side effects of the pill by giving oral contraceptives to some of the women and placebos to the others. The placebo was a dummy pill similar in appearance to the contraceptive pill but lacking its medical properties; of course, placebos are only useful in research if the subjects to whom they are prescribed are unaware that they are placebos. Whatever the side effects of the patients to whom the contraceptives were prescribed, the more noticeable and predictable effect was shown by the women who were given placebos: ten of them became pregnant. The physician accepted no financial responsibility for the babies, saying that if only the law permitted he could have aborted those pregnant (Bok, 1974: 17). Sissela Bok makes the point that the physician was not particularly heartless but that placebos were so widely used in experimental research that the investigation he conducted was normal in its setting. In Bok's analysis, researchers are products of a professional culture in which some practices are approved and others disapproved. In this case the collective function of codes and controls, debate on ethical issues and ethics as a component of professional training will be to affect the norms of that culture.

What we must now assess in the light of all that has been said above is the professional culture of social researchers. Have they got it right? In particular, would the adoption of ethical principles current in the profession guarantee appropriate safeguards and help establish the reputation of social researchers as a morally responsible profession? Have we achieved as reasonable a balance as possible between the individual entitlements of human subjects and the desirability of public knowledge?

What has emerged is that the science of developing moral principles as applications to social research is poorly developed. In some instances this is because the conflict of values is more direct in social research than in medicine: the medical profession operates a distinction – problematic though it may be – between therapeutic and non-therapeutic research whereas social researchers are inclined or committed to represent all findings in some kind of published form: the practice of investigating aspects of the behaviour of individuals merely for their own information is rare in social research, educational evaluation and appraisal being possible exceptions.

And not only is the science undeveloped but its outcomes are barely respected. We have observed that applications of moral principles in ethical codes or guidelines invite professionals to play their own system. The professional culture is at best never more moral than its codes and professionals are encouraged to believe that they are behaving in a morally responsible way if they observe the letter of the law. Loopholes abound and textbook counsel on field methods is often ethical without being moral. The moral principles observed to have been dishonoured in 'ethical' practice include the privacy of the human subject, the autonomy of the individual, the well-being of subjects and the public right to know.

One of the reasons for these inadequacies is that the formulation of ethical principles for the practice of social research has been widely prompted not by the moral convictions of those practising it but by professional self-interest, such as the dependence of commissions and cooperation upon a favourable public profile. At worst, ethical practice is only counselled because of the likely consequences of unethical practice. Ethical conduct is often to be seen as a grudging subscription to expedient principles: but the notion of a professional implies an attitude that is altogether more heartfelt.

In suggesting and operating this dichotomy of ethics and morality, we observe that there is little talk of morality in the literature treating the ethics of social research. Where one finds reference to the morality of a researcher, it is normally to the set of values and dispositions which he or she brings to the situation of research. It contrasts with the set of applications or ethics which are then found to be more or less agreed within the profession. A researcher may like the method of participant observation but draw the line at house-breaking or some other invitation to engage in criminal activity. A researcher such as Richard Jenkins (1987: 155–6) might feel a moral obligation to confront incidents of racism and then have to square the impulse to report with guarantees of anonymity. Orlans develops a notion of professional integrity which respects the morality of the researcher who is urged not to get involved in the first place with projects in which the compromise of moral beliefs cannot be justified in the consideration of long-term interests. In particular, Orlans notes that in times less competitive than the present researchers have declined and boycotted certain funding programmes such as military and security agencies (Orlans, 1967: 8). In the current economic climate there are relatively few who would endorse Orlans' firmly moral view:

> In the sphere of research financing the conclusion that follows is: if you disagree with the objectives of an agency, don't decry the morality of its staff but try to change their objectives and, in the interim, don't take their money (Orlans, 1967: 5).

The problem that arises, of course, is that if moral scruples prevent one researcher from accepting a particular contract, that project may then be taken up by a less scrupulous practitioner. Professionals can undercut one another with their moralities as they can with their ethics. They may do so in the belief that they are selling their own time and skills. The need for a professional morality is argued in recognition that individuals for hire trade upon and offer the reputation and integrity of the profession and this may be sold irretrievably. Barnett (1983) takes the case of a survey commissioned by an agency for the American government to measure opinions on defence and nuclear weapons: the questions were said to have been loaded to produce the responses desired. A contributor to the *Newsletter* of the Market Research Society had expressed the view,

If a research company takes a commission to accept biased questions in surveys knowing that they will be used for publication, then it must retain the right to do so.

In Barnett's comment 'Never mind the quality . . . Will it give us the answers we want?', he insists that professionalism and pride become meaningless sentiments when a research agency allows its clients to dictate the wording or sequencing of questions (Barnett, 1983: 1104).

We have several times explained that professional control by codes and sanctions is a far off prospect for social research because its practitioners are so diverse and the obligation of formal membership is not a realistic expectation. Meanwhile, there is an urgent need for quality control and for a commitment to truth and knowledge comparable with the moral obligation of medical professionals to the maintenance and quality of human life. This implies in the context of social research, as it has done in medicine, an educational initiative. We cannot afford to prepare students for work in the research field with so little attention to the fundamental values on which social research is established.

BIBLIOGRAPHY AND REFERENCES

Abse, D. (1973) *The Dogs of Pavlov*, Valentine, Mitchell

Aitken, M., Bennett, S. N. and Hesketh, J. (1981) Teaching styles and pupil progress: A re-analysis, *British Journal of Educational Psychology*, 51, 170–86

Akeroyd, A. V. (1984) Ethics in relation to informants, the profession and government. In Ellen, R. F. (ed.) *Ethnographic Research: A Guide to General Conduct*, pp. 133–54

American Anthropological Association (1971) *Principles of Professional Responsibility*

American Sociological Association (1968) Toward a code of ethics for social researchers, *American Sociologist*, 3, pp. 16–18

American Sociological Association (1989) *Code of Ethics*

Amrine, M. and Sanford, F. H. (1956) In the matter of juries, democracy, science, truth, senators and bugs, *American Psychologist*, 11, pp. 54–60

Annas, G. J., Glantz, L. H. and Katz, B. F. (1977) *Informed Consent to Human Experimentation: The Subject's Dilemma*, Cambridge, Mass., Ballinger

Azrin, N. H., Holtz, W., Ulrich, R. and Goldiamond, I. (1961) The control of the content of conversation through reinforcement, *Journal of the Experimental Analysis of Behavior*, 4, pp. 25–30

Ball, S. J. (1985) Participant observation with pupils. In Burgess, R. (ed.) *Strategies of Educational Research: Qualitative Methods*, pp. 23–53

Barbour, R. (1979) The ethics of covert methods, *Network*, 15, 9

Barnes, J. A. (1963) Some ethical problems in modern fieldwork *British Journal of Sociology*, 14, pp. 118–34

Barnes, J. A. (1977) *The Ethics of Inquiry in Social Science*, Delhi, Oxford

Barnes, J. A. (1979) *Who Should Know What? Social Science, Privacy and Ethics*, Harmondsworth, Penguin

Barnes, J. A. (1981) Professionalism in British sociology. In Abrams, P., Deem, R., Finch, J., Rook, P. (eds) *Practice and Progress: British Sociology 1950–1980*, London, Allen and Unwin, pp. 13–24

Barnes, J. A. (1983) Lying: A sociological view, *Australian Journal of Forensic Science*, 15, pp. 152–8

Barnett, S. (1983) Never mind the quality . . . Will it give us the answers we want? *Social Research Association News*, November, 1–2

Baumrind, D. (1964) Some thoughts on ethics of research: After reading Milgram's 'Behavioral study of obedience', *American Psychologist*, 19, pp. 421–3

Baumrind, D. (1971) Principles of ethical conduct in the treatment of subjects: Reaction to the Draft Report of the Committee on Ethical Standards in psychological research, *American Psychologist*, 26, pp. 887–96

Beattie, G. (1983) *Talk: An Analysis of Speech and Non-verbal Behaviour in Conversation*, Milton Keynes, Open University

Beauchamp, T. L. and Childress, J. F. (1983) *Principles of Biomedical Ethics*, 2nd edn, New York, Oxford

Beauchamp, T. L. and Perlin, S. (1978) *Ethical Issues in Death and Dying*, Englewood Cliffs, NJ, Prentice-Hall

Becker, H. S. (1964) Against the code of ethics, *American Sociological Review*, 29, pp. 409–10

Beckford, J. A. (1985) *Cult Controversies: The Societal Response to the New Religious Movements*, London, Tavistock
Bell, C. and Newby, H. (eds) (1977) *Doing Sociological Research*, London, Allen and Unwin
Belson, W. A. (1975) *Juvenile Theft: The Causal Factor*, New York, Harper and Row
Bennett, C. C. (1967) What price privacy? *American Psychologist*, 22, pp. 371–6
Bennett, N. (1976) *Teaching Styles and Pupil Progress*, London, Open Books
Bentham, J. (1789) *An Introduction to the Principles of Morals and Legislation*, Burns, J. H., Hart, H. L. A. (eds) (1982), London, Methuen
Bettelheim, B. (1943) Individual and mass behavior in extreme situations, *Journal of Abnormal and Social Psychology*, 38, pp. 417–52
Black, D. J. and Reiss, A. J. (1970) Police control of juveniles, *American Sociological Review*, 35, pp. 63–77
Blumer, H. (1967) Threats from agency-determined research: The case of Camelot. In Horowitz, I. L. (ed.) *The Rise and Fall of Project Camelot*, Cambridge, Mass: MIT Press, pp. 153–74
Boas, F. (1919) Scientists as spies, *The Nation*, 109 (20 December). Reprinted in Weaver, T. (ed.) *To See Ourselves: Anthropology and Modern Social Issues*, Clenview, Ill., Scott Foresman, pp. 51–2
Boddy, A. (1988) *DHSS Research Contracts*, Society for Social Medicine
Bok, S. (1974) The ethics of giving placebos, *Scientific American*, 231, 5, pp. 17–23
Bok, S. (1978) *Lying: Moral Choice in Public and Private Life*, New York, Pantheon
Bok, S. (1984) *Secrets: On the Ethics of Concealment and Revelation*, Oxford, Oxford University Press
Bridges, D., Brown, S., Adelman, C., and Torrance, H. (1988) What constitutes a fair research agreement? Paper presented to the British Educational Research Association conference at Norwich
British Association Study Group (1974) Does research threaten privacy or does privacy threaten research? Reprinted in Bulmer, M. (ed.) (1979) *Censuses, Surveys and Privacy*, London, Macmillan, pp. 37–54
British Psychological Society (1978) Ethical principles for research with human subjects
British Psychological Society (1985) A code of conduct for psychologists, *Bulletin of the British Psychological Society*, 38, pp. 41–3
British Sociological Association (1974) Professional Ethics Sub-committee [Terms and conditions of employment]
British Sociological Association (1982) Statement of ethical principles and their application to sociological practice
Bulmer, M. (ed.) (1979) *Censuses, Surveys and Privacy*, London Macmillan
Bulmer, M. (ed.) (1980) *Social Research and Royal Commissions*, London, Allen and Unwin
Bulmer, M. (ed.) (1982a) *Social Research Ethics*, London, Macmillan
Bulmer, M. (1982b) The research ethics of pseudo-patient studies: A new look at the ethics of covert ethnographic methods, *Sociological Review*, 30, pp. 627–46
Bulmer, M. (1982c) How safe is the census? Some reflections on legal safeguards for social research. In Raab, C. D. (ed.) *Data Protection and Privacy: Proceedings of a Conference*, London, Social Research Association, pp. 13–20
Bulmer, M. and Warwick, D. P. (eds) 1983 *Social Research in Developing Countries: Surveys and Censuses in the Third World*, Chichester, Wiley
Burgess, R. G. (1980) Some fieldwork problems in field-based research, *British Educational Research Journal*, 6, 2, pp. 165–173
Burgess, R. G. (ed.) (1982) *Field Research: A Sourcebook and Field Manual*, London, Allen and Unwin

Burgess, R. G. (1984) *In the Field: An Introduction to Field Research*, London, Allen and Unwin

Burgess, R. G. (ed.) (1985) *Strategies of Educational Research: Qualitative Methods*, Lewes, Falmer

Burgess, R. G. (ed.) (1989) *The Ethics of Educational Research*, Lewes, Falmer

Calomiris, A. (1950) *Red Masquerade*, Philadelphia, Lippincott

Carlson, R. O. (1967) The issue of privacy in public opinion research, *Public Opinion Quarterly*, 31, pp. 1–8

Cassell, J. and Wax, M. L. (eds) (1980) Ethical problems of fieldwork, *Social Problems*, (Special issue), 27, pp. 259–378

Caudill, W. (1958) *The Psychiatric Hospital as a Small Society*, Cambridge, Mass., Harvard University Press

Caudrey, A. (1988) When politicians tune the researchers' pipes, *The Independent*, 8 March, p. 12

Cavendish, R. (1982) *Women on the Line*, London, Routledge

Chagnon, N. A. (1983) *Yanomamö: The Fierce People*, 3rd edn, New York, Holt Rinehart

Clift, S. M. (1988) Lesbian and gay issues in education: A study of the attitudes of first-year students in a college of higher education, *British Educational Research Journal*, 14, 1, pp. 31–50

Cohen, S. and Taylor, L. (1970) The experience of time in long-term imprisonment, *New Society*, 31 December, pp. 1156–9

Cohen S. and Taylor, L. (1977) Talking about prison blues. In Bell, C., Newby H. (eds) *Doing Sociological Research*, Allen and Unwin, pp. 67–86

Cohen, S. and Taylor, L. (1981) *Psychological Survival*, 2nd edn, Harmondsworth, Penguin

Committee of Directors of Polytechnics (n.d.) *Data Protection Act 1984: Code of Practice for Colleges and Polytechnics*

Council for National Academic Awards (1986) Development Fund Sub-Committee: Guidelines for Development Fund projects (9 October) 526e

Cross, M. (ed.) (1980) *Social Research and Public Policy: Three Perspectives*, London, Social Research Association

Dale, A., Arber, S., and Procter, M. (1988) *Doing Secondary Analysis*, London, Unwin Hyman

Dalenius, T. (1982) Privacy and statistics: Some potential research topics. In Raab, C. D. (ed.) *Data Protection and Privacy*, Social Research Association, pp. 26–30, followed by discussion by Peter Fisk

Daniel, W. W. (1963) A consideration of individual and group attitudes in an expanding and technically changing organisation. Unpublished MSc (Tech) thesis, University of Manchester

Data Protection Registrar (1989) *Data Protection Act 1984: Guidelines 1–8*, 2nd series

Davis, A. and Horobin, G. (eds) (1977) *Medical Encounters: The Experience of Illness and Treatment*, London, Croom Helm

Davis, A. J. and Aroskar, M. A. (1983) *Ethical Dilemmas in Nursing Practice*, 2nd edn, Norwalk, Ct, Appleton-Century-Crofts

Deloria, V. (1980) Our new research society: Some warnings for social scientists, *Social Problems*, 27, 3, pp. 265–72

Denzin, N. K. and Erikson, K. T. (1982) On the ethics of disguised observation: An exchange. In Bulmer, M. (ed.) (1982a) *Social Research Ethics*, London, Macmillan, pp. 142–51

Department of Education and Science (1985) (Revised) Standard Contract Form P2 (FP)

Dicker, R. and Gilbert, J. (1988) The role of the telephone in educational research, *British Educational Research Journal*, 14, 1, pp. 65–72

Diener, E. and Crandall, R. (1978) *Ethics in Social and Behavioral Research*, University of Chicago Press

Dingwall, R. (1977) *The Social Organisation of Health Visitor Training*, London, Croom Helm

Dingwall, R. (1979) Covert observation: A question of ethics: Correspondence with Ronald Frankenberg, *Network*, 14, 7

Dingwall, R. (1980) Ethics and ethnography, *Sociological Review*, 28, 4, pp. 871–91

Ditton, J. (1974) The fiddling salesman: Connivance at corruption, *New Society*, 28 November, pp. 535–7

Ditton, J. (1977) *Part Time Crime: An Ethnography of Fiddling and Pilferage*, London, Macmillan

Ditton, J. (1979) Baking time, *Sociological Review*, 27, 1, pp. 157–67

Douglas, J. D. *et al.* (1977) *The Nude Beach*, Sage

Downie, R. S. and Calman, K. C. (1987) *Healthy Respect: Ethics in Health Care*, London, Faber and Faber

Doxiadis, S. (ed.) (1987) *Ethical Dilemmas in Health Promotion*, Chichester, Wiley

Economic and Social Research Council (1984) Research Funding

Eggleston, J., Dunn, D. and Anjali, M. (1986) *Education for Some: The Educational and Vocational Experience of 15 to 18 Year old Members of Minority Ethnic Groups*, Stoke-on-Trent, Trentham

Ellen, R. F. (ed.) (1984) *Ethnographic Research: A Guide to General Conduct*, London, Academic Press

Elliott, J. (1989) Towards a code of practice for funded educational research, *Research Intelligence*, 21, British Educational Research Association

Emerson, J. (1973) Behaviour in private places: Sustaining definitions of reality in gynaecological examinations. In Salaman, G., Thompson, K. (eds) *People and Organisations*, London, Longman, pp. 358–71

Erikson, K. T. (1967) A comment on disguised observation in sociology, *Social Problems*, 14, pp. 366–73

Festinger, L., Riecken, H. W. and Schachter, S. (1964) *When Prophecy Fails: A Social and Psychological Study of a Modern Group that Predicted the Destruction of the World*, New York, Harper and Row (First published by University of Minnesota 1956)

Fielding, N. (1981), *The National Front*, London, Routledge

Fielding, N. (1982) Observational research on the National Front. In Bulmer, M. (ed.) (1982a) *Social Research Ethics*, London, Macmillan, pp. 80–104

Finch, J. (1984) 'It's great to have someone to talk to': The ethics and politics of interviewing women. In Bell, C. and Roberts, H. (eds) *Social Researching: Politics, Problems and Practice*, London, Routledge, pp. 70–87

Fine, G. A. (1980) Checking diamonds: Observer role in little league baseball settings in the acquisition of social competence. In Shaffir, W. B., Stebbins, R. A. and Turowetz, A. (eds) *Fieldwork Experience: Qualitative Approaches to Social Research*, New York: St Martin's Press, pp. 117–32

Fine, G. A. and Glassner, B. (1979) Participant observation with children: Promise and problems, *Urban Life*, 8, 2, pp. 153–74

Fletcher, J. (1978) Medical diagnosis: Our right to know the truth. In Beauchamp, T. L. and Perlin, S. (eds) *Ethical Issues in Death and Dying*, Englewood Cliffs NJ, Prentice-Hall, pp. 146–56

Foster, J. and Sheppard, J. (1980) Archives and the history of nursing. In Davies, C. (ed.) *Rewriting Nursing History*, London, Croom Helm, pp. 200–14

Fredson, E. (1964) Against the code of ethics, *American Sociological Review*, 29, pp. 410

Friedl, E. (1962) *Vasilika: A Village in Modern Greece*, New York, Holt Rinehart

Gaiman, D. (1977) A Scientologist's comment. In Bell C. and Newby, H. (eds) *Doing Sociological Research*, London, Allen and Unwin, pp. 168–9

Gallaher, A. (1961) *Plainville Fifteen Years Later*, New York, Columbia University Press

Gallaher, A. (1964) Plainville: The twice-studied town. In Vidich, A., Bensman, J., and Stein, M. (eds) *Reflections on Community Studies* New York, Harper and Row, pp. 285–303

Galliher, J. F. (1973) The protection of human subjects: A reexamination of the professional code of ethics, *American Sociologist*, 8, 3, pp. 93–100

Galliher, J. F. (1974) Professor Galliher replies, *American Sociologist*, 9, pp. 159–60

Gardner, G. (1978) *Social Surveys for Social Planners*, Milton Keynes, Open University

Gibson, A. with Barrow, J. (1986) *The Unequal Struggle: The Findings of a Westindian Research Investigation into the Underachievement of Westindian Children in British Schools*, Centre for Caribbean Studies, London

Gilsenan, M. (1976) Lying, honor and contradiction. In Kepferer, B. (ed.) *Transaction and Meaning: Directions in the Anthropology of Exchange and Symbolic Behavior* Philadelphia: Institute for the Study of Human Issues

Goffman, E. (1971) *Relations in Public: Microstudies of the Public Order*, London, Allen Lane

Griffin, J. H. (1977) *Black Like Me*, 2nd edn, Boston, Houghton Mifflin

Gulleford, K. (1986) *Data Protection in Practice*, London, Butterworths

Hakim, C. (1979) Census confidentiality in Britain. In Bulmer, M. (ed.) *Censuses, Surveys and Privacy*, London, Macmillan, pp. 132–57

Hargreaves, D. (1967) *Social Relations in the Secondary School*, London, Routledge

Häring, B. (1972) *Medical Ethics*, Slough, St Paul

Harris, M. (1984) The strange saga of the Video Bill, *New Society*, 26 April, pp. 140–2

Hartley, S. F. (1982) Sampling strategies and the threat to privacy. In Sieber, J. E. (ed.) *The Ethics of Social Research: Fieldwork, Regulation and Publication*, New York, Springer, pp. 167–89

Health Education Authority (1987) Rules Governing the Payment of Grants, London, Health Education Authority

Heasman, M. (1982) Confidentiality and health service records. In Raab, C. D. (ed.) *Data Protection and Privacy: Proceedings of a Conference*, London, Social Research Association, pp. 34–41

Heilman, S. C. (1980) Jewish sociologist: Native-as-stranger, *American Sociologist*, 16, pp. 100–8

Henle, M. and Hubble, M. B. (1938) Egocentricity in adult conversation *Journal of Social Psychology*, pp. 227–34

Henry, S. (1978) *The Hidden Economy: The Context and Control of Borderline Crime*, London, Martin Robertson

Herdt, G. (1987) *The Sambia: Ritual and Gender in New Guinea*, Holt Rinehart

Hite, S. (1977) *The Hite Report: A Nationwide Study on Female Sexuality*, London, Tammy Franklin

Hobbs, D. (1988) *Doing the Business: Entrepreneurship, the Working Class and Detectives in the East End of London*, Oxford, Clarendon

Holdaway, S. (1982) 'An inside job': A case study of covert research on the police. In Bulmer, M. (ed.) *Social Research Ethics*, London, Macmillan, pp. 59–79

Homan, R. (1978) Interpersonal communication in pentecostal meetings, *Sociological Review*, 26, 3, pp. 499–518

Homan, R. (1980) The ethics of covert research, *British Journal of Sociology*, 31, pp. 46–59

Homan, R. (1981) Crises in the definition of reality, *Sociology*, 15, pp. 210–24

Homan, R. (1986) Observations on the management of mood in a neurological hospital, *British Medical Journal*, 293, pp. 1417–19

Homan, R. (1990) Institutional controls and educational research *British Educational Research Journal*, 16, 3, pp. 237–48

Homan, R. and Bulmer, M. (1982) On the merits of covert methods: A dialogue. In Bulmer, M. (ed.) *Social Research Ethics*, London, Macmillan, pp. 105–21

Homans, G. C. (1946) The small warship, *American Sociological Review*, 11, pp. 294–300

Horowitz, I. L. (ed.) (1967) *The Rise and Fall of Project Camelot: Studies in the Relationship between Social Science and Practical Policy*, Cambridge, Mass. MIT Press

Horowitz, I. L. and Katz, J. E. (1975) *Social Science and Public Policy in the United States*, New York, Praeger

Humphreys, L. (1975) *Tearoom Trade: Impersonal Sex in Public Places*, Chicago, Aldine

Ianni, F. A. J. and Reuss-Ianni, E. (1972) *A Family Business: Kinship and Social Control in Organized Crime*, London, Routledge

Jahoda, M. (1981) To publish or not to publish? *Journal of Social Issues*, 37, 1, pp. 208–20

Jarvie, I. C. (1982) The problem of ethical integrity in participant observation. In Burgess, R. (ed.) *Field Research: A Sourcebook and Field Manual*, London, Allen and Unwin, pp. 68–72

Jenkins, D. (1980) An adversary's account of SAFARI's ethics of case study. In Simons, H. (ed.) *Towards a Science of the Singular: Essays about Case Study in Educational Research and Evaluation*, University of East Anglia: CARE Occasional Publications, 10, pp. 147–59

Jenkins, R. (1987) Doing research into discrimination: Problems of method, interpretation and ethics. In Wenger, G. C. (ed.) *The Research Relationship: Practice and Politics in Social Policy Research*, London, Allen and Unwin, pp. 144–60

Johnson, C. G. (1982) Risks in the publication of fieldwork. In Sieber, J. E. (ed.) *The Ethics of Social Research: Fieldwork, Regulation and Publication*, New York, Springer, pp. 71–91

Jorgensen, J. G. (1971) On ethics and anthropology, *Current Anthropology*, 12 June, 321–34. Reprinted in Weaver, T. (ed.) (1973) *To See Ourselves: Anthropology and Modern Social Issues*, Glenview, Ill., Scott Foresman, pp. 19–26

Josephson, E. (1979) Resistance to community surveys. In Bulmer, M. (ed.) *Censuses, Surveys and Privacy*, London, Macmillan, pp. 96–111. First published in *Social Problems*, 1970

Jowell, R. (1982) Ethical concern in data collection. In Raab, C. D. (ed.) *Data Protection and Privacy: Proceedings of a Conference*, London, Social Research Association, pp. 43–53

Karhausen, L. (1987) From ethics to medical ethics. In Doxiadis, S. (ed.) *Ethical Dilemmas in Health Promotion*, Wiley, pp. 25–33

Katz, J. (ed.) (1972) *Experimentation with Human Beings*, New York, Russell Sage Foundation

Kinsey, A. C. Poleroy, W. B. and Martin, C. E. (1948) *Sexual Behavior in the Human Male*, Philadelphia, Saunders

Klockars, C. (1975) *The Professional Fence*, London, Tavistock. First published in the United States by the Free Press, 1974

Knerr, C. R. (1982) What to do before and after a subpoena of data arrives. In Sieber, J. E. (ed.) *The Ethics of Social Research: Surveys and Experiments*, New York, Springer, pp. 191–206

Levi, K. (ed.) (1982) *Violence and Religious Commitment: Implications of Jim Jones's People's Temple Movement*, University of Pennsylvania

Linguistic Minorities Project (1983) *Linguistic Minorities in England: A Report by the Linguistic Minorities Project for the Department of Education and Science*, University of London Institute of Education

Lofland, L. H. (1972) Self management in public settings. Parts I and II, *Urban Life* pp. 193–208 and 217–231

Lofland, J. and Lejeune, R. A. (1960) Initial interaction of newcomers in Alcoholics Anonymous: A field experiment in class symbols and socialization, *Social Problems*, 8, pp. 102–11

Lofland, J. and Lofland, L. H. (1984) *Analyzing Social Settings: A Guide*, Qualitative Observation and Analysis, 2nd edn, Belmont, Ca., Wadsworth
Lurie, A. (1978) *Imaginary Friends*, Harmondsworth, Penguin. First published by Heinemann (1967)
Lynd, R. S. and Lynd, H. M. (1929) *Middletown*, New York, Harcourt Brace
McCloskey, J. C. and Grace, H. K. (1981) *Current Issues in Nursing*, Oxford, Blackwell
McCrossan, L. (1985) *A Handbook for Interviewers: A Manual of Social Survey Practice and Procedures of Structured Interviewing*, London, Her Majesty's Stationery Office
MacDonald, B. and Walker, R. (1974) *Information, Evaluation, Research and the Problem of Control* SAFARI Working Paper 1. Centre for Applied Research in Education
MacDonald, B. (1976) Evaluation and the control of education. In Tawney, D. (ed.) *Curriculum Evaluation Today: Trends and Implications*, London, Macmillan, pp. 125–36
McNeill, P. (1985) *Research Methods*, London, Tavistock
Madian, A. L. (1969) Knowledge for what? The Camelot legacy: The dangers of sponsored research in the social sciences, *British Journal of Sociology*, 20, 3, pp. 326–30
Malamuth, N. M., Feshbach, S. and Heim, M. (1980a) Ethical issues and exposure to rape stimuli: A reply to Sherif, *Journal of Personality and Social Psychology*, 36, 3, pp. 413–5
Malamuth, N. M., Heim, M. and Feshbach, S. (1980b) Sexual responsiveness of college students to rape depictions: Inhibitory and disinhibitory effects, *Journal of Personality and Social Psychology*, 38, 3, pp. 399–408
Malinowski, B. (1929) *The Sexual Life of Savages in North-western Melanesia*, London, Routledge
Market Research Society (1986) *Code of Conduct*, London
Marsh, C. (1982) *The Survey Method: The Contribution of Surveys to Sociological Explanation*, London, Allen and Unwin
Martin, F. M. (1982) Lindop and after. In Raab, C. D. (ed.) *Data Protection and Privacy: Proceedings of a Conference*, Social Research Association, pp. 1–8
Martin, J. (1987) Organization of ethical control. In Doxiadis, S. (ed.) *Ethical Dilemmas in Health Promotion*, Chichester Wiley, pp. 185–212
Mead, M. (1959) *An Anthropologist at Work: Writings of Ruth Benedict*, Boston, Houghton Mifflin
Mead, M. (1969) Research with human beings: A model drawn from anthropological field practice, *Daedalus*, Spring, pp. 361–86
Measor, L. (1985) Interviewing: A strategy in qualitative research. In Burgess, R. G. (ed.) *Strategies of Educational Research: Qualitative Methods*, Lewes, Falmer, pp. 55–77
Michael, J. (1984) Privacy. In Wallington, P. (ed.) (1984) *Civil Liberties* 1984, London, Martin Robertson, pp. 131–50
Milgram, S. (1963) Behavioral study of obedience, *Journal of Abnormal and Social Psychology*, 67, pp. 371–8
Milgram, S. (1964) Issues in the study of obedience: A reply to Baumrind, *American Psychologist*, 19, pp. 848–52
Milgram, S. (1974) *Obedience to Authority*, London, Tavistock
Mill, J. S. (1975) *Three Essays*, Oxford, Oxford University Press
Moore, R. (1977) Becoming a sociologist in Sparkbrook. In Bell, C. and Newby, H. (eds) *Doing Sociological Research*, London, Allen and Unwin: pp. 87–107
Morgan, D. H. J. (1972) The British Association scandal: The effect of publicity on a sociological investigation, *Sociological Review*, 20, 2, pp. 185–206
Mullan, B. (1980) *Stevenage Ltd: Aspects of the Planning and Politics of Stevenage New Town 1945–78*, London, Routledge
Niblett, B. (1984) *Data Protection Act 1984*, London, Oyez-Longman

Nixon, J. (ed.) (1981) *A Teachers' Guide to Action Research: Evaluation, Enquiry and Development in the Classroom*, London, Grant McIntyre

Norris, N. (1988) The contractual control of social inquiry: The terms and conditions of funded research. Paper presented to British Educational Research Association conference, Norwich, 31 August

Oakley, A. (1981) Interviewing women: A contradiction in terms. In Roberts, H. (ed.) *Doing Feminist Research*, London, Routledge, pp. 30–61

O'Connor, M. E. and Barnes, J. A. (1983) Bulmer on pseudo-patient studies: A critique, *Sociological Review*, 31, pp. 753–8

Open University (1987) Communication and education: The Bennett report (video format)

Orlans, H. (1967) Ethical problems in the relations of research sponsors and investigators. In Sjoberg, G. (ed.) *Ethics, Politics and Social Research*, Cambridge, Mass., Schinkman, pp. 3–24

Øyen, Ø. (1976) Social research and the protection of privacy: A review of the Norwegian development, *Acta Sociologica*, 19, 3, pp. 249–62

Patrick, J. (1973) *A Glasgow Gang Observed*, London, Eyre-Methuen

Payne, G., Dingwall, R., Payne, J. and Carter, M. (1981) *Sociology and Social Research*, London, Routledge

Phillips, M. and Dawson, J. (1985) *Doctors' Dilemmas: Medical Ethics and Contemporary Science*, London, Harvester

Platt, J. (1976) *Realities of Social Research: An Empirical Study of British Sociologists*, London, Chatto and Windus

Platt, J. (1981) On interviewing one's peers, *British Journal of Sociology*, 32, 1, 75–91

Polsky, N. (1969) *Hustlers, Beats and Others*, Harmondsworth, Penguin. (Previously New York, Aldine (1967))

Pond, D. (Chair) (1987) *Report of a Working Party on the Teaching of Medical Ethics,* Institute of Medical Ethics

Pring, R. (1984a) The problems of confidentiality. In Skilbeck, M. (ed.) *Evaluating the Curriculum in the Eighties*, London, Hodder and Stoughton, pp. 38–44

Pring, R. (1984b) Confidentiality and the right to know. In Adelman, C. (ed.) *The Politics and Ethics of Evaluation*, London, Croom Helm, pp. 8–18

Pryce, K. (1979) *Endless Pressure: A Study of West Indian Life-styles in Bristol*, Harmondsworth, Penguin

Raab, C. D. (ed.) (1982) *Data Protection and Privacy: Proceedings of a Conference*, Social Research Association

Rainwater, L. and Pittman, D. J. (1967) Ethical problems in studying a politically sensitive and deviant community, *Social Problems*, 14, pp. 357–66

Rees, J. G. (1985) *John Stuart Mill's 'On Liberty'*, Oxford, Clarendon

Reiss, A. J. (1979) Conditions and consequences of consent in human subject research. In Wulff, K. M. (ed.) *Regulation of Scientific Inquiry: Social Concerns with Research*, American Association for the Advancement of Science, pp. 161–84

Rex, J. and Moore, R. (1967) *Race, Community and Conflict*, Oxford, Oxford University Press

Reynolds, D. K. and Farkerow, N. I. (1976) *Suicide: Inside and Out*, Berkeley, University of California Press

Reynolds, P. D. (1979) *Ethical Dilemmas and Social Science Research: An Analysis of Moral Issues Confronting Investigators in Research Using Human Participants*, San Francisco, Jossey-Bass

Reynolds, P. D. (1982) *Ethics and Social Science Research*, Englewood Cliffs, NJ, Prentice-Hall

Rhodes, G. (1980) The Younger committee and research. In Bulmer, M. (ed.) *Social Research and Royal Commissions*, London, Allen and Unwin, 110–21

Richardson, E. (1973) *The Teacher, the School and the Task of Management*, London, Heinemann

Richardson, J. T. (1980) People's Temple and Jonestown: A corrective comparison and critique, *Journal of the Scientific Study of Religion*, 19, pp. 239–55

Richardson, S. A., Dohrenwend, B. S. and Klein, D. (1965) *Interviewing: Its Form and Functions*, New York, Basic

Rosenhan, D. L. (1973) On being sane in insane places, *Science* 179, 19 January, 250–8. (Reprinted in Bulmer, M. (ed.) 1982, *Social Research Ethics*, London, Macmillan, pp. 15–37)

Roth, J. (1962) Comment on 'secret observation', *Social Problems*, 9, 283–4

Sadler, P. (1980) Personal decisions in classroom research ethics *Classroom Action Research Network Bulletin*, 4, pp. 78–81

Sagarin, E. (1973) The research setting and the right not to be researched, *Social Problems*, 21, pp. 52–65

Salaman, G. and Thompson, K. (eds) (1973) *People and Organisations*, London, Longman

Savage, N. and Edwards, C. (1984) *A Guide to the Data Protection Act 1984*, Financial Training, London

Schuler, H. (1982) *Ethical Problems in Psychological Research*, trans Woodruff, M. S. and Wicklund, R. A., New York, Academic Press

Shaffir, W. B., Stebbins, R. A. and Turowetz, A. (eds) (1980) *Fieldwork Experience: Qualitative Approaches to Social Research*, New York, St Martin's

Shapley, D. (1974) Jury selection: Social scientists gamble in an already loaded game, *Science*, 185, 20 September, pp. 1033–4, 1071

Sherif, C. W. (1980) Comment on ethical issues in Malamuth, Heim and Feshbach's 'Sexual responsiveness of college students to rape depictions: Inhibitory and disinhibitory effects' *Journal of Personality and Social Psychology*, 38, 3, pp. 409–12

Sieber, J. E. (ed.) (1982a) *The Ethics of Social Research: Fieldwork, Regulation and Publication*, New York, Springer

Sieber, J. E. (ed.) (1982b) *The Ethics of Social Research: Surveys and Experiments*, New York, Springer

Simons, H. (1979) Suggestions for a school self-evaluation based on democratic principles *Classroom Action Research Network Bulletin*, 3, pp. 49–55

Simons, H. (ed.) (1980) *Towards a Science of the Singular: Essays about Case Study in Educational Research and Evaluation*, University of East Anglia: CARE Occasional Publications 10

Simons, H. (1981) Conversation-piece: The practice of interviewing in case study research. In Adelman, C. (ed.) *Uttering, Muttering: Collecting, Using and Reporting Talk for Social and Educational Research*, London, Grant McIntyre, pp. 27–50

Simons, H. (1984) Guidelines for the conduct of an Independent evaluation. In Adelman, C. (ed.) *The Politics and Ethics of Evaluation*, London, Croom Helm, pp. 87–92

Singer, E. (1978) Informed consent: Consequences for response rate and response quality in social surveys, *American Sociological Review*, 43, 2, pp. 144–62

Sissons, M. (1971) The psychology of social class. In Open University *Understanding Society: A Foundation Course Units 14–18: Money, Wealth and Class*, 111–31

Sjoberg, G. (ed.) (1967) *Ethics, Politics and Social Research*, Cambridge, Mass., Schinkman

Social Research Association (1980) *Terms and Conditions of Social Research Funding in Britain*, London, Social Research Association

Social Research Association (n.d.) *Ethical Guidelines*, London

Spector, M. (1980) Learning to study public figures. In Shaffir, W. B., Stebbins, R. A. and Turowetz, A. (eds) *Fieldwork Experience: Qualitative Approaches to Social Research*, New York, St Martin's, pp. 98–109

Stacey, M. (1959) *Methods of Social Research*, Oxford, Pergamon. (Reprinted 1980)

Sudman, S. and Bradburn, N. M. (1982) *Asking Questions: A Practical Guide to Questionnaire Design*, San Francisco, Jossey-Bass

Sullivan, M. A., Queen, S. A., and Patrick, R. C. (1958) Participant observation as employed in the study of a military training program, *American Sociological Review*, 23, pp. 660–7

Sutherland, A. (1975) *Gypsies: The Hidden Americans*, London, Tavistock

Tanke, E. D. and Tanke, T. J. (1982) Regulation and education: The role of the Institutional Review Board in social science research. In Sieber, J. E. (ed.) *The Ethics of Social Research: Fieldwork, Regulation and Publication*, New York, Springer, pp. 131–49

Tornabene, L. (1967) *I Posed as a Teenager*, New York, Simon and Schuster

Turner, A. G. (1982) What subjects of survey research believe about confidentiality. In Sieber, J. E. (ed.) *The Ethics of Social Research: Surveys and Experiments*, New York, Springer, pp. 151–65

Udry, J. R. and Billy, J. O. G. (1987) Initiation of coitus in early adolescence, *American Sociological Review*, 52, pp. 841–55

Verma, G. A. K. (1986) *Ethnicity and Educational Achievement in British Schools*, London, Macmillan

Verplanck, W. S. (1955) The control of the content of conversation: Reinforcement of statements of opinion, *Journal of Abnormal and Social Psychology*, 55, pp. 668–76

Vidich, A. J., Bensman, J. and Steen, M. R. (eds) (1964) *Reflections on Community Studies*, New York, Harper and Row

Vidich, A. I. and Bensman, J. (1968) *Small Town in Mass Society: Class, Power and Religion in a Rural Community*, Princeton University Press

Vinacke, W. E. (1954) Deceiving experimental subjects, *American Psychologist*, 9, April, 155

Wade, N. (1976) I.Q. and heredity: Suspicion of fraud beclouds classic experiment, *Science*, 194, pp. 916–9

Walker, A. G. and Atherton, J. S. (1971) An Easter pentecostal convention: The successful management of a 'Time of blessing', *Sociological Review*, 19, pp. 367–87

Walker, M. (1977) *The National Front*, New York/London, Fontana/Collins

Walker, R. (1985) *Doing Research: A Handbook for Teachers*, London, Methuen

Wallis, R. (1973) Religious sects and the fear of publicity, *New Society*, 24, 7 June, pp. 545–7

Wallis, R. (1976) *The Road to Total Freedom: A Sociological Analysis of Scientology*, London, Heinemann

Wallis, R. (1977) The moral career of a research project. In Bell, C. and Newby, H. (eds) *Doing Sociological Research*, London, Allen and Unwin, pp. 149–67

Warren, C. A. B. (1977) Fieldwork in the gay world: Issues in phenomenological research, *Journal of Social Issues*, 33, Fall, 93–107

Warwick, D. P. (1974) Who deserves protection? *American Sociologist*, 8, pp. 158–9

Warwick, D. P. (1982) Tearoom Trade: Means and ends in social research. In Bulmer, M. (ed.) *Social Research Ethics*, London, Macmillan, pp. 38–58

Warwick, D. P. (1983) The politics and ethics of field research. In Bulmer, M. and Warwick, D. P. (eds) *Social Research in Developing Countries: Surveys and Censuses in the Third World*, Chichester, Wiley: pp. 315–30

Wax, M. L. and Cassell, J. (1981) From regulation to reflection: Ethics in social research, *American Sociologist*, 16, 4, pp. 224–9

Wax, M. L. (1982) Research reciprocity rather than informed consent in fieldwork. In Sieber, J. E. (ed.) *The Ethics of Social Research: Fieldwork, Regulation and Publication*, New York, Springer, pp. 33–48

Weaver, T. (ed.) (1973) *To See Ourselves: Anthropology and Modern Social Issues*, Glenview, Ill. Scott Foresman

Wells, G. (1981) *Learning through Interaction: The Study of Language Development*, Cambridge, Cambridge University Press
Wenger, G. C. (1987) *The Research Relationship: Practice and Politics in Social Policy Research*, London, Allen and Unwin
West, J. (1945) *Plainville, USA*, Columbia University Press
West, S. G., Gunn, S. P. and Chernicky, P. (1975) Ubiquitous Watergate: An attributional analysis, *Journal of Personality and Social Psychology*, 32, 1, pp. 55–65
Westin, A. F. (1970) *Privacy and Freedom*, Oxford, Bodley Head
Whyte, W. F. (1951) Observational field-work methods. In Jahoda, M., Deutsch, M. and Cook, S. W. (eds) *Research Methods in Social Relations. Part Two: Selected Techniques*, New York, Dryden
Wiener, R. S. P. (1970) *Drugs and Schoolchildren*, London, Longman
Willmott, P. (1980) A view from an independent research institute. In Cross, M. (ed.) *Social Research and Public Policy: Three Perspectives*, Social Research Association, pp. 1-13
Wilson, B. (1961) *Sects and Society: A Sociological Study of Three Religious Groups in Britain*, London, Heinemann
Wulff, K. M. (ed.) (1979) *Regulation of Scientific Inquiry: Social Concerns with Research*, American Association for the Advancement of Science
Younger, K. (Chair) (1972) *Report of the Committee on Privacy*. Cmnd 5012, London, Her Majesty's Stationery Office
Zaslavsky, V. and Brym, R. J. (1978) The functions of elections in the USSR, *Soviet Studies*, 30, pp. 362–71
Zweig, F. (1948) *Labour. Life and Poverty*, London, Gollancz

INDEX